M000311909

Between State and Synagogue

A thriving, yet small, liberal component in Israeli society has frequently taken issue with the constraints imposed by religious orthodoxy, largely with limited success. However, as this thoughtful new book by Guy Ben-Porat suggests, in recent years, in part because of demographic changes and in part because of the influence of an increasingly consumer-oriented society, dramatic changes have occurred in the secularization of significant parts of public and private lives. Even though these fissures often have more to do with lifestyle choices and economics than with political or religious ideology, the demands and choices of a secular public and a burgeoning religious presence in the government are becoming ever more difficult to reconcile. The evidence, which the author has accrued from numerous interviews and a detailed survey, is nowhere more telling than in areas that demand religious sanction, such as marriage, burial, the sale of pork, and the operation of businesses on the Sabbath. This book makes an important and timely contribution to the study of contemporary Israeli society as new alliances are being forged in the political arena.

Dr. Guy Ben-Porat has been with the Department of Public Policy and Administration at Ben-Gurion University since 2001. He is the author of *Global Liberalism, Local Populism: Peace and Conflict in Israel/Palestine and Northern Ireland* (2006); a co-author of *Israel Since 1980* (2008); and co-editor of *The Contradictions of Israeli Citizenship: Land, Religion and State* (2011).

Cambridge Middle East Studies

Editorial Board

Charles Tripp (general editor)
Julia Clancy-Smith
F. Gregory Gause
Yezid Sayigh
Avi Shlaim
Judith E. Tucker

Cambridge Middle East Studies has been established to publish books on the nineteenth- to twenty-first-century Middle East and North Africa. The series offers new and original interpretations of aspects of Middle Eastern societies and their histories. To achieve disciplinary diversity, books are solicited from authors writing in a wide range of fields including history, sociology, anthropology, political science, and political economy. The emphasis is on producing books affording an original approach along theoretical and empirical lines. The series is intended for students and academics, but the more accessible and wide-ranging studies will also appeal to the interested general reader.

A list of books in the series can be found after the index.

Between State and Synagogue

The Secularization of Contemporary Israel

GUY BEN-PORAT

Ben-Gurion University, Israel

CAMBRIDGE
UNIVERSITY PRESS

CAMBRIDGE UNIVERSITY PRESS
Cambridge, New York, Melbourne, Madrid, Cape Town,
Singapore, São Paulo, Delhi, Mexico City

Cambridge University Press
32 Avenue of the Americas, New York, NY 10013-2473, USA

www.cambridge.org
Information on this title: www.cambridge.org/9780521176996

© Guy Ben-Porat 2013

This publication is in copyright. Subject to statutory exception
and to the provisions of relevant collective licensing agreements,
no reproduction of any part may take place without the written
permission of Cambridge University Press.

First published 2013

Printed in the United States of America

A catalog record for this publication is available from the British Library.

Library of Congress Cataloging in Publication data

Ben-Porat, Guy.
Between state and synagogue : the secularization of contemporary Israel / Guy Ben-Porat.
  p. cm. – (Cambridge Middle East studies)
Includes bibliographical references and index.
ISBN 978-1-107-00344-6 (hardback) – ISBN 978-0-521-17699-6 (paperback)
1. Judaism – Israel.   2. Judaism and state – Israel.   3. Secularism – Israel.
4. Jews – Israel – Identity.   5. Israel – Politics and government.   I. Title.
BM390.B428   2012
322'.1095694–dc23   2012023185

ISBN 978-1-107-00344-6 Hardback
ISBN 978-0-521-17699-6 Paperback

Cambridge University Press has no responsibility for the persistence or accuracy of URLs
for external or third-party Internet websites referred to in this publication and does not
guarantee that any content on such websites is, or will remain, accurate or appropriate.

Contents

Figures and Tables

Figures

Tables

Preface and Acknowledgments

A study of secularization in Israel may seem strange considering the fact that a separation of religion and state is unlikely in the near future, only Orthodox Judaism is recognized by the state, religious parties hold significant political power, and a 2009 survey indicates that more Jewish Israelis described themselves as "religious" or "very religious" than they did 10 years ago and fewer describe themselves as "secular." Religion in Israel is welded into the essence of nationality that is built into the Jewish definition of the state and is institutionalized through religious institutions that have a direct bearing on individual lives on intimate issues such as marriage and divorce. The prolonged and lingering failure of secular Israelis to change any of the above was a reason why scholars were dismissive of Israeli secularism:

Most of the issues in the struggle for control of the public domain are usually relatively marginal.... Most of the public defined as secular have no interest in these subjects unless the issues affect a specific community directly and generally speaking the tendency is to separate them from the general and comprehensive context, apparently owing to the absence of a consolidated ideology and a secular Jewish organized philosophy ever since the disappearance of etatism. The major reason for the marginality of the struggles over the public sphere . . . is the inability of the state and the majority of the majority of the Jewish population to engage with the major problem . . . separating nationhood from religion and the encompassing character of Jewish identity in Israel. (Kimmerling, 2004: 256)

Studies of religion and politics in Israel may have been right to regard secularism as weak but seemed to have missed important developments that suggest secularization may be part of contemporary life. The expansion of commerce on the Sabbath, a thriving nonkosher culinary culture, marriages performed without Orthodox rabbis, civil burials, and even an annual lively gay pride parade, all relatively new developments, allude that the religious hold on public and private life may be changing. What is unique about these developments, and why they remained below the radars of social scientists, is, first, the fact that they are not necessarily related to a secular ideology; second, that they occur alongside a religious resurgence; and, third, that they advance outside of formal political processes. These developments fall far short of religious freedom or a full-fledged liberal order, but since the early 1990s secular Israelis have gained new freedoms and choices that defy religious authority.

Thus, while religion remains a strong force in Israeli society and has formally conceded little if any of its authority, since the 1990s secular spaces for marriage, burial, nonkosher establishments, and commerce on the Sabbath have been established across the country. These changes can be explained neither by a growth in the number of Jewish Israelis who define themselves as secular, nor by political struggles that ended in secular legislation. Considering the overall weakness of secularism as an identity or a political force, what can explain these developments? How could these changes have emerged when religious institutions maintained their formal power? Who are the initiators and the beneficiaries of these changes? How should we expect these changes to have an impact on religious power in the near future?

Secularization, as the experience from Israel and elsewhere demonstrates, can evolve even when significant aspects of state and society remain religious and secularism as an identity is embraced only by a minority. This complexity in which secular and religious are not mutually exclusive suggests that modern secularity may be a more puzzling phenomenon than many of the religious explosions of fundamentalism (Berger, 1999). In order to explain these paradoxes as they manifest themselves in Israel this book offers a different perception and interpretation of secularization that rests on five main premises. First, secularization implies the decline of religious authority rather than of religiosity per se (Chaves, 1994). Second, secularization as a process is separated from secularism, a comprehensive worldview associated with a liberal ideology of equality and freedom. Third, rather than the ideological change associated with liberalism, secularization can be the result of economic and demographic changes. Fourth, secularization is a multidimensional process measured in identity, beliefs, values, and practices. And, fifth, secularization advances not only through organized and openly declared ideological struggles against the Orthodox monopoly in the political arena but also through practical and individual choices related to everyday life.

The disaggregation of the concept of secularization opens up new possibilities for research on both the declining role of religion in society vis-à-vis other systems (political and economic) and the role religion continues to hold in individual lives (beliefs, practices, and values). Accordingly, the focus here is shifted from ideological transformations and political struggles to social and economic changes, both global and local, that create new incentives and to the groups and individuals that take advantage of these changes and become secular entrepreneurs. The secular entrepreneurs identified in the book are agents whose actions, intentionally or not, undermine existing religion–state arrangements. Entrepreneurs can have wide and far-reaching goals of separation of church and state or concrete goals for change, and be motivated by a secularist ideology with commitment to liberal values or by individual economic motivations. Their goals, as the research reveals, are not always clear, mutually exclusive, and available for categorization. Moreover, the goals and their justifications may change according to constraints and opportunities available. The study of structural changes, entrepreneurs, and their targeted followers or clientele provides a nuanced, multidimensional, and dynamic account of Israeli secularization.

Secularization: Theoretical Context

The historical narrative of secularization presents itself as an ideological victory of liberalism that ended in a pluralist public sphere with a shared and neutralized language that secures individual freedom. The more critical accounts of secularization, engaged in this book, argue that it has often been a consequence of changes in social structure and technology and the endorsement of rational procedures in modern social systems, rather than an ideological change related to liberal values. Although secularists often challenged church dogma and the dominance of religion in society, the factors that stimulated the secularization of society owe more to socioeconomic change that has "occurred involuntarily as an autonomous and largely endogenous process, and as an unintended and perhaps unanticipated consequence of that more fundamental process of change" (Wilson, 2001: 39). In the same vein, tolerance associated with secularism was, more often than not, the result not of an ideological-liberal transformation but rather of the application of rational principles of social organization that no longer saw religion as reinforcing political authority and legitimacy (ibid., p. 46).

The economy – in particular, the global economy and the expanding consumer culture – is expected to influence secularization by creating new choices and incentives that defy the traditions and practices associated with religion and the religious hold over public life. But, although consumer culture often clashes with some religious practices and traditions, it does not necessarily undermine deep-seated religious beliefs and values, and the secularization it underscores may be detached from liberal values and political commitments. Whereas globalization brings forth new motivations and opportunities that, implicitly or explicitly, foster secularization, at different levels, counterforces that resist secularization also make their mark and allow religions in some realms and areas to maintain their stance or even expand. Secularization, therefore, unfolds in different changes, is measured in a decline of religious authority, and is often driven by nonideological forces, and, consequently, its contribution to a liberal order can be limited. Finally, these caveats do not suggest that secularization is marginal. Rather, the different changes and forces, ideological and nonideological, uncoordinated and with different goals, can constitute an institutional change. What exactly is being secularized, by whom, and how, therefore, is context bound and requires an empirical study. These theoretical tools allow an analysis of Israeli secularization and coming to term with its gaps, inconsistencies, and contradictions.

Secularization: Israel as a Case Study

The four issues studied in the book – civil marriage, civil burial, sale of pork, and commerce on the Sabbath – demonstrate dramatic changes that have occurred in the past three decades. These changes, as the study demonstrates, can at most be partially attributed to a secular ideology and to an organized secular struggle. Religious-inspired rules and political compromises between secular and religious elites (known as the status quo), institutionalized in early statehood, restricted private choices of nonreligious Jewish Israelis. Jewish Orthodoxy was granted a monopoly over marriage and burial of Jews, and various restrictions have limited commerce on the Sabbath and the sale of nonkosher meat. Secular Israelis, until the late 1980s, waged different struggles against the status quo that largely failed to challenge the arrangements. Two developments in the past three decades have changed the balance of power: the large immigration from the former Soviet Union (FSU) and economic growth that included globalization, a neoliberal order, and a consumer society. These changes, together with traditional liberalism and new demands for recognition by non-Orthodox groups, enabled the emergence of a new and different secularization.

Not only have the pace and extensity of secularization in Israel changed, but its underlying rationale and legitimacy have changed as well. Early secularization combined arguments of liberal rights with republican claims that underscored the secular contribution to the public good and the rights this contribution supposedly entailed. In the new secularization, conversely, these arguments have not disappeared but are overshadowed by arguments of market rationality and everyday practical choices that render religious restrictions irrelevant. Motivations, likewise, vary between a secularist ideology with commitment to liberal values and economic goals compatible with market rationality. However, as the research reveals, goals, strategies, and justifications are dynamic and contextual. In each of the four case studies selected – marriage, burial, the sale of nonkosher meat, and commerce on the Sabbath – the status quo agreements (and others that followed) granted Jewish Orthodoxy authority and included restrictions on personal choices.

The changes described earlier and elaborated on in the book have made it difficult to maintain these restrictions as new needs and demands have emerged and different entrepreneurs have attempted to foster change, in both formal and nonformal channels. Although struggles for civil marriage and burial can be described as "ideological" and those for the sale of nonkosher meat and commerce on the Sabbath as "commercial," in practice these distinctions have often collapsed in the process of change. Entrepreneurs, as this study demonstrates, employ a variety of motivations, goals, ideologies, and strategies that do not necessarily fall into neat categories.

As elsewhere, secularization in Israel is a multifaceted process that interacts with religion rather than eliminates it from public and private realms. Religious institutions retain some of their powers and regain new powers, religious organizations struggle against secularization, and individuals oscillate between religious and secular choices. Rather than adopt a coherent religious or secular identity, the majority of Jewish Israelis continue to maintain at least some beliefs, identities, and practices that can be described as religious – often alongside secular ones. Regardless of the meaning individuals attribute to their desires, choices, demands, and

actions, in practice those may defy religious authority. This dynamic reality, described sometimes as "post-secular," presents challenges to political
systems in countries when the old rules of the game cannot contain the
new and often conflicting demands. In Israel, this dynamic reality has
stood in stark contrast to a deadlocked political system unable either
to maintain the old rules of the game or to establish new agreed rules.
Consequently, the religious–secular struggles gradually shifted to other
realms we explore in the following chapters.

Main Argument and Methodology

The main argument developed in this book can be summarized as follows. Institutional arrangements of religion and state (the status quo)
in Israel are challenged by contemporary changes – economic, political,
and demographic – so that a discrepancy emerges between the formal
authority of religious institutions and new needs and demands that stem
from these changes. Secular entrepreneurs, with different motivations
and goals, attempt to provide solutions not only through formal political struggles, but also, when facing a deadlocked system, through the
legal system and initiatives that take place outside formal politics. The
latter, often taking advantage of changes associated with globalization,
circumvent rather than confront existing institutional arrangements and
gradually alter them. Institutional changes, therefore, take place either
through alternative channels of political struggle or through personal
choices devoid of an explicit political goal. Studying these developments
requires, first, mapping and tracing secular entrepreneurs and their goals,
strategies, and actions, and, second, examining how these initiatives cor-
respond with popular needs and demands.

A combined methodological approach, using both qualitative and
quantitative measures, is used in this empirical study of secularization.
The first part of the research is a mapping exercise based on secondary
materials: newspaper archives, the Internet, and published works. Specifically, this part of the research (a) traces, through media reports and
Internet sources, the main agents involved; (b) studies the different organizations and the initiatives taken by them; and (c) detects critical political
and judicial decisions relevant to these initiatives. This mapping provides
for the second part of this work, a series of about forty in-depth interviews of the agents identified (see the Bibliography for a list of interviewees quoted in the book). These open-ended interviews with "secular entrepreneurs" provided (a) information about the background of
the agents/entrepreneurs and their worldviews and perceptions of church

and state relations, (b) information about the goals and strategies of their operation, (c) reports of their relations with state and religious institutions and how those influence the strategies chosen, (d) details of the constituencies at which their initiatives aim and of attempts to widen their influence, (e) reports of their subjective assessment of their impact and future potential among new constituencies, and (f) details of their perceptions of other agents/entrepreneurs and of the overall impact that secularization initiatives have on Israeli state and society. The interviews, combined with archival sources and media coverage, provide a rich description of the perceptions, actions, and relations between different entrepreneurs and initiatives.

The third part of the research, a detailed survey of the Israeli Jewish public conducted in April 2009, complements the interviews with an overview of the public's perception of different aspects of religion and state in Israel. Respondents were asked about the different aspects of beliefs, preferences, and practices related to religion and the role of religion in public life. The empirical data enable the analysis of the different categories of secularization and present a multidimensional picture of what it means to be secular in Israel. The survey data are supplemented by other surveys conducted by different agencies – most importantly, the Israeli Central Bureau of Statistics. Following the survey, another set of twenty in-depth interviews was conducted with people surveyed to add depth to the statistical data.

Five central questions occupy every one of the empirical chapters of the book. (1) What is the institutional setting (or the "rules of the game") formed in early statehood and what restrictions does this setting imply? (2) What challenges did demographic and economic changes present to this institutional setting? (3) Which secular entrepreneurs attempted to answer new needs and demands against the status quo? (4) What strategies were adopted by secular entrepreneurs? (5) What was their impact on existing institutions and public perceptions? These rather specific questions help explain, first, how new secular motivations and strategies emerge and, second, whether this multidimensional process of secularization is likely to be followed by secularism, namely, a liberal and tolerant societal order.

Outline of the Book

The theoretical framework for the book is set in the following chapter to resolve, theoretically, the puzzles and paradoxes that the study of secularization in Israel presents and to provide a comparative view of

Israeli secularization. This requires "unpacking" secularization by three theoretical distinctions. First, *secularization* as a process is distinguished from *secularism* as a worldview or ideology. Second, secularization as the decline of religious authority is distinguished from a personal decline in religious belief and identity. Third, institutional change is extended beyond formal political channels to various society-level initiatives and the incremental impact of personal changes. This secularization – the result of external economic and nonprincipled societal transformations – is loosely related to principled liberal values, a coherent secular identity, and liberal political commitments, but amounts to a significant challenge to religious authority. Following Ulrich Beck the focus is shifted from the formal to new political channels of influence "outside and beyond the representative institutions of the political system of nation-states" (Beck, 1996:18).

Chapter 2 merges the theoretical framework developed in the previous chapter with the history of religion and the state in Israel and the contemporary discrepancy between arrangements formed in early statehood and a dynamic secularization process. The general trajectory of secularization is explained by forces that emerged – neoliberalism and consumer society, the mass immigration from the FSU, and various cultural demands for recognition. These new demands and desires were often loosely related to an ideological secularism or a secular identity and more to everyday life needs and desires. The struggle between those forces and counter-religious forces (new and old) translated to various subpolitical actions that occurred outside formal political channels. This general framework is replicated in the following four chapters. Each chapter describes the institutional setting and religious restrictions and the "mismatch" between the rules of the game and new developments. Secular entrepreneurs, detailed in each case, take action to promote change in formal political channels or through the courts. Eventually, however, as demonstrated in each chapter, actions take advantage of loopholes, circumvent rules and regulations, and undermine religious authority.

Marriage patterns and their change are the subject of Chapter 3. Marriage is not only a private choice of two individuals but also, defined and regulated by religious and political authorities, an institution that guarantees the right to a domain of privacy, which itself is defined by public policy (Josephson, 2005). The modern state not only provides an official seal for marriage, but is also involved in its regulation through licensing, distributing benefits, and overseeing duties of the marriage, as well as the process of its dissolution (Eichner, 2006). As with other societal institutions, however, marriage in the Western world has also been affected by changes in recent years, losing its mandatory status and becoming more flexible. In Israel, marriage controlled by Orthodoxy is a major source of resentment for secular Israelis and a practical problem for a large number of Russian immigrants not recognized as Jews, who therefore cannot marry in Israel. Some secular entrepreneurs have attempted to change existing laws through legislation and the courts, but have so far achieved little. However, new initiatives, based on ideological or economic motivations, provide alternatives of marriage abroad, contractual marriage, and secular or non-Orthodox ceremonies that challenge religious authority and provide an outlet for a growing number of Israelis.

Chapter 4 explores the changes in burial and funeral arrangements, another issue related to the secular demand to choose and design significant rituals. The modern state, as part of the nation-building process, became a party to the design of the rituals of funeral and burial as well as for more mundane responsibilities of the public provision of services and resources required. In Israel, the state entrusted funeral and burial services to religious authorities that enforced an Orthodox procession on the Jewish public and limited alternative rituals. The Orthodox monopoly over burial was another source of resentment for secular Israelis who demanded to take charge of their own funerals or those of their loved ones. This included both the rituals and ceremonies and the aesthetic aspects of the burial, especially the demand to be buried in a coffin, forbidden by Jewish Orthodoxy in Israel. The growing, but still small, demand of secular Israelis to be buried the way they chose was supplanted by the concrete needs of non-Jewish immigrants who were refused burial by the Orthodox cemeteries. Struggles in the political and legal spheres were partially successful in this case, but no less important was the rise of a private burial industry that provided the aesthetic needs and ritual freedoms for those who could afford the price.

For many years, pork was all but banned in Israel as a result of religious objections and limited demand. This began to change in the 1990s, as Chapter 5 shows, when the FSU immigration and a growing connoisseur culture raised the demand for nonkosher products, including pork. Secular entrepreneurs until the 1990s found different loopholes that allowed them to produce and sell pork and struggled with religious attempts to restrict their operations. Whereas the incentive to operate was economic, the political struggles to prevent their closure were couched in the language of liberal freedoms and republican rights, pitted against what was described as "religious coercion." Since the 1990s, the high demand for pork and the neoliberal setting have rendered the political struggle unnecessary. Even though the formal rules have not changed, the loopholes proved sufficient, as the number of supermarkets and restaurants that serve pork attest. Struggles, initiated by religious entrepreneurs, have shifted to local arenas in an attempt to keep the sale of pork outside religious neighborhoods.

Commerce on the Sabbath, the subject of Chapter 6, is a marked indication of the erosion of the status quo and the growing rift between religious and nonreligious Israelis who hold different interpretations of the Sabbath. The regulation of the day of rest is a challenge for secularizing and multicultural societies when differences between groups on the day and its public meaning are contested. The declaration of the Sabbath as the official day of rest was one of the tenets of the status quo that restricted commercial activity on the Sabbath. Struggles until the 1980s were largely about secular demands to allow cultural activities on the Sabbath. However, the expansion of consumer culture encouraged secular entrepreneurs to find different loopholes that enabled the operation of businesses on the Sabbath, catering to the desires of many Israelis. Consequently, commerce on Sabbath, like the trade in pork, was powered by economic considerations, but its expansion required even less political action or legal protection. Rather, as the change in perceptions toward the Sabbath included a majority of Israelis and as the decision to shop was almost completely separated from ideology, entrepreneurs could operate almost without interference and the Sabbath, in practice and despite religious objections, became a day for shopping.

Contrary to the stagnant political sphere, in which rules and regulations hardly change, a vibrant civil society in Israel was the setting for various secular alternatives that shift the debates and struggles to new arenas. Secular marriage, secular cemeteries, the sale of pork, and commerce on the Sabbath are all evidence of changes that occur in Israeli public life, all with limited political involvement or interference. But what is the overall impact of this process? And, more important, what are its limitations? In Chapter 7, the concluding chapter of this work, the gap between secularism and secularization will be discussed, reflecting on the findings detailed throughout the book.

Acknowledgments

This research was a long journey – probably longer than I expected. Several institutions and individuals have provided the financial, intellectual, and moral support that made it possible. The field research was supported by research grants from the Israel Foundations Trustees, the Israel

Science Foundation (grant 1041–07), and the Posen Foundation. Their support that has made this research possible is highly appreciated. I was fortunate to have Omri Shamir as my research assistant for this project. His meticulous work, precision, and common sense were of great value to me. Maurice Herman translated parts of this work from Hebrew to English, and his professional work and questions helped reshape some of the concepts discussed here. Fany Yuval helped me make sense of the data collected, often seeing more than I did.

About fifteen years ago, while I was a graduate student at Johns Hopkins, I attended a course by William Connolly titled "Why I Am Not a Secularist." I am, in spite of this course, (still) very much a secularist but also deeply indebted to Bill for exposing the shaky ground on which secularism often stands and the constant need for critical self-reflection. I came back to this topic a few years later as a lecturer at Ben-Gurion University. A sabbatical year at the University of California, Davis, enabled me to put together my initial thoughts and turn the collected data into a manuscript. Not only the tranquility of California, but also the support of my colleagues – Diane Wolf, David Beale, and Zeev Maoz – contributed to the work. In Israel, my own department of Public Policy and Administration was a strong base of support. I want to thank my colleagues, past and present: Shlomo Mizrahi, Arye Naor, Fany Yuval, Miki Malul, Eran Manes, Ofir Rubin, Ruhama Reshef, and Liel Shalev. Colleagues from the business faculty have often been puzzled over this research but nevertheless have been supportive. My work at the Van Leer Institute in Jerusalem has been immensely important and intellectually rewarding, and the research groups I was involved with provided inspiration and new ideas.

I have had the fortune to present this research at several international conferences. Usually, Jeff Haynes was there. His insights and friendship are appreciated. Yariv Feniger provided valuable assistance and many insights at different stages of this project. Many friends and colleagues have contributed in the various stages of this research: Yochi Fischer, Michael Shalev, Mark Blyth, Bryan Turner, Barry Kosmin, Gad Barzilai, Uri Ram, Jonathan Anson, Yossi Yona, Jose Casanova, Manfred Brocker, Gideon Katz, Michael Philippov, Menny Mautner, Orna Sasson-Levy, Zeev Shavit, Yagil Levy, Ioannis Grigoriadis, Istar Gozaydin, and John Hall. Their advice and insights were invaluable. The responsibility for this book is entirely mine.

A special thanks for the team at Cambridge University Press. Marigold Acland supported this project from its start, and her professional manner and that of the rest of the staff were both helpful and encouraging.

Moral support comes from the ones closest to you. I am grateful to Rachel, Amir, Anat, Nadav, Segev, and Erez for being there. My loving and lovely daughters, Shira and Talia, always provide just enough distraction to make work enjoyable. Above all, I am fortunate to have my partner, Neta, whose love and patience enabled this work and so many other things.

In my third year of graduate school at Johns Hopkins, Giovanni Arrighi joined the department of sociology and agreed to be my dissertation adviser. His wisdom and intellect could have been paralyzing, if not for his grace, patience, collegiality, and good humor. Giovanni passed away in 2009. As always, I hope this work lives up to his standards.

I

Unpacking Secularization

Almost half a century ago, the theologian Harvey Cox made the important distinction between secularization and secularism:

Secularization implies a historical process, almost certainly irreversible...
[whereas] secularism...is the name for an ideology, a new closed world-view
which functions very much like a new religion. (Cox, 1965: 20)

The irreversibility of secularization envisioned by Cox, and other scholars of that period, was somewhat premature, as religious persistence and vitality proved in the following decades. However, theorizing secularization in terms of a secularizing social process rather than in terms of an ideology of secular liberalism (Cady, 2005) provides for a better understanding of the multidimensionality and the inherent contradictions of the process. Most important, it may enable one to comprehend how seemingly religious societies can be secularizing or how religion remains significant in seemingly secularizing societies. As discussed in the following chapters, Israel provides a fascinating example of secularization in a state in which religion maintains a significant formal role over public and private life and a society in which secularism (measured in a liberal worldview and commitment) remains rather weak. Some of the developments in Israel, however, have parallels elsewhere, if at different paces and intensities. This chapter sets the theoretical framework for the rest of the book by unpacking the concept of secularization, the forces and motivations behind it, and the way it unfolds.

Studies of secularization have tended to focus on ideological–liberal struggles for freedom and on changes of formal political arrangements that institutionalize religious authority. Secularization for this work is first and foremost a decline of religious authority (Chaves, 1994) measured in an institutional change that may or may not be registered in formal political processes. The replacement of religious authority by political and economic institutions – the modern state and the capitalist economy – involved struggles that led to institutional arrangements in which labor and authority were divided between religious and secular organizations. But the stability of these institutions was often temporary as – following social, political, and economic changes – new struggles and challenges emerged. Globalization, neoliberalism, and consumer culture are especially important, as they create not only new and stronger motivations to challenge existing and limiting institutions, but also new opportunities for "secular entrepreneurs" to promote change. This secularization, the result of external, economic, and nonprincipled societal transformations, is loosely related to core liberal values, a coherent secular identity, and liberal political commitments, but nevertheless amounts to a significant challenge to religious authority.

The decline of religious authority is neither complete nor linear. Rather, religions across the world maintain hold over significant aspects of private and public life, and religious organizations continue to struggle, often successfully, over political power. Secularization, however, often based on the changes described above advances not necessarily through social–political struggle, underpinned by a coherent ideology, and not necessarily through formal political changes. Yet, this secularization can undermine both religious authority and the institutional arrangements that secure it.

Five arguments developed in this chapter set the theoretical framework for the rest of this book. First, in contrast to a uniform and coherent secularism, secularization unfolds in inconsistent sets of beliefs, practices, and values. Second, secularization is driven not only by an ideology, but often also through "practices of everyday life" when people engage in leisure activities and consumption habits that violate religious codes but, at the same time, often refuse to define themselves as secular. Third, globalization and the expanding consumer culture challenge existing religion–state arrangements and encourage secular entrepreneurs and individuals to contest religious-imposed limitations. Fourth, although secularization is a political process that involves an institutional change, it is not necessarily a "political project" that involves coherent goals and a coordinated strategy. Rather, it is made of different initiatives and choices of entrepreneurs and individuals with different goals, strategies, and commitments.Finally, fifth, as a result of contemporary developments, this secularization often takes place outside formal politics and, therefore, might be overlooked by observers who underestimate its significance.

Secularization: from Inevitable to Debatable

The death of religion was envisioned by many Western intellectuals and by the founding figures of sociology who predicted a world in which religion will lose its hold over public and private lives. C. Wright Mills succinctly summarized the expectations: "Once the world was filled with the sacred – in thought, practice and institutional form. After the reformation and the Renaissance, the forces of modernization swept across the globe and secularization, a corollary historical process, loosened the dominance of the sacred. In due course, the sacred shall disappear altogether except, possibly, in the private realm" (Mills, 1959: 32; quoted in Hadden, 1987). Secularization, derived from the Latin *saeculum*, meaning an era and later "the world," came to be associated, following Max Weber, with the process of the rationalization of action coupled with modern-world rationality (Swatos and Christiano, 1999). In some accounts, known as "secularization theory," secularization was almost the inevitable outcome of modernization that would necessarily lead to the decline of religion, both in society and in the minds of individuals (Berger, 1996).

Embedded in the broader theoretical framework of modernization theory, secularization theory proposed that as industrialization, urbanization, rationalization, and religious pluralism increased, religiosity would decline, both in society and in the minds of individuals (Berger, 1996; Hadden, 1987; McClay, 2001). Dynamics of rationalization, a process in which social spheres operate according to their own standards, undermines transcendentally anchored worldviews and institutions (Lechner, 1991). Alongside the Weberian rationalist argument a related explanation, originating from the work of Emile Durkheim, attributed secularization to a process of functional differentiation (Norris and Inglehart, 2004: 9). Functional differentiation of modern industrialized societies entails the evolution of professionals and organizations that perform tasks previously provided by churches. Stripped of their core social purposes, Durkheim predicted, religious institutions will gradually waste away in industrial societies, left with only specific, and often not binding, responsibility for performing the formal rites of births, marriages, and deaths, and the observance of special holidays (Norris and Inglehart, 2004: 9).

Bereft of its privileged, dominant position, religion is to become only one institution among others (Dobbelaere, 1981) as many of its traditional responsibilities are carried out by "professionals" or state bureaucrats. Bureaucratized states that assume power exercise rational-legal authority, no longer rest on religious legitimacy, separate civil and ecclesiastical spheres, and control resources previously managed by churches. The political community's boundaries are also not necessarily based on religious exclusiveness as inclusion on the basis of citizenship has transformed the meaning of membership. Finally, whereas in the past religious institutions and elites maintained clear standards of transcendent belief relevant to all spheres of cultural activity, in modern life science, art and morality no longer require any religious grounding (Lechner, 1991: 1104). Overall, the disengagement of religion from the public sphere, political life, and aesthetic life and its retreat to a private world would limit its authority to its followers (Bell, 1980).

Secularization theory came under attack from scholars who found its claims and predictions unsubstantiated. Religion was hard to ignore or to be dismissed as a private matter as, since the 1970s, new and old religious movements were growing across the world and religion emerged (or reemerged) as a vital force in world politics. The Moral Majority in the United States, the Iranian revolution, or Pentecostalism in South America were a few of the indications that religion continued to play an important role in public and private lives and in politics. In the so-called third world, religious resurgence was explained by the failure of modern secular ideologies and of the new regimes associated with these ideologies (Jurgensmeyer, 1995), but the salience of religion was not confined to one part of the world. Religion, religious identity, and religious behavior manifested themselves in different places not only in relation to the supernatural but also through national and ethnic identities providing a sense of "primordial continuity" (Demerath, 2000; Mitchell, 2006). Consequently, religious politics and tensions remained potent and became one of the characteristics of the post-Cold War era (Jurgensmeyer, 1995). Furthermore, in some cases religious institutions maintained their significance as "vicarious religion" when active minorities performed religious rituals, embodied moral codes, and offered a religious space for a larger number of citizens (Davie, 2007) who continued to identify with religion and to seek religious services in significant or critical periods of their lives. Most important, politically, since the 1980s scholars have been witnessing the de-privatization of religions that refused to accept a marginal and privatized role and often became a significant political force (Casanova, 1994: 5).

The strongest criticism of secularization theory was leveled by research findings that indicated the significant role religion continued to hold over individual lives, leading scholars to argue that secularization never happened, or at most was confined to Western Europe. The supply-side or religious economics model defines secularization as a decline in aggregate levels of religious demand, yet to be found. In the United States, the strongest evidence against secularization theory was found in the numbers of Americans who report they believe in God, church attendance, and prayer, so that "no evidence to support a decisive shift either towards or away from religion" was found (Hadden, 1987). These findings, it was argued, not only undermine secularization theory – because the United States was indisputably modern but not secular – but also explain the stable demand for religion. In the United States, according to the economic model, separation of church and state led to pluralism, competition, specialization, recruitment efficiency, and higher demand, not to secularization. The secularization of Europe, the real anomaly, was explained by the lack of a free market, or the existence of monopolies, that limited choices and participation (Iannaccone, 1995). Moreover, even in the secular Europe, where church membership was low, more than two-thirds of people described themselves as "a religious person" (Stark and Finke, 2000: 33; see also Berger, 1996; Keddie, 2003; Wallis and Bruce, 1989). The fact that religion remained a potent social force therefore underscored the suggestions that secularization as a concept be abandoned altogether and dropped from all theoretical discourse (Stark, 1996, Stark and Iannacone, 1994: 231). Even Peter Berger, one of the leading scholars of secularization theory, admitted in 1999 that the assumption that we live in a secular world is false and that counter-secularization is at least as important a phenomenon in the current world as secularization (Berger, 1999: 6).

Defenders of secularization theory relied not only on other empirical evidence that indicated the erosion of religion in individual lives and in political influence (Voas and Crocket, 2005; Kosmin and Keysar, 2009) but also on theoretical premises that argued that critics of the theory failed to grasp its essential value. Secularization theory, they argued, does not predict a demise of individual religiosity but a decline of religious authority (Chaves, 1994). Consequently, the persistence of individual religiosity in itself does not rule out secularization when the latter is measured in the functional significance of religion. Secularization and religiosity, therefore, are not mutually exclusive. Rather, first, secularization and secularity are always relative to some definition of religion or the religious (Swatos and Christiano, 1999). Second, religious ideas and practices can be present even when they are "neither theologically pure nor socially insulated" (Ammerman, 2007: 6) and are held and practiced in different ways and with varying levels of commitment. Third, similarly, secularization can be present even when individuals remain believers or continue to practice religion in specific ways.

Complex and nuanced frameworks have been developed that treat secularization as a multidimensional process and distinguish different levels of analysis (Gorski and Altmordu, 2008): *macro-level processes of differentiation* (sometimes described as *laicization*) in which religion loses its primary overarching status over other institutional spheres such as politics and the economy and the latter are "emancipated" from religious institutions and norms (Casanova, 2006; Dobbelaere, 1999); *meso-level processes* (internal secularization) in which religious organizations adapt to the secular world and a "religious market" emerges in which religions compete for the souls of people; and *micro, individual-level* changes in beliefs, identities, affiliations, and practices, often with internal inconsistencies or even contradictions (Beckford, 2002; Dobbelaere, 1999; Norris and Inglehart, 2004; Swatos and Christiano, 1999). On the micro, individual level, the deregulation of the religious realm, combined with a cultural emphasis on freedom and choice, leads to intermingled and interfused forms of religion or a "bricolage" of beliefs, practices, and values. Studies in Europe demonstrate that, on one hand, a reduction in church attendance does not necessarily lead to the adoption of secular alternatives and, on the other hand, most people who perceive themselves as religious do not feel any obligation to attend church on Sunday (Davie, 1994). "Believing without belonging" and an individual patchwork of beliefs or a "religion à la carte" are all examples of the religious bricolage that defines contemporary Western societies that enables both individual and religious institutions to borrow, pick, choose, and imitate (Beckford, 2007; Dobbelaere, 1999; Lambert, 1999).

The disaggregation of the concept of secularization opens up the possibility of a more nuanced and empirical study of both the declining role of religion in society vis-à-vis other systems (political and economic) and the role of religion in individual lives (measured by beliefs, practices, and values). Moreover it allows, coming to a full circle, an understanding of the complexities of modernization as a multifaceted process, of plural and multiple modernities (Eisenstadt, 2000) with varying relations to religion and religiosity. Modernization, in other words, can influence, generate, and contain both secularization and religious revival. The complexity of contemporary religious–secular relations is a reminder that modernity does not necessarily bring about secularization, but can bring pluralism (Berger, Davie, and Fokas, 2008: 12). This pluralism, intensified by globalization, creates a religious market that, on one hand, can strengthen individual religiosity but, on the other hand, can undermine the authority of traditional religious institutions. We may, as several scholars suggested, be entering a post-secular age in which religious and secular worldviews and ways of life coexist (Gorski and Alinordu, 2008) alongside struggles for power and influence. In this age, more than before, "religious" and "secular" are not zero-sum realities (Ammerman, 2007: 9), so religion can continue to play a role in society regardless of its formal standing (Davie, 2007) and vice versa.

What then, is being secularized? Secularization, as Mark Chaves suggests, is most productively conceived as a "decline in religious authority" and the decrease in the influence of religious values, leaders, and institutions over individual behavior, social institutions, and public discourse (Chaves, 1994). The influence of these processes on individual indicators of religiosity – belief or practices – remains an open question, but secularization need not imply that most individuals relinquish all their interest in religion (Chaves, 1994; Lechner, 1991). Religion, according to this argument, may still have a hold on private beliefs and practices, but secularization will unfold in societal changes that involve a decline of religious authority over significant spheres of life. It is hard to imagine that societal change could occur without individual change or that it would not affect individual change, and vice versa. These changes, however, in spite of their interrelatedness, may occur at different paces and depths and be driven by different forces, as discussed later. Secularization, by this definition, is neither universal, linear, nor deterministic. Rather, the multiple trajectories of religious and secular with their particular histories and politics can be conceived as an institutional change that pertains to political authority.

Secularization, Religion, and Politics: a Neoinstitutional Framework

Scholars of political science had tended to neglect the study of religion until it assumed new prominence in the late 1970s, but even then they tended to focus on specific events or groups that drew attention by their actions (Wald, Silverman, and Fridy, 2005). As a social phenomenon that extends beyond individual belief and private spiritual preferences, religion is always political to some degree and, accordingly, requires a general theory of its political roles and its politicization (ibid.). Religious institutions in search of power can become "political," politicians in search of support can turn to religion, and religious and political institutions can compete as both claim to give authoritative answers to important questions in "oughts" and terms of commands (Haynes, 1998; Heclo, 2001). In *Politics and Religion*, Steve Bruce includes in "politics" the nature and actions of states and governments, political parties, actions of groups intended to influence governments, and the basic liberties states are supposed to protect (Bruce, 2003: 9). In these debates, church (or any other religious organization) and state may stand in a mutual supportive relationship to one another or religious and political authorities can assume opposed or independent roles (Jelen and Wilcox, 2002: 7).

Explanations for the decline and resurgence of religion in politics tend to rely on ideational factors (Gill and Keshavarzian, 1999) and focus on the formal aspects of politics and decision-making processes where states create rules and enforce them. This focus may be limited, as identifying politics, religious or other, solely with the state and its institutions might overlook negotiations, interactions, and resistances that occur elsewhere (Migdal, 2001: 15). Understanding of the dynamics of politics and political change must widen the scope of and locus of politics so political activity is not only what is openly declared and visible and observed in direct engagements between rulers and elites (Singerman, 1995:14). Changes in religion's role in and authority over public life are the result not only of direct initiatives registered as "political" but also of incremental changes of practices, nonideological choices, and of initiatives outside the "formal" political sphere. Neoinstitutional theory provides a convenient framework for understanding the complex dynamics of religion and politics and the different realms of secularization. The theory

> bridges the gap between the macro-level (structural) and micro-levels (individual behavior and beliefs) of social life by examining how institutions and their myths create social roles, the authority adhering to these roles, and the scripted behavior and knowledge of individuals who enact them. (McMullen, 1994: 711)

Institutions, in this framework, refer to the systems of values, norms, and practices that exist in every society and influence preferences, choices, and actions of groups and individuals, acting as a "set of cultural rules that give generalized meaning to social activity and regulate it in a patterned way" (Meyer, Boli, and Thomas, 1987: 36). Institutions include not only formal government and overarching state structures but also the normative social order that (together with formal institutions) provide the context in which individuals and groups interact with authorities, make choices and strategies, and wage political struggles. Institutionalization, then, is a set of processes that make authority and rules seem natural and taken for granted and eliminate alternative interpretations and regulations (ibid.). The scope of control exercised by religious authority (Chaves, 1994), therefore, can be described in institutional terms that pertain to "formal rules, compliance procedures and standard operating practices" (Hall, 1986: 19). Similarly, secularization, a challenge that undermines religious authority, can be understood as an institutional change.

Institutions are explained as the result either of a deliberate choice of rational agents interested in efficient and stable rules of the game or as an unintended outcome of the interaction between agents, interests, ideas, and existing institutions. Established at particular moments in history, in response to particular needs, demands, and compromises, institutions tend to persist (Ikenberry 1988: 31) so that they provide a context in which most "normal politics is conducted" (Hall, 1986). Institutions are associated with stability, order, and "path dependency" that structure actions and reactions of agents. But, because institutions emerge at different times and out of different historical configurations they may not "fit together into a coherent, self-reinforcing, let alone functional, whole" (Thelen, 1999). These internal contradictions allow for institutional change when opportunities for those disadvantaged by existing institutional arrangements are opened. Alterations in domestic and international environments may undermine stability (Krasner, 1984: 224) by shaking institutions' material and ideational foundations. These alterations signal to involved parties that the rules of the game have become less binding and encourage them to change their preferences, goals, and strategies. A careful analysis is required not only of ideas that drive the change, but also of the "larger social, economic and political context in which these ideas are situated" (Peters, Pierre, and King, 2005). Change can be the result either of moments when institutions lose their grip and rapid change occurs in what has been described as "punctuated equilibrium" (Krasner, 1984) or from incremental change and shifts of context that are less dramatic but no less significant in outcomes.

The role of religion in social and political life is institutionalized through processes of struggles, negotiations, and political compromises that establish religious authority and define its scope. These political compromises are often endowed with specific formal institutional designs that define the division of authority between the religious and the political but also translate into informal rules that define norms and structure choices and behavior of individuals. These institutions, like others, can be challenged when their material and ideational foundations are shaken. Foundations differ from one state to another and, consequently, differ in their resilience to external changes and internal pressures. In addition, secularization within states unfolds differently along ethnic and other identities in which religion performs different roles. Incremental changes of beliefs, values, and practices may gradually lead to institutional change. Significant institutional changes can occur outside formal political processes and institutions so a gap is formed between the formal rules and everyday behavior. Thus, historical processes and conditions have institutionalized rules and norms, religious or secular, which differ from place to place. Changes – economic, cultural, and demographic – create new incentives and opportunities for groups and individuals to challenge the status quo, as the Israeli case studied here demonstrates.

Political Arrangements: Religion and the State

The *cuius regio, eius religio* (as the ruler, so the religion) principle has turned into a tenet of religious tolerance and state neutrality toward privatized religion (Casanova, 1994: 22). The secularization of the modern state advanced as states freed themselves from dependency and obligations toward religious authorities. Not only did the modern state take over many of the functions of religious institutions and limited the role of religion in public life, but it also found new sources of legitimacy independent from religious institutions. This secular state, in Poggi's words, "disclaims any responsibility for fostering the spiritual wellbeing of its subjects/citizens or the welfare of religious bodies, and treats as irrelevant for its own purposes the religious beliefs and the ecclesiastical standing of individuals" (Poggi, 1990: 20). Politically, secularization could be observed in several transformations in the basic relationship between politics and religion. *Constitutionally*, the official character of the state is no longer defined in religious terms. In *policy terms*, the state ceases to regulate society on the basis of religious criteria and expands its policy domains to areas previously controlled by religious institutions. *Institutionally*, religious institutions lose their political significance as pressure groups, parties, and movements. In *agenda settings*, needs and problems cease to have an overt religious content. Finally, *ideologically*, values and belief systems used to evaluate the political ream are no longer couched in religious terms (Moyser, 1991: 14–15).

The weakening of the institutional status of religion and the privatization of religion have supposedly turned politics into a secular realm of rational decision making that limits the chances for religious contentions and saves society from religious wars. Religious agendas, when they exist, are promoted by democratic means and, therefore, reflect the general will (Safran, 2003). Because most democracies are formally secular, their modern bureaucracies "managed national systems of education, social control and social welfare that paid little attention to religious affiliation and claimed little by way of divine approval" (Bruce, 2003: 1). The churches that remained "established" within states often found themselves caught between a secular state that no longer needed them and between people no longer confined to churches and able to make private choices regarding their religious needs (Casanova, 1994: 22).

Religion, however, as discussed previously, often remains important in modern states, so religious organizations hold political power and authority, formal and informal. States often deviate from the secular formula of church–state separation and grant religion official status and roles, give preferential treatment to some or all religions, place restrictions on minority religious practices, fund and regulate religious institutions, and legislate on religious affairs (Fox, 2008). Religious institutions, in turn, often hold informal authority through their affiliations with ethnicity, political power, or moral order, as well as formal authority through the responsibilities allocated to them by the state. The role of religion and religious institutions in politics reflects not only the mere presence of religious voices in the political debates but also the impact of religious actors on the enactment and application of religious (or religious-influenced) laws (Yamane, 1997).

Religious authority over public and private lives is the outcome of particular struggles, negotiations, and compromises that set the institutional "rules of the game." This institutional arrangement establishes the formal relations between religious organizations, the state, and its citizens. They include the roles that religious organizations perform in public life and their authority over different spheres (family life, rituals, or education) and individuals (religious or secular). This institutional order, however, can destabilize and change when social, political, and economic contexts change and with them the preferences of groups and individuals. These changes, as discussed in the following text, may or may not be part of a coherent secular ideology.

Between Secularism and Secularization

Secularization is often presented as a struggle and an ideological victory of liberalism that ended in a pluralist public sphere with a shared and neutralized language that secures individual freedom. This description, gladly adopted by secularists, seems to conflate secularization as a process with secularism (or secularity), an ideology or a worldview (Cox, 1965), a political project, or the outcome of a completed secularization process. Secularization, in this narrative, is a story of freedom and progress in which science, arts, the economy, and politics are released from religion's control and a neutral public sphere guarantees those freedoms. In the same vein, politically, secularization is a separation of church and state by a "wall" protecting liberties and equalities (Walzer, 1984) that secures a democratic, free society committed to individual rights, respect, and tolerance. In Sartori's (1995) words:

Secularization occurs when the realm of God and the realm of Caesar – the sphere of religion and the sphere of politics – are separated. As a result, politics is no longer reinforced by religion: it loses both its religion-derived rigidity (dogmatism) and its religious-like intensity. Out of this situation arise the conditions for the taming of politics. By this I mean that politics no longer kills, is no longer a warlike affair, and that peacelike politics affirms itself as the standard *modus operandi* of a polity.

Adopting the secular narrative of liberty and freedom overlooks the possibility that secularization was also a consequence of socioeconomic change that "occurred involuntarily as an autonomous and largely endogenous process and as an unintended and perhaps unanticipated consequence of that more fundamental process of change" (Wilson, 2001). This overlooked aspect of secularization separates it from secularism – an ideology – and is significant both for identifying the forces behind secularization and the consequences of the process. Secularization, as an institutional change measured by the decline of religious authority, advanced not only as an ideological battle between tolerance and liberalism but also as a set of practices associated with, on one hand, economic interests of entrepreneurs and, on the other hand, individual choices described as "practices of everyday life" (Ben-Porat and Feniger, 2009). The engagement in economic activities, leisure, and consumption can violate religious codes and defy religious authority, but does so without adoption of a secular identity or a commitment to a secular political project.

Liberalism and tolerance, the supposed outcome of secularization, are also questionable, as even secular ideology may fall short of its liberal promise. Secular ethics and institutions often bear the traces of their theological or ecclesiastical origins (Gorski and Alinordu, 2008), and Western secularism is often bound up with more generic characteristics of Christian culture than most of its proponents are willing to acknowledge (Ben-Porat, 2000). Thus, the tolerance associated with secularism, more often than not, was the result not of an ideological-liberal transformation but rather the application of rational principles of social organization that no longer saw religion as reinforcing political authority and legitimacy (Wilson, 2001: 46). The gap between secularism and liberal tolerance is often observed in national secular movements that adopt, explicitly or implicitly, religious symbols and, more important, religious boundaries. National movements, even explicitly secular ones, often display low levels of liberal tolerance in their quest for territorial sovereignty. Civil religions (Bellah, 1967), at times an alternative to "old" religions, provide nations with a sense of cohesion and solidarity as well as a moral understanding. They carry sets of sacred rights and symbols that resemble traditional religious ones, are impregnated with biblical imagery, and are embedded in religious moral understandings (Cristi and Dawson, 2007).

Nationalism and religious belief have much in common in their conception of purity, boundaries, and order. The affinity can underscore competition for authority between religion and the state but also provides a common ground of understanding and a mutual interest in protecting boundaries and punishing deviant or disloyal behavior. Secularism, in its liberal-national version, often ends up either redrawing the boundaries set by religion or invoking religion to demarcate boundaries that exclude and establish hierarchies. Consequently, when the national imagination is embedded in religion, regardless of contemporary religiosity, boundaries are likely to persist and liberal tolerance and equality may be secondary to state and societal commitment to those boundaries. Secularism, under these circumstances – and, even more so, secularization – will be at most loosely committed to a comprehensive and inclusive liberal political project.

The decline of religious authority, therefore, is often partial and nonlinear and is the result not only of a liberal, politically active and coordinated secularism but also of a changing context that affects existing institutions and forms the "opportunity structures" for their development (Safran, 2003: 10). To follow this nonideological secularization and the ways it undermines religious authority, focus must be shifted, first, from the political to the economic sphere and, second, from formal to informal political arenas.

All That Is Solid? Religion, Economy, and Secularization

The differentiation of modern societies along functional lines allowed the creation of independent domains with their own logic, emancipated from religious institutions and norms (Casanova, 2006). Especially significant was the functional rationality (Dobbelaere, 1999) of the economy that broke loose from religious constraints and later also from political ones. Unlike early capitalism that could coexist with religion, especially Protestantism, the modern capitalist economy disembedded itself from subordination to politics and religion. The capitalist market was proven unsusceptible to moral regulations; the modern economy, therefore, was a secularizing force that offset existing church–state institutional arrangements, rendering religious restrictions costly to maintain as capitalist markets become unsusceptible to moral regulation (Casanova, 1994: 23). Capitalism, as Karl Marx observed, was a revolutionizing but also a secularizing force that "melts all that is solid into air and profanes all that is holy" (Marx and Engels, 1848).

Religion and the economy often interact, as religion extends over major aspects of life and sets systems of beliefs, values, and practices that also influence economic transactions. Similarly, economic development sets rules that cannot avoid the contact with a dominant religion, and economic development can affect religious participation and belief (McCleary and Barro, 2006). Conflict between religious and economic institutions can be avoided when the limits religion places on economic activity do not interfere with economic development or are accepted by economic entrepreneurs as legitimate or unavoidable. Max Weber's *Protestant Ethic* articulated a possible compromise between religion and the emerging capitalist economy that benefited both and underscored an "intimate relationship" (Weber, 1958: 42). The Protestant ethic preached hard work, frugality, and investment not for the fulfillment of hedonist desires but as a moral duty of every individual, so acquisition becomes an end in itself. The work and profit under this spirit were perceived as a duty or a calling and private profit was a sign of virtue for if God "shows one of His elect a chance of profit, he must do it with a purpose" (ibid: 162).

The spirit of early capitalism combined a devotion to the earning of wealth and the legitimacy of profit with avoidance of the use of income for personal enjoyment (Giddens, 1971: 126). Taking advantage of the opportunity provided by God did not imply a life of idleness, leisure, or enjoyment, but rather the continuation of hard work that increases the glory of God and manifests his will (Weber, 1958: 157). This combination of restraints and opportunities, according to Weber, has provided capitalism with legitimacy, motivations, stability, and the ability to expand:

When the limitation of consumption is combined with this release of acquisitive activity, the inevitable result is obvious: accumulation of capital through ascetic compulsion to save. The restraints which were imposed upon the consumption of wealth naturally served to increase it by making possible the productive investment of capital. (Weber, 1958: 172)

This "moment" of asceticism and divine guidance, however, was soon replaced with modern capitalism and mechanical conformity to the economic and organizational exigencies of industrial production (Giddens, 1971: 130). Capitalist secularization, as Casanova (1994: 23), following Weber, explains, first shifted from the early puritan phase to the utilitarian phase, in which irrational compulsion turned into "sober economic virtue." Second, when capitalism began to rest on "mechanical foundations," it no longer needed religion and began to penetrate and colonize the religious sphere and subjected it to the "logic of commodification." The rising capitalism freed itself from the restrictions imposed by religion and undermined the power of the church as capitalism turned into a "liberated territory" with respect to religion (Berger, 1969: 129). In Weber's words:

Since asceticism undertook to remodel the world and to work out its ideals in the world, material goods have gained an increasing and finally an inexorable power over the lives of men as at no previous period in history. To-day the spirit of religious asceticism – whether finally, who knows? – has escaped from the cage. But victorious capitalism, since it rests on mechanical foundations, needs its support no longer . . . the pursuit of wealth, stripped of its religious and ethical meaning, tends to become associated with purely mundane passions, which often actually give it the character of sport. (Weber, 1958: 182)

The puritan capitalism based on modesty and frugality was replaced by a new capitalism disembedded from religious constraints and was overrun by the emerging consumer society. Modern consumerism, the cause and consequence of many social changes, had an adverse affect on the status of religion in economic and public life. The birth of consumer society in the eighteenth century meant the emergence of a demand side of the Industrial Revolution (McCracken, 1990: 4–5). The increase of prosperity brought by the economic growth meant new earnings available to larger groups of people, new goods offered, and new marketing procedures that used enticing methods to lure the new consumers (Stearns, 2006: 28–9).

Consumption, satisfying basic needs, was replaced by consumerism, a continued expansion of wants and intensity of desires (Bauman, 2007: 31) and a societal preoccupation with guilt-free purchase of goods for pleasure rather than survival or fulfillment of essential needs (Gabrial and Lang, 2006: 96).

The institutions established to regulate religion and politics, were challenged by a consumer culture often indifferent or intolerant to religious restrictions (Barber, 1992). Consumerism expanded from the old aristocracy to, first, the emerging bourgeoisie and, later, the working class with its new purchasing power and expanding desires to emulate the upper classes. By the eighteenth century, as the variety of available goods widened, needs and aspirations were redefined and the number of items people regarded as necessities began to expand (Stearns, 2006: 22). "Luxuries," in the emerging consumer society, came to be seen as mere "decencies," and "decencies" came to be seen as "necessities" (McKendrick, 1982: 1). Consequently, consumption "was beginning to take place more often, in more places, under new influences, by new groups, in pursuit of new goods, for new social and cultural purposes" (McCracken, 1990: 22). Consumerism began to spread to other aspects of life: leisure activities, holidays, exchanges of gifts, childbearing, and even emotional life (Stearns, 2006: 51–53). People in the new consumer society were offered not only what they needed, but also what they desired – and desires and needs were soon difficult to separate (Miles, 1998: 7).

These contradictions and tensions became ever more salient in the late twentieth century, when consumer culture became part and parcel of globalization. Shopping in the late twentieth century, to quote Benjamin Barber (1992), "has little tolerance for blue laws, whether dictated by pub-closing British paternalism, Sabbath-observing Jewish Orthodox, or no-Sunday liquor-sale Massachusetts Puritanism." Global consumer society offers a greater variety of commodities, more difficult to regulate, whose consumption is associated with lifestyle, pleasure, individual free choice, hedonism, comfort, and immediate gratification that erode religion's hold on public life when individual religious commitment is substituted for "consumer heaven" (Bauman, 1992: 50; Turner, 2008).

Globalization: New Game, New Rules?

The complex relations between the state, the economy, religious institutions, and secularization processes described previously are embedded in the past two decades in overarching changes described as *globalization*. Globalization has become a part of everyday lives, affecting (although in different ways and on different levels) each major aspect of social reality (Archer, 1990). A general description of globalization defines it as "a process (or set of processes) which embodies a transformation in the spatial organization of social relations and transactions – assessed in terms of their extent, intensity, velocity and impact – generating transcontinental or interregional flows and networks of activity, interaction, and the exercise of power" (Held et al., 1999:16). Globalization entails political–economic changes and the disembedding of markets from the hold of political institutions in favor of a neoliberal order and a self-regulating market. The neoliberal order underscores the erosion of borders and, possibly, adoption of flexible identities required to take advantage of the opportunities the global world offers. Old political institutions such as the state, according to this logic, will either disappear or (more likely) undergo significant change if they interfere with economic interests and individual desires. Consequently, allegiance to nation and state would be replaced or (more likely) challenged by a liberal cosmopolitan identity (Kobrin, 1998; Omhae, 1995; Rosecrance, 1996).

Religious institutions and religious–state institutional arrangements could be another victim of globalization and of an expanding global consumer culture in particular. Global culture has intensified both production and consumption, offering a seductive supply of a variety of goods, many of them produced and marketed by multinational companies often oblivious to "local" restrictions and sensitivities. On the demand side, global culture constantly creates new global consumers with desires (presented as needs) that may conflict with religious mores. Days of rest (see Chapter 6), for example, under pressures from consumers and business owners, can turn into shopping days instead of days devoted to prayer and religious activity.

Globalization, however, is not a linear secularization process (underscored by consumer culture) that erodes religion (Shamir and Ben-Porat, 2007). Flows across boundaries of people, technology, finance, images, and ideas, rather than being homogeneous and homogenizing, are, to use Appadurai's term, "disjunctured" (Appadurai, 1990), so that globalization does not "pound everything in the same mold" (Mittleman, 2000). Thus, globalization is a potential secularizing force that sets different challenges to religious authorities, but at the same time it provides motivation and opportunities for religious agents and groups to organize, use new information technologies to deliver their messages and bring together believers in the virtual space, and offer new religious identities based on beliefs and practices once thought of as incompatible (Hunt, 2005: 34–5). The new opportunities opened up for religion in the global world do not necessarily imply a peaceful adaptation and coexistence. Rather, sharp differences between religious and secular worldviews, and the refusal of religion to privatize, translate to sharp conflicts between religious and secular ways of life.

Religious identity, as do other "old" identities – ethnic, national or class – remain significant for many people (Gans, 1994; Mitchel, 2006) and organized religions struggle in a globalizing world to protect their turf and expand (Thomas, 2005: 27). Already in the 1980s "old" religions, assumed to have lost their stance, revitalized and "de-privatized," refusing to accept the marginal and privatized role reserved for them. Religions were part of movements that challenged secular spheres such as the state and market economy, took on themselves public and political roles, and demanded the reinstatement of religious considerations in the public policy decision-making process (Casanova, 1994: 5–6; Shup and Hadden, 1989). By the 1990s the clash between religion and secularization accentuated so that the post-Cold War world appeared to be a site of struggle between religious civilizations or between secular forces and religious fundamentalism (Haynes, 2006), raising the specter of a "culture war" (Hunter, 1991: 42–44).

The specter of culture war might be offset by the fact that secularization is driven not only by a coherent liberal ideology but also by economic incentives and the consumer culture. The consumer culture might conflict with religious restrictions but, because it is based on comfort and immediate gratification, it is questionable whether it carries the political commitment sufficient for a culture war. This gap, however, does not diminish the significance of religious–secular conflicts resulting either from religious reactions against global consumer culture or from struggles of secular ideologists to ensure liberal freedoms. Those struggles, even if they fall short of a culture war, are likely to continue and expand across the globe and challenge existing rules of the game. These conflicts will, first, focus on existing institutions – regulating relations between religious and secular and between church and state – no longer able to contain social and economic changes and demands. Second, conflicts will involve different entrepreneurs who do not necessarily describe themselves or their goals as "secular." And, third, they may extend beyond the scope of conventional political channels that are no longer found suitable to engage these struggles.

Secular Entrepreneurs

Globalization and the changes embedded in the process provide new incentives and opportunities to challenge existing arrangements – but secularization, defined as institutional change, could not evolve without agency or entrepreneurship, even if the latter do not explicitly identify themselves as secular. Economic entrepreneurs discover and exploit market opportunities in order to earn profits (Schneider and Teske, 1992). Political entrepreneurs require a more complicated utility function that includes terms related to policy success and status (ibid.) but also those related to political agendas that can be described as "ideological." These entrepreneurs, "individuals whose creative acts have transformative effects on politics, policies and institutions" (Sheingate, 2003), use available resources and political expertise to foster change in directions they favor. Political entrepreneurs can come either from within the political system (politicians or bureaucrats) or from outside (social movements or lobbyists), in both cases seeking a change of the political status quo (Meydani, 2010). Consequently, studies of political entrepreneurship focus on agenda setting, cost–benefit calculations, strategic manipulation, and success measured by the ability to change the direction and flow of politics and of existing institutions. The ability of entrepreneurs to promote desired institutional change depends on the resources at their disposal, the social setting in which they operate, and, accordingly, their influence over politicians and/or the public.

Entrepreneurs can have different motivations and use different strategies to solve what they perceive as social problems or inadequacies of existing rules, or to promote private economic and political interests that are impeded by existing regulations. Secular entrepreneurs are defined here as entrepreneurs who offer services that challenge (intentionally or unintentionally) existing religious–state institutions. These entrepreneurs have different interests, ideologies, commitments, and strategies that are loosely related and, at times, difficult to define or categorize. Secular entrepreneurs are defined here by their actions rather than by identities and declared goals; they include individuals who may not identify themselves or their intentions as "secular" but nevertheless are a part of a secularization process. Categories of economic entrepreneurs motivated by profits and political entrepreneurs committed to political goals and ideologies are ideal types rather than descriptions of reality. Secular entrepreneurs who operate to remove religious restrictions on economic matters may use ideological liberal discourse of freedoms to legitimize their demands. Similarly, secular principled and ideological struggles may rely on economic means and tactics to achieve their goals.

The category of secular entrepreneurs is expanded here and includes individuals and groups that, in their choices and actions, undermine existing religious authority. The use of the word "actions" is not incidental, as these entrepreneurs vary in their worldviews or aspirations. Regardless of their ideologies or declared goals, these entrepreneurs respond to new opportunities to promote political and social change or increase profits. These include struggles in the formal political sphere, in which "ideological" secularists attempt to change existing rules, and take various actions outside the formal political sphere, in which everyday life practices, particular interests, and ideological initiatives challenge institutional settings. Here, again, the division between formal and informal political channels may be too rigid and binding, as secular (and religious) entrepreneurs may respond to what they perceive as the inability of governments to govern effectively by shifting between conventional political participation and alternative channels of political action.

Globalization and Governance: What Game? What Rules?

The study of religion and politics tends to focus naturally on the formal political realm where religious and secular actors attempt to shape the public sphere and control resources through legislation. In the formal political realm, "religious" and "secular" describe political parties, agendas, and often ideologies that guide them. Accordingly, when religious or secular issues turn "political," they are part of a struggle over the public sphere and the "common good." Conversely, when religious or secular issues are "de-politicized," they move out of the public and political into the private sphere. This description seems to miss two important developments described earlier: first, secularization based on individual choices that are part of everyday life practices, devoid from a political agenda or commitment, yet having significant public and political impact; and, second, a functional weakening of the state associated with globalization that diminishes the dominance of conventional political participation and encourages new forms of participation. Secularization, therefore, may occur through different combinations of noncoordinated and nonideological choices of citizens/consumers and through alternative political channels of influence not registered in formal accounts of political change.

The rich negotiations, interactions, and resistance that make up what is called politics cannot be confined to the state and its institutions (Migdal, 2001: 15). Understanding politics and the dynamics of political change requires a wide scope so that political activity is not only what is openly declared and visible and not only the direct engagement with rulers and elites (Singerman, 1995:14). The expansion of the "political" is essential for grasping social changes in a period in which traditional forms of politics lost their appeal and the future of democracy became uncertain. Growing distrust of politics and politicians was found in many contemporary democracies since the late twentieth century (Arian et al., 2008; Boggs, 2000), reflected in the withdrawal of citizens from party affiliation, and a general decline of political involvement (Dalton, 2004). Citizens' trust in and satisfaction with the government and their representative politicians have declined (Dalton, 2004; Norris, 1999; Nye, 1997), feelings of alienation from political institutions and leaders have grown (Diamond and Gunther, 2001), and election turnouts have fallen (Hay, 2007; Pharr and Putnam, 2000). The decline of trust in governments and politicians has diminished the capacity of traditional governance (Pierre, 2000) and further undermined trust in governments.

The decline in the significance of formal politics and political institutions, however, is not necessarily equal to political apathy or a decline of politics. Researchers, as the German sociologist Ulrich Beck (1997) argues, may be looking for politics in the "wrong places" – namely, the formal arena – when "real" politics happens elsewhere. Social discontent and needs and aspirations of groups and individuals manifest themselves in different channels often not registered as "politics." Citizens dissatisfied with the government's performance and skeptical of the regular democratic means of protest can certainly withdraw from politics but can also search for new political channels of influence and opt for what Beck (1996) defined as "subpolitics," a noninstitutionalized form of politics "outside and beyond the representative institutions of the political system of nation-states," which may be replacing traditional forms of participation (Beck, 1996: 18; see also Holzer and Sorensen, 2001). Practices of subpolitics can be traced outside the formal political system of the state – in supermarkets, schools, media, and the streets (Beck, 1997) – anywhere citizens seek to fill the political vacuum and take responsibility for matters in their everyday, individual-oriented life arena that cuts across the public and private sphere (Holzer and Sorensen, 2001). In Beck's words:

"[A]ctive sub-politics" implies the taking of Sub-politics, means "direct politics... ad hoc individual participation in political decisions, bypassing the institutions of representative opinion-formation (political parties, parliaments) and often even lacking the protection of the law. In other words, subpolitics means the shaping of society from below... sub-politics sets politics free by changing the rules and boundaries of the political so that it becomes more open and susceptible to new linkages – as well as capable of being negotiated and reshaped. (Beck, 1999: 39–40)

When states lose control over the authoritative allocation of values in society, new arenas for political participation are sought (Stolle, Hooghe, and Micheletti, 2005). "Alternative politics," a proactive course of action taken by citizens to supply, at times illegally, a public good or governmental services they find missing (Lehman-Wilzig, 1991; 1992), compels politicians to change the policy in accordance with the demands made by the public (Mizrahi and Meydani, 2003). The political vacuum, therefore, opens new spaces and channels for political action available for both groups and individuals dissatisfied with existing institutional settings.

Political actions involve entrepreneurs who seek to promote change they perceive will benefit not only them, the group they claim to represent, or society at large, but also individuals freed from previous constraints. This original description of contemporary politics can be widened and used for our purpose here by taking into account two more possibilities. First, actions of different groups with different goals and contradicting ideologies can, without planning or coordination, combine to change existing arrangements or combat existing institutions. The anti-globalization movement, for example, is an amalgam of different groups and ideologies that have little in common besides being against globalization. Second, while subpolitics refers to the conscious action of groups and individuals, purposeful and coordinated, toward changing existing rules of the game, this does not rule out other possibilities. Politics is composed not only by conscious and ideological action, but also by everyday choices and actions of individuals. Individual choices of leisure, intimate relations, performance of life rituals, or consumption can often not be identified with ideology, nor are they explicitly politically driven. However, in the aggregate, behind the backs of individuals and possibly separated from their political desires, these everyday choices may end in institutional change.

Secularization and Globalization: Local Unfolding

Secularization must be contextualized and understood in relation to what is being secularized and to where religion remains significant. The demographic and economic changes globalization carries are often associated with a process of unrelenting secularization, the unleashed market forces said to significantly undermine previous arrangements involving religion, state, and society, while supposedly allowing greater individual choice, including religious choice. But, while globalization is a universal change that affects social structures and institutions, it affects them in different ways, through particular interactions with local settings. Similarly, secularization unfolds in a political and cultural context, between and within states with differential effects. A study of secularization, therefore, posits a basic question: What exactly is being secularized? (Lyon, 1985). The question can be answered by differential measurements not only of different aspects of secularization as discussed earlier, but also of specific types of secularization constituted by particular histories of interactions between religion and other identities.

Religion has different meaning and significance in local or national settings where it provides ideological concepts that blend with cultural and historical contexts and, therefore, can be adopted or maintained by members of the ethnic group who are not religiously devout or even partially secularized. Consequently, its decline, even in secularized societies, may be limited or partial, held back by religions' ongoing contribution to individual identity and group solidarity (Sharot, Ayalon, and Ben-Eliezer, 1986). Ethnic assimilation, for example, often parallels religious secularization (Hammond and Warner, 1993), but religion may remain significant in different ways and resurface in specific contexts.

When religion is embedded in national and ethnic identities, secularization, driven by global changes and economic incentives, will unfold not only through individual choices and personal biographies, but also through collective identities that influence or delay changes in beliefs, rituals, and values. Secularization, therefore, will appear as an uneven process that unfolds in hybrid forms of beliefs, practices, and values. But this hybridity is not necessarily arbitrary or individualized. Rather, national and ethnic identities provide a framework within which secularization occurs and shapes particular paths of secularization. Consequently, although ethnic (and other identity) groups may be affected by similar secularizing forces, those forces will have different impacts and translate to different paths of secularization manifested in beliefs, practices, and values.

Explaining Secularization: An Alternative Model

Secularization may have not met the expectations of twentieth-century sociology that predicted religion's disappearance from public life, yet the general debate on secularization seems almost meaningless without a proper definition of the process, its measurements, and the context in which it takes place. Conversely, unpacking the concept opens up the possibility of a more nuanced and empirical study of both the declining role of religion in society vis-à-vis other systems (political and economic), the role of religion in individual lives (beliefs, practices, and values), and, most important, understanding secularization as an institutional change that varies according to the context in which it unfolds. Neoinstitutional theory, adopted in this work, suggests that we conceptualize secularization as a set of processes influenced by individual and group choices and actions that change the rules of the game, not necessarily according to the desires or intentions of those involved. From this theoretical discussion, a few general principles underpin this study of secularization:

(1) Secularization is measured, first and foremost, by the general decline of religious authority and challenges to existing religious institutions.

(2) Secularization is driven not only by ideological but also by practical preferences and everyday life choices that respond to economic and social changes.

(3) Secularization unfolds in a bricolage of changing beliefs, practices, and affiliations that do not always move in lockstep with one another.

(4) The exact pace, form, motivating forces, and outcomes of secularization depend also on particular, local conditions that constitute the institutional setting.

Secularization is influenced, globally and locally, by social, economic, and political changes that structure incentives, choices, and actions of individuals and groups. Although these decisions and actions may not count as "political" when measured by intention, commitment, or organized political endeavor, they are political when measured by their impact on existing institutions. Specifically, based on the previous discussion, we can theorize the following principles of the development of secularization in the early twenty-first century:

(1) Relations between religion and the state, between religious and secular ways of life, and between religion and the economy have found different compromises and settlements manifested in institutional arrangements best understood as established rules of the game.

(2) Changes associated with globalization create new preferences and choices that conflict with existing rules of the game and new opportunities for secular entrepreneurs to challenge the rules.
(3) Secularization is advanced by ideological-liberal and economic entrepreneurs with different motivations and strategies to change the rules of the game.
(4) Secular initiatives (and religious ones) shift from the formal political realm perceived inadequate to other realms that secular entrepreneurs find more rewarding.
(5) Individuals who respond to and take part in secular initiatives contribute, at times regardless of their orientations and purposes, to the secularization of the public sphere.

The theoretical framework developed in this chapter provides for an analysis of secularization not only as a complex process that unfolds in different ways, but also as a political transformation that occurs outside the realm of formal politics in different group and individual choices and actions. Contrary to the stagnant political sphere in which rules and regulation may hardly change and significant political actions of citizens are not registered, a vibrant civil society exists in which various secular (and religious) struggles take place but also seemingly nonpolitical choices and actions affect existing institutions. In different "practices of everyday life" people engage in leisure activities and consumption habits that violate religious codes but, at the same time, may refuse to define themselves as secular, maintain their relation to religion either through personal beliefs or through other practices, and remain indifferent or hostile to liberal ideologies. Consequently, this secularization process is expected to have the following effects and outcomes:

(1) Secularization will be limited to specific parts of the public sphere in which economic incentives, coupled with political-ideological commitments, will change the rules of the game.
(2) Secular entrepreneurs are likely to be more successful outside the formal political sphere and likely to choose strategies that avoid conflict and confrontation.
(3) Citizens responding to secular entrepreneurship (and some of the entrepreneurs) will associate their choices with practical everyday choices rather than with a coherent secular commitment.
(4) Institutional changes resulting from entrepreneurial actions and individual choices will often not be registered in formal change but will nevertheless be evident in specific secularized spaces created.

(5) Secularization is likely to be loosely related to the adoption of a secular-liberal worldview and, consequently, will have a very limited impact on liberal reforms related to equality and rights.

The unpacking of secularization enables us to come to terms with the contradictions and limitations of secularization in Israel and elsewhere. Understanding secularization as an institutional change reflected in the decline of religious authority can suggest why religion and religiosity remain significant. Shifting the focus from formal politics to subpolitics incorporates secular activities and initiatives not registered elsewhere. And, finally, distinguishing secularization from secularism, a coherent worldview associated with liberalism, can explain why the secularization of Israel is not only limited in scope but also develops independently from secularism. The dynamics, contradictions, and limitations of this secularization will be demonstrated in the following chapters.

2

Israel

From Status Quo to Crisis

Religion continues to play an important and disputed role in both private and public life in Israel. The debate over the status of *halakhah* (Jewish religious law) in the conduct of public and private life has occupied the largely secular Zionist movement from its very beginnings. The secular–religious debate became more concrete and acute first, once the pre-state entity became a sovereign state faced with essential questions relating to daily life and the nature of the public domain and, second, when the institutions established in early statehood to resolve the dilemmas could no longer provide solutions in the face of a changed reality. Secularization in this work, as elaborated in the previous chapter, refers to a decline in religious authority and a process in which religion loses its hold over public life. In Israel, it refers specifically to the erosion of the status quo as an institutional arrangement and, specifically, to the erosion of the authority of the Orthodox rabbinical establishment over daily life. When we turn to examining the forces behind secularization, this definition incorporates different secularizing projects carried out by entrepreneurs with different ideologies, objectives, and strategies.

The late writer and journalist Israel Segal, a secularist who left the ultra-Orthodox world years ago, provided a pessimistic account of a secular defeat in a culture war: "In my view, the full-scale war has already ended in defeat for the secular people.... [W]e are living under a regime of occupation imposed by a *haredi* (ultra-Orthodox) minority and this occupation is growing more intensive" (Segal, 1999: 140). An assessment of the reality of religious power more than a decade later, suggests a more complex picture, where, alongside religion, secularization can be identified in private and public life. This secularization, following the framework developed in the previous chapter, is measured in the decline of religious authority rather than by individual levels of religious belief and practices, is underpinned by both ideological and nonideological forces, does not diminish the presence of religion in public life, and, consequently, its impact is significant but restricted.

Until the 1980s, most of the disputes between religious and secular populations were resolved by the authority of religious institutions, a commitment to a basic consensus, and the ability of state institutions to circumvent contentious issues and avoid controversial decisions. However, an accelerated secularization process backed by the spread of globalization, as outlined in the previous chapter, met a counter-process of religionization and a religious struggle to maintain the existing arrangements undermined existing institutions and radicalized the public debate.

Neither the study of the political system nor surveys of individual religiosity capture the full picture of secularization. Politically, the power of religious parties seems unshaken, and formal changes in religious policies and legislation are few and minor. Individually, a large number of Israelis maintain their attachment to Jewish religion in beliefs and practices and many have become more religious in various ways. Moreover, the consensus among the Jewish majority that Israel is and must remain a "Jewish state" guarantees the all-but-permanent importance of religion in public life. However, economic and demographic changes in the past two decades have created new incentives and opportunities for secular entrepreneurs and, following their actions, for individual Israelis to challenge existing institutions. These incremental changes, not registered in formal political channels, establish the partial, yet significant, secularization of Israel.

Israelis, regardless of the way they define their religiosity, can (as a result of these changes) choose how they want to spend the Sabbath (Saturday), what they wish to eat, and how they arrange the significant ceremonies in their lives with limited interference of religious institutions. These secularized spaces are created less by liberal ideological struggles and more by practical, everyday-life secularization, economic entrepreneurship, and private individual choices. These choices are not necessarily "political" in terms of affiliation and participation and not necessarily "secular" in their goals. However, they are political and secularizing in their overall effects. To explain these changes, the theoretical framework detailed in the previous chapter will be linked to the tangible Israeli reality, in which secularization processes are taking place in the context of socioeconomic and demographic changes that enable secular actions, underscored by different motives, to reshape the public domain in Israel.

Nationality, Sovereignty, and the Status Quo

Zionism established itself as a national movement led by Jews who rebelled against the Orthodox leadership and followed the modernization of Jewish life that began in the eighteenth century. European Jews that sought modern education and professions gradually stepped out of their closed communities and integrated into the surrounding societies, without religious conversion. Emancipated and modernized Jews in Europe began to carve new forms of Jewish identity. The growing rupture between those Jews and their traditional societies enabled the creation of different interpretations of Jewish commandments and new sources of authority (Yovel, 2007). Zionism, which appeared toward the end of the nineteenth century, was one form of modern Jewish identity, related to the growing national sentiment across Europe and to the anti-Semitism that threatened to undermine Jewish emancipation. The solution to the "Jewish problem," argued Zionist leaders, was not emancipation but territorial sovereignty that would "normalize" Jewish existence.

Jewish nationalism, on one hand, was a secular ideology, but, on the other hand, could not completely detach itself from its religious roots. As a secular ideology, Zionism challenged religious authority that held the view that Jewish redemption would come about with the advent of the Messiah. As a national ideology, religion was indispensable to Zionism as a marker of boundaries and a mobilizing force. This ambivalence toward religion could hardly be resolved, as secular nationalists would often have to acknowledge. Simon Dubnow (1860–1941), a Russian Jew, a historian, and a forerunner of modern Jewish nationalism, explained:

> By aspiring to secularism, by separating the national idea from religion, we are only aiming at negating the supremacy of religion, but not at eliminating it from the store house of our national cultural treasures. If we wish to preserve Judaism as a cultural-historical type of nation, we must realize that the religion of Judaism is one of the integral foundations of national culture and that anyone who seeks to destroy it thereby undermines the very basis of national existence (quoted in Abramov, 1979: 58).

Zionism not only had to challenge religious institutions by presenting its national destiny, but also had to separate itself from what religiosity symbolized. National revival implied a break with the past and the attempt to replace Judaism, a religion identified with the old world, with Jewishness, a modern identity based on culture, ethnicity, a historical sense of belonging to the Jewish people and a proactive approach toward the future. For Theodor Herzl, a secularized Jew, the main drive for Jewish sovereignty was anti-Semitism that welded the Jewish people together (Abramov, 1979: 60). In his programmatic book, *The Jewish State*, he outlined a vision for a secular entity with a separation of religion and state:

Shall we end by having a theocracy? No. Faith unites us, knowledge gives us freedom. We shall therefore prevent any theocratic tendencies from coming to the fore on the part of our priesthood. We shall keep our priests within the confines of their temples in the same way as we shall keep our professional army within the confines of their barracks.

Politics, according to this vision, must be freed from religion and ruled by knowledge, which provides freedom. Faith, however vaguely defined, is what unites the Jewish people and therefore must necessarily remain part of the secular order. In practice, Herzl's approach to religion and the religious was pragmatic, concerned mostly with the unity of the Zionist movement, and he was willing to compromise to secure religious support and avoid a cultural debate. Unlike Herzl's "political Zionism," which focused on diplomacy and organizational work, spiritual Zionism, formulated by Ahad Ha'Am, emphasized Jewish identity and a vision of a future Jewish state as a spiritual secular Jewish center. For others, such as Micah Joseph Berdichevsky, Jewish revival meant emancipation of the Jew from Orthodoxy and the discipline of the *halakhah* (Abramov, 1979: 323). The debate between political-pragmatic compromises and cultural struggles would continue to occupy secular Zionists even after statehood and attested to the power of religion in Jewish political life.

The territorial debate was exemplary of the power of religion and religious symbols, as attempts to find territorial solutions outside Palestine, the historical land of Israel, encountered strong opposition. Herzl's plan to take advantage of an offer made by Joseph Chamberlain, British Secretary of State for the Colonies, to settle Jews in Kenya encountered strong opposition. The plan that came to be known as the "Uganda Plan" was brought before the Zionist Congress in 1903 and encountered fierce resistance, leading Herzl to affirm his commitment to Palestine and declare, quoting the Psalms, "If I forget thee, O Jerusalem, may my right hand wither." Only the historic Land of Israel (*Eretz Israel*), it was acknowledged, could evoke sentiments among a critical mass of Jews, sentiments mediated through traditional religious symbols (Ben-Porat, 2000). Not only for internal purposes was the symbolic value of the Land of Israel significant. Externally, the Zionist claim to this specific territory combined a historical relation with a reference to God's promise that granted the land to the Jewish people.

In the nation-building process, religious symbols have played a major instrumental role. Zionism developed the classic features of organic nationalism, producing its own cult of ancient, biblical history, the contact with the soil and the desire to strike roots in it, and the "sanctification" of the territory where the ancient biblical heroes lived and fought (Sternhell, 1998). Secular Zionism was cultivated by the messianic enthusiasm and adopted religious symbols (Shapira, 1992) so that, beneath a thin veneer of secularism, a Jewish tradition never ceased to exist. The Hebrew culture adopted by Zionists and the civil religion it created reinterpreted religious texts and borrowed from traditional Jewish culture so that almost all its symbols, rites, and myths bore a religious significance (Don-Yehia and Liebman, 1984). The Bible and Jewish religious tradition, after selection and reinterpretation, provided for Zionism a narrative of continuity of nationhood, connection to the land, culture, and a calendar for national life. This calendar included the Jewish day of rest on the Sabbath and Jewish holidays emptied of their old religious Jewish content, which were replaced with symbols of new national experience and expectations, turning them into celebrations of national liberation (Ben-Porat, 2000; Liebman and Don-Yehia, 1984; Ram, 2008). As a result, Zionism could lend religion its own interpretation but never completely detach itself – as it continued to be directed by powerful religious structures (Ben-Porat, 2000; Raz-Krakotzkin, 2000) – and share "a common ideological mantle" with religion and the religious (Elam, 2000).

Both symbolic and practical political questions kept Jewish religion inside the political life of the nation and, later, of the state. First, the Zionist movement also included religious groups that shared with secular Zionists the desire to establish sovereignty. Second, more important, the Zionist claim to speak on behalf of the Jewish people encouraged the movement to seek wide support and forced it to make compromises on practical religious questions. Third, religion has always remained in the background as a legitimating force for territorial claims. This ambivalence of secular Zionism toward religion and the pragmatic approach of secular Zionist leaders translated into different formal and informal agreements and was put to the test in 1947 when the UN Special Committee on Palestine was debating the future of Palestine toward the end of the British Mandate. The Zionist leadership, concerned that the ultra-Orthodox community would undermine its position, pledged to continue and respect the religious agreements in the administration of the sovereign state after it was established.

Zionism was a secular movement in the challenge it presented to religious authority but, as elsewhere, religion remained a significant force in social and political life. This significance, established in the formative period described previously, when religion was acknowledged as the underlying foundation of belonging and solidarity, allowed it to continue to perform the role of a gatekeeper (Ben-Porat, 2000; Connolly, 1999). This role, explored later, rested on the political power that the religious parties accumulated and the choice of mainstream, secular Zionist parties to compromise. However, the ambivalence of secular (or rather, nonreligious) Israelis toward the role of religion, religious symbols, and boundaries ensured the continued presence of religion in public and private life.

Statehood and the Status Quo

The letter sent by David Ben-Gurion to the ultra-Orthodox party Agudat Israel before the visit of the UN Special Committee on Palestine became a cornerstone of religious–secular arrangements known as the status quo. The commitments in the letter were somewhat vague, but the status quo, further developed after statehood, laid down a basic agreement on the Jewish character of the state of Israel that enabled secular and religious political elites to formulate compromises and avoid conflicts (Don-Yehia, 2000). Two of the components of the status quo dealt largely with duties and obligations. First, ultra-Orthodox yeshiva students were exempted from military service, meaning that the burden of defense in a country with universal conscription would not be equally shared. Second, the government granted autonomy to the ultra-Orthodox school system, a decision that raised debates over issues of curricula and funding. Three other components had a more direct effect on the lives of secular Jews: the designation of Saturday, the Sabbath, as the day of rest, with the mandatory closing of stores and public services; the required observance of Jewish dietary rules (kashrut) in public institutions; and the Orthodox monopoly over burial, marriage, and divorce.

The status quo operated as a guideline for religious–secular negotiations during the first decades of statehood (Susser and Cohen, 2000). State laws based on the status quo included the jurisdiction of rabbinical courts over marriage and divorce, educational autonomy for religious groups, and declaration of the Sabbath as the official day of rest. Beyond legislation and formal institutions regulating private lives, the status quo included informal institutions that helped overcome disagreements. These included refraining from making formal and binding decisions over controversial matters, favoring of coalition partnerships over majority rule, allowing religious autonomy in specific areas, and attempting to shift disputes from national-political to judicial and local arenas.

The ability of the status quo to remain effective for almost three decades can be explained by the general desire to avoid conflict that would divide Jewish society, concrete political interests of political parties, and a general ambivalence toward secularism in Israeli society. The desire for consensus that created the status quo continued after statehood. The leading political parties, as well as the majority of Jewish Israelis, were occupied with challenges of state building and concerned with external security threats that marginalized secular–religious differences. The approach adopted, known as *mamlahtiyut*, placed the state at the center of collective life of the Jewish nation and upheld the functionality of the status quo for the reinforcement of consensus with respect to the state. The consensus was secured by political interests and cooperation between the dominant Labor Party and the major religious party (Mizrahi). This cooperation allowed the Labor Party to dominate foreign policy and security policy in return for Orthodox monopoly over significant aspects of public life.

The stability of the status quo in the first three decades could also be attributed to the support of the majority of nonreligious Israelis who continued to relate to codes, values, symbols, and a collective memory that could hardly be separated from Jewish religion (Kimmerling, 2004: 354). The gap between religious groups and a large proportion of the secular population was narrowed not only by common symbols but also by the widespread loyalty shared to the idea of a "Jewish state" and the instrumentality of religion for maintaining boundaries. The secular idea of a Jewish state referred to ethnicity or culture, but religion was called up as the gatekeeper to provide the criteria for inclusion and exclusion (Ram, 1998b). Thus, the citizenship law defined criteria to obtain citizenship not in secular-nationalist terms but in religious ones, stating that a Jew entitled to citizenship is a person born of a Jewish mother, or who has converted to Judaism, and is not a member of another religion. In a society yet to be exposed to consumer culture and occupied with a state-building project, the differences separating religious and secular Israelis were relatively small and of secondary importance.

The status quo emerged in a period when the compromises it entailed were feasible, thanks to favorable political circumstances, concrete political interests, a desire for consensus, and an ambivalent secularism. This

institutional framework, however, was subjected to challenges and crit-
icisms as religious–secular compromises had their price, especially for
some groups. State laws provided religious orthodoxy with authority
over major milestones in society, ranging from marriage and divorce to
burial. Secular groups and individuals who felt disadvantaged or wronged
by the Orthodox order, and those opposed in principle to the religious
monopoly, all voiced their resentments and demands. Needless to say, this
compromise among the Jewish majority excluded the non-Jewish minority, which remained marginal in the political process. Then again, as long
as the sociopolitical context did not change dramatically, the status quo
arrangements withstood the challenges.

Secularism and the Status Quo: Demands for Religious Freedom

The authority vested in the hands of the religious establishment was
resented by declared secularists. While the majority of non-religious
Israelis, for the reasons described previously, accepted the status quo
as a given, a minority of secularists attempted to challenge it, demanding religious freedom. "Ideological" secularism that advocated freedom –
described in terms of religion–state separation, freedom from religion, or
religious freedom – has been part of political life since the rise of Zionism.
Roots of this secularism can be found in different historical, social, and
ideological sources that include the Jewish Enlightenment movement,
which appeared toward the end of the eighteenth century and attempted
to bridge the gap between Jewish identity, modern science, and citizenship
of the nation-state. Zionism, strongly influenced by the Enlightenment,
championed a secular worldview that marginalized the role of religion
and rebelled against religious authority. The young pioneers, members of
the second and third *Aliyahs* (waves of immigrants), who settled in Palestine adopted a secular way of life that fused rejection of the Diaspora
with the rejection of religiosity (Abramov, 1976: 326).

Secular ideas and ideologies that continued to develop engaged with
both theoretical dilemmas of Jewish identity and practical political questions of rights and obligations. Influenced by the ideas of the Enlightenment, some secularists attempted to merge their Jewishness with liberal-
humanistic perspectives, universal moral principles, support of individual
liberties, and rationality held above religious commandments. Secular-
humanistic Jews describe themselves as individuals who "wish to belong
to the Jewish people and continue the tradition of the Jewish people completely free of any supernatural authority. They believe in the sanctity of

the human personality and the inviolability of dignifying human honor and integrity" (Bauer, 2005). The universal secular humanism developed alongside, and at times against, more particularist secular visions of Jewish cultural-ethnic identity and concrete demands for religious freedom, independent from universal-liberal visions. The different attempts to define Jewish identity in cultural rather than religious terms implied the rejection of religious authority and resistance to the ultra-Orthodox monopoly over significant aspects of public life. In practical political terms, they implied the vision of a secular public domain where religion would exercise its authority only over those who choose to accept it.

Secular challenges to the status quo in the early years of statehood, described in detail in the following chapters, were few, and mostly local and short-lasting. One exception was the League against Religious Coercion, formed in the 1950s, which developed a comprehensive agenda and explained it would:

distribute among the general public the idea that a man's convictions are his own private affair and so in Israel it is essential to struggle for the separation of religion and state, freedom of religion, belief and conscience; to encourage and support any individual who feels that he himself has been damaged...by religious restrictions. (Tzur, 2001: 220)

Assisted by the organizational resources of the kibbutzim, the league struggled for civil marriage, easing the requirements for conversion to Judaism, and for ending the restrictions on activities on Shabbat ("Shabbat without chains"). In 1955, the league submitted a petition with 100,000 signatures to the Knesset (Parliament), demanding a referendum on the authorization of civil marriage (Tzur, 2001: 212). The league, however, failed to mobilize the general public, and its cooperation with the secular parties did not yield any significant results either. Its activities gradually declined until it disappeared after the 1967 war.

Secularism: The Limits of an Ideology

The secular-liberal political agenda that advocated religious pluralism and freedom of choice instead of the status quo and the religious monopoly appealed only to a small group with marginal political power. For the majority of Israelis, the support or acceptance of the role of religion in public life resulted from pragmatic political attitudes, the continued attachment to religious symbols and rituals, and a "traditional" self-identity located between religious and secular. Surveys carried out between 1969 and 1985 have found that 15 to 25 percent of the population defined themselves as Orthodox (*dati*), 40 to 45 percent as traditional (*masorti*), and another 35 to 45 percent as nonreligious (Kedem, 1991). Many Israelis, including those who defined themselves as nonreligious, took part in religious rituals during holidays (Passover) or private events (marriage, burial, and circumcision). Jewish Orthodoxy, therefore, acted as what Grace Davie (2007) described elsewhere as a vicarious religion: "performed by an active minority but on the behalf of a much larger number, who (implicitly at least) not only understand, but, quite clearly, approve of what the minority is doing." The role religion played in private lives and its role as a gatekeeper of the national boundaries have rendered the possibility of separating state and religion unlikely, even for those who described themselves as "nonreligious."

The "traditional" category many Israelis choose to describe their religiosity is not necessarily a comfortable middle position, but is also an identity rooted in the ethnicity and culture of immigrants from the Middle East and North Africa (Mizrahim) and their descendants. The state's secular elite attempted to secularize these immigrants as part of a modernization process that showed little regard for the immigrants' traditions. However, the Mizrahim resisted secularization and developed a strategy of cultural accommodation, steering a religious path midway between Ashkenazi Orthodoxy and Ashkenazi secularism that they describe as "traditional" or *masorti* (Shokeid, 1984). The traditional model open to variations in beliefs and practices and an oral tradition (different from Ashkenazi formality and its written tradition) was an "imported" pattern that developed among Jews in Muslim countries, who, like the Muslim majority in their countries of origin, continued to perceive religion and religious authorities as significant even as they went through a modernizing process. This pattern is sustained in the second and third generation of Mizrahim in Israel as well. Although flexible in some of its practices, the group maintains a conservative position regarding the role of religion in its community and is strict in its observance of rituals (Leon, 2009).

Conservatism and the acceptance of the rules of the game as a given were shared until the 1980s by the majority of Israelis. Consequently, secularism as an ideology could hardly drive a process of secularization that would challenge the religious authority vested in the status quo. Not only religious Israelis, but also traditional and nonreligious ones, showed no desire for change. Specifically, the restrictions on marriage and burial choices, activities on the Sabbath, and the sale of nonkosher meat were accepted by the majority of Jewish Israelis. These restrictions were perceived by the majority as constitutive to the Jewish character of the state or their own Jewish identity, part of a necessary compromise between religious and secular, or simply an issue of minor importance that did not affect their everyday lives enough to justify its politicization.

Secularization: New Challenges to the Status Quo

Secularization, a process of societal change and a decline of religious authority, could not advance in Israel by secularism, an ideology and a worldview shared by a small minority. The status quo, as described earlier, in spite of the authority it vested in the hands of the minority religious Orthodox over the lives of nonreligious Jews, maintained its institutional stability. The priority of state building, the desire for consensus, and the importance religion continued to hold for public and private lives ensured the legitimacy of the political compromise and the stability of the status quo. In the 1980s, however, the consensus began to wane and secular resentment toward religious orthodoxy and especially the ultra-Orthodox (*haredim*) strengthened. Beyond the resentment, discussed later, three important changes provided new grounds for secularization and the opportunities for secular entrepreneurs to challenge the status quo: a neoliberal economy, the immigration of a million Jews from the former Soviet Union, and the emergence of religious and spiritual alternatives.

Globalization, Neoliberalism, and Consumer Society

The modest collectivist ethos and the limited material resources available in early statehood provided a protective shield for the status quo. Life in Israel in the 1950s was rather simple, influenced by the pioneering ethos of state building and the limitations of a developing economy. In the period immediately after the war of 1948, the government initiated a policy of austerity. This policy, well suited to the egalitarian ideology of the new state, dominated by the Labor Party, was an attempt to manage the pressures caused by war and the mass immigration (Rivlin, 2010: 36). Tight control of the economy began to relax in the 1950s, as various measures of liberalization were gradually introduced. A rapid growth of the Israeli economy continued until 1972 (with a recession in the 1960s), largely the result of inflows of labor and capital and appropriate economic policies (Rivlin, 2010: 42). Despite economic growth and liberalization (the latter accelerating after the Labor Party was ousted from power in 1977), the economy remained dominated by the government. Similarly, in

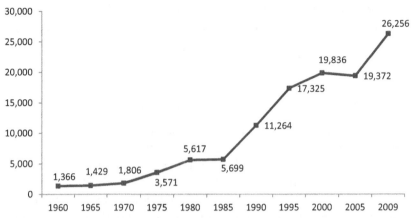

FIGURE 2.1. Economic growth, measured by gross domestic product. *Source:* Data from World Bank Last updated: March 30, 2012, http://www.google.co.il/ publicdata/explore?ds=d5bncppjof8f9_&met_y=ny_gdp_pcap_cd&idim= country:ISR&dl=en&hl=en&q=israel+gdp+per+capita.

spite of the relaxation of government policies, consumerism was lagging behind the developments in the Western world.

Liberal economic policies took a more dramatic turn in the 1980s and set in motion the rapid rise of a consumer society similar to, and aspiring to be even more similar to, other Western countries. A decade of economic instability, hyperinflation, deterioration of the balance of payments, and foreign debt reached its climax in 1985 and led to a stabilization program initiated by a national unity government. The plan included the reduction of government intervention by cutting subsidies and services. Economic growth that began after the plan was initiated exploded in the 1990s, influenced by immigration, the peace process, and the high-tech industry. Israel's economic leap matched those of the "tiger" countries of Southeast Asia, and the standard of living in Israel, especially for the upper and middle class, measured by ownership of consumer goods, increased almost to the level of the industrialized Western states. State-led economic policies were replaced by neoliberal policies that encouraged privatization, increased socioeconomic gaps between rich and poor, and underscored what can be described as a "consumer revolution" (Figure 2.1).

Economic growth brought with it the new possibilities and desires that characterize a consumer society – and the new lifestyles rendered the restrictive arrangements of the status quo difficult to maintain. Shopping malls and large stores, many of them American or global, began to emerge in the 1980s, offering a variety of commodities and a new shopping

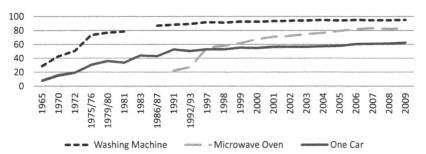

FIGURE 2.2. Ownership of appliances. *Source:* Israel Central Bureau of Statistics, Social Survey, and Statistical Yearbook.

experience. Israelis were spending more and more on housing, transportation, and communication and less on food and clothing. Similarly, their affluence and consumerism were attested to by the increase in the number of motor vehicles, electrical appliances (Figure 2.2), and, later on, mobile phones and Internet access (Ram, 2008a).

The Ashkenazi middle class, previously the carriers of the collective pioneering ethos, was now the leader of the new individual ethos of self-fulfillment and quest for the good life. However, individualism and the consumer culture extended well beyond ethnic and class boundaries and applied to many spheres of life. Like the transition described in the previous chapter from the old to the new capitalism, the shift from the state-led to the neoliberal capitalism also had cultural significance. Economic growth was accompanied by cultural changes often described as "Americanization" – imitation of the American lifestyle and the import of American goods. This processes gained momentum during the 1990s, owing to globalization and the initiation of a peace process that added to the economic growth and opened up new parts of the world to Israel and to Israeli consumers (Ben-Porat, 2005).

The collective ethos of frugality was replaced by individualism, hedonism, and a consumerism around which the Israeli middle class organized its daily life (Carmeli and Applebaum, 2004: 6). Consumption was not only a process of "fitting in" but also, supposedly, an attempt to define individuality through choice. The consumerist desire for new experiences and the new leisure patterns were often incompatible with the religious restrictions of the status quo. For religious people, also influenced by consumer culture, the religious rules held firm although some challenges to religious authority have emerged, in relation to the use of the Internet or mobile phones for example. However, secular Israelis (and, to a lesser

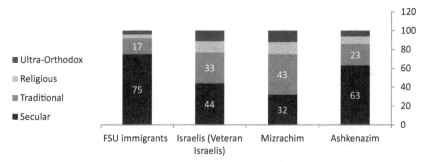

FIGURE 2.3. Religiosity and ethnicity. *Source:* Diagram 3, Israelis' Secularism in Guttman Institute Surveys, 1990–2008, at http://www.idi.org.il/GuttmanCenter/ SurveyArticle/Pages/The_Guttman_Center_Surveys_Articles_4.aspx.

extent, traditional ones) were ready to transgress the restrictions they no longer saw fitting. The growth of commerce on the Sabbath (Chapter 6) and the sale of nonkosher meat (Chapter 5) demonstrate the impact of consumer society on the status quo.

FSU Immigrants and the Changing Demography

The one million immigrants who arrived in Israel from the former Soviet Union (FSU) between 1989 and 2000 constitute the largest single country-of-origin group among the Jewish population of Israel (Al Haj, 2002).Although this large group is not homogeneous, its members do share some general characteristics, including a secularization process they underwent during the communist regime, leaving them with only vague notions about Judaism (Ben-Rafael, 2007; Leshem, 2001). In Russia it was not uncommon for Jews to attend Orthodox Christian services and *halakhic* (pertaining to Jewish religious law) regulations concerning "who is a Jew" were often completely disregarded. As a result, owing to intermarriage, about one-fourth of the immigrants do not meet the Orthodox criteria of Jewishness (Ben-Rafael, 2007). Consequently, immigrants were granted citizenship under the Law of Return (1970)[1] but were not considered Jewish by the Orthodox establishment[2] unless they would go through an Orthodox conversion process. FSU immigrants, as Figure 2.3 demonstrates, are far more secular in their identities than all other ethnic groups in Israel.

[1] The law grants Israeli citizenship to "the child or grandchild of a Jew, the spouse of a Jew, and the spouse of a Jewish child or grandchild."

[2] According to Jewish Orthodoxy, a Jew is "someone who was born to a Jewish mother, and who does not belong to another religion, or someone who converted to Judaism."

The sheer scale of this immigration produced a critical mass of demand for Russian culture and imported cultural products, as well as economic initiatives to provide a response to those demands (Kimmerling, 2004: 411). The immigrant community created a "Russian niche" in which the Russian language was preserved and links with the country of origin were maintained, thanks to the supply of products, services, and cultural performances from the old homeland. Newspapers, television channels, and various cultural enterprises provided immigrants with a cultural environment that enabled them to maintain their identity. Russian food stores, mostly owned by immigrants, selling nonkosher and other imported food products were established in cities where Russian immigrants settled (Gvion, 2005). FSU immigrants were quick to organize politically at both the local and the national levels, at times clashing with the religious and *haredi* sectors who insisted on maintaining the Jewish character of the state and of their neighborhoods (Peres and Ben-Rafael, 2007: 167).

The status quo agreements and the Orthodox monopoly caused considerable difficulties for the immigrants, especially for those not recognized as Jews who, among other difficulties they experienced, could not marry in Israel. This reinforced their tendency to remain as a separate community but also strengthened the political demands for change in the current state of affairs and, most important, initiatives that undermined the status quo. FSU immigrants had influence not only on the developments of alternative marriage (Chapter 3) and burial (Chapter 4), but also on the restrictions on pork production and sale (Chapter 5). FSU immigrants' contribution to secularization, however, developed separately from that of veteran Israelis for two main reasons. First, the political orientation of the immigrants, described as "pragmatic-secular-rightist and ethnic" (Al Haj, 2002), was different from the more liberal political stance of most secular Ashkenazim. FSU immigrants, as a result of their Soviet experience (Shumsky, 2001 and 2004), adopted an ethnocentric approach that prevented cooperation with secular left-wing parties. Second, the FSU immigrant imported a "passive citizenship" approach (Philipov and Bystrov, 2011) and a preference for practical solutions, often provided by "Russian" entrepreneurs or their political representatives, rather than for a struggle for comprehensive political change.

Jewish but Not Orthodox: Cultural Alternatives

Alongside material changes, ideational developments also took a new turn of challenging the Orthodox monopoly, demanding that alternative

Jewish identities be recognized by the state and receive an equal stance to
Jewish Orthodoxy.

The Reform (Israeli Movement for Progressive Judaism) and Conservative (Masorti) movements became sharp critics of the status quo,
demanding religious pluralism. The Reform movement, which established
its first congregation in Israel in 1958, raised the banner in the struggle
for freedom of religious practice and conscience as well as a commitment
to equality of the sexes, including women in the various religious ceremonies. The Conservative movement, founded in Israel in 1979, also
began to provide religious services for the general public, including weddings and other ceremonies that did not receive official recognition from
the Orthodox establishment and the state. Although the Reform and
Conservative communities remained small and based mainly on immigrants from English-speaking countries, they received substantial back-
ing from their related communities in the United States, which defended
their status and enabled them to function without government funding
for religious institutions, a budget that was controlled by the Orthodox
establishment.

Beginning in the 1990s, an additional trend developed in Israel and
became known as the "fourth stream," or secular Judaism. It is difficult
to characterize this trend, which was influenced by "New Age" orientations, the search for a Jewish identity, and the hope for a religious–
secular dialogue, especially in the aftermath of Itzhak Rabin's assassina-
tion in 1995. These groups frequently insisted on distinguishing themselves from Reform Jews, whom they associate with immigrants from
English-speaking countries, and prefer to define their group as a deeply
rooted Israeli development. For many of those who associate with secular
Judaism, belonging includes the right for appropriation and reinterpretation of scriptures and the adaptation of Jewish rituals to modern life and
to universal values:

[A]bundant and rich Jewish civilization, that also includes those parts of our
people's culture, which rabbinic Judaism refused to accept and rejected out of
hand.... [W]e [also] regard ourselves as sharing in the global culture, and therefore are quite justified in stating that "our ship" carries a broad and profound
Jewish humanistic culture, which also includes the "fully laden wagon" of the
Jewish religion. (Itzhaki, 2000: 51–2)

Secular Judaism's popularity among the middle-class and educated populations was expressed in the organization of major festivals of Jewish

identity, as well as secular *batei midrash* (centers of Jewish
and secular yeshivot (colleges of higher Jewish learning), in
ish scriptures are studied and questions of belonging and
debated. Initially, this secular interest in Judaism and Jewish ᴗᴗᴗ,
seemed to bring secular Jews closer to religion and the religious. However, the open and critical reading of texts and, more important, the
reinterpretation of rituals and commandments directly challenged religious orthodoxy and the status quo. Specifically, secular interpretations
of rituals and the design of new Jewish life-cycle ceremonies evolved
to alternative marriage (Chapter 3) and burial ceremonies (Chapter 4),
undermining religious authority.

The new forces behind secularization in the 1990s did not change the
inherent ambivalence of Israeli secularism and, except for the minority
seeking a cultural or religious alternative to Jewish orthodoxy, its lack of
depth:

> The lack of depth of Jewish secular culture following its transition, within a
> short span of time, from rejection of the contents of Jewish heritage to their
> adoption; from a collectivist worldview, which considers the good life to consist
> of contributing to the national project, to an individualistic worldview that sees
> life as a project of personal self-determination; and from social-democracy to
> capitalism and neo-liberalism. (Mautner, 2011: 2)

Thus, while a minority of secular Israelis were occupied in a cultural
and political struggle, for many Israelis secularization was about lifestyle
and practical decisions related to everyday life. Religious authority, in
the form of the rabbinate and affiliated institutions, however, was losing its authority not only because of the secular demands for religious
freedom or practical individual decisions but also because of a tarnished
image. Allegations of corruption, insensitivity, rigidity, and poor service
were often waged against religious authorities and incorporated in the
demands of secular entrepreneurs for change (Chapters 3 and 4). In a
survey conducted by a popular website, 41 percent of the respondents
agreed with the statement that the chief rabbinate is no longer necessary
(YNET, 6/11/07). In a wider survey, only 45 percent of Jewish Israelis
expressed trust in the chief rabbinate, a low score similar to those for political institutions such as the parliament or the government (IDI, 2007).
The negative – and, at times, hostile – attitude of secular Israelis toward
the rabbinate undermined its privileged position, its legitimacy, and its
ability to exert authority.

Religion in the Private and the Public Spheres: Counter-Secularization

As elsewhere, secularizing trends in Israel have met counter-forces of religion fundamentalism fighting to defend their way of life and fashion the public realm surrounding it. Even though religious revival often looks to tradition, it is also a modern phenomenon (Eisenstadt, 2000) with a multiplicity of sources, motives, strategies, and goals that draw on contemporary developments. Contrary to secularist attempts to privatize and allow individual choice, the goal of religious fundamentalism is to subject everything to exclusive religious authority. Three important developments in religious revival have occurred in Israel alongside (and against) secularization: secular and traditional Jews adopting a religious way of life, the rise of a new and powerful ultra-Orthodox religious party, and a Zionist revival led by religious Jews. What is common to these three developments is the desire to strengthen the authority of religion over both private and public domains.

Born-Again Jews

The movement encouraging Jews to return to a religious way of life (*hazarah be-teshuvah*) dates back to the crisis that affected Israeli society in the wake of the 1973 Yom Kippur war (Beit-Hallahmi, 1992) as well as to the 1960s, when it was one among other spiritual trends (Caplan, 2007). This trend received considerable attention, especially when secular celebrities embraced an Orthodox religious way of life and denounced their former lives. The return to religion has been orchestrated by religious entrepreneurs who specialized in finding ways to the hearts of nonreligious Jews, using different strategies. Secular Ashkenazi Jews are regarded as those whose fathers slipped away from religion for ideological reasons, whereas Mizrahim are considered as Jews who have no ideological objection to religion but simply have adopted a less strict level of religious observance. Even though there are many sound reasons to doubt this division, it has nevertheless resulted in the use of different strategies that range from threats and promises that relate to reward and punishment in the afterlife to attempts to battle the authority of science and the status of scientific rationalism (Caplan, 2007: 105–9), or demonstrate that science in its entirety may be found already in the holy scriptures, in keeping with the adage in Ecclesiastes, "There is nothing new under the sun" (Goodman, 2003: 34).

The religious campaign included yeshivot dedicated to the *hozrim be-teshuvah* (those returning to a religious way of life) alongside various additional institutions that organized seminars and lectures and produced learning materials for general circulation. The number of secularists who turned religious is unknown; *haredi* spokesmen mention numbers reaching into six figures, but researchers estimate their number at around 40,000 and that the overall influence of the *hozrim be-teshuvah* on the size of the *haredi* society is minor (Caplan, 2007: 101–2). Among Mizrahim, however, the shift was less radical. Unlike secular Ashkenazim who returned to religion (*hozrim be-teshuvah*), the more traditional Mizrahim describe themselves as becoming stronger in faith (*mit'hazkim*). The adoption of a more Orthodox way of life, or the "*haredi* upsurge" (Leon, 2009), includes Torah lessons with a *haredi* orientation for both women and men, as well as the emergence of a new media domain with *haredi* radio stations and audiotapes and discs.

SHAS: Religious and Political Revival

The most important development in the upsurge of religiosity among Mizrahim was SHAS, a political party that gained prominence from the 1980s onward. Combining ethnicity and religiosity, SHAS advocated a return to tradition against the secularization forced on Mizrahi immigrants. Becoming a significant political force, the party was successful in channeling Mizrahi resentment not against the Ashkenazi element, being loyal to Jewish unity and the state, but rather against the secular element (Peled, 1998). SHAS organized its activities using an extensive network of educational and welfare institutions, constituting a substitute for the receding welfare state and thereby reinforcing the party's standing with both the state, which used it as an intermediary, and with its voters, who became more dependent on this party network (Levi and Amreich, 2001). Through its extensive educational and welfare network, SHAS became an important player in promoting religious (and anti-secular) Jewish identity. The party's constituency was not necessarily *haredi*, as its voters often identified with its social and ethnic message, but the vote for SHAS was a vote for a more religious state or even for a *halakhic* state (Susser and Cohen, 2000: 120).

Unlike Ashkenazi *haredi* parties, SHAS entered Israeli politics not only to defend the interests of a specific public and advance the cause of Jewish *halakhic* legislation, but also to implement a far-reaching change in the social agenda and the Israeli collective identity (Ben-Rafael and Leon, 2006: 309). If at the outset SHAS aimed at rectifying the discrimination against Mizrahim, from the 1990s onward the party championed a religious revolution and a spiritual revival aimed at changing the balance of power between the secular majority and the religious minority (Tessler, 2003: 167). The party became the political proponent of a *haredi* model that rejects the secular philosophy and seeks to mold the public domain as a religious one, bound as much as possible by the rules of *halakhah*. SHAS's electoral power, enhanced by its education and social network, enabled it to promote different proposals to curb the secularizing trends. Although many of those proposals have never materialized, they have strengthened the party's status as the authentic representative of Jewish identity.

Zionist Revival: The Jewish Way

Religious Zionism was part of the Zionist movement but, until the late 1960s, it settled for the secondary role of managing the religious institutions and protecting their monopoly. A younger generation of religious Zionists who took power after the war of 1967, however, was no longer willing to accept its marginal role. Gush Emunim ("Bloc of the Faithful"), which appeared on the scene during the 1970s, constituted an attempt by the religious Zionists to make headway into a position of leadership while fusing religion, politics, and territoriality (Schwartz, 1999: 83). Religious Zionists came to believe that secular Zionism has "fulfilled its mission and finished its role" (Karpel, 2003: 15), and it was now their turn to assume leadership and settle the new territories occupied in the war to ensure they would become part of a larger Israel. Gush Emunim's ideologists associated the reluctance and hesitation of secular Israelis to settle the territories with a general weakening of mainstream Zionism, as the movement's platform explained:

[W]e are unfortunately witnessing a series of events indicating a process of degeneration and retreat from realizing the Zionist idea...a trend that is a shoddy imitation of the western culture...a mood featuring a quest for the "easy and comfortable life, high standard of living and after luxury items." (Shafat, 1995, appendix 1).

The settlement of the territories – areas with historical and religious significance – was for religious Zionists the fulfillment of both religious commandments and national duty. The national revival that Gush Emunim offered replicated many of the symbols and practices of secular Zionism, but instilled them with religious meaning. Hiking the land, community life, Hebrew culture, and, especially, pioneering became the markers of the new movement (Ben-Porat, 2000). This settlement project, led by the movement in the occupied territories, often bending the rules and ignoring restrictions to create "facts on the ground," received (at least in its early stages) sympathy and support from secular Zionists who identified with the renewal of Zionism and the pioneering collectivist spirit behind the movement. But, Gush Emunim's settlement enterprise contradicted the ideology of a growing number among the secular public that opposed the occupation of the territories acquired and set their sights on territorial compromise and peace. This schism intensified in the 1990s when Israel and the Palestinians began negotiating a future peace and Gush Emunim intensified its settlement project to prevent a territorial compromise.

The three counter-secularization developments – *hazarah be-teshuvah*, the growth of the SHAS party, and Gush Emunim – shared a common agenda to protect, first, what they describe as "the Jewish character of the state" and, second, the authority of religion in public and private lives. These developments indicated that a privatization of religion was unlikely and that religion would remain a significant political force in years to come.

Religious and/or Secular – The Numbers

Secularization theory, discussed in the previous chapter, would predict an increase in the number of secular people in Israel, with a corresponding retreat of religion into the private domain. However, in Israel, the numbers, when measured by self-identity, have not changed radically, as many Israelis continue to describe themselves in surveys as "religious" or "traditional." The middle category of "traditional" (or, when available, "nonreligious") rather than "secular" (see Table 2.1) can express either some religious attachment or a reluctance to identify as secular because of the relation between a secular identity and other political and ethnic orientations (see Figure 2.4).

Measured by self-identity, differences among religious, traditional, and secular Israelis can be discerned (see Table 2.2). Secular Israelis tend to be more educated, Ashkenazi, and politically identified with the left, and tend to describe themselves as upper-middle class. The "traditional" category is popular among Mizrahim. Furthermore, religiosity strongly correlates with a rightist political orientation.

Secularization is not indicated in the numbers of self-identified secularists but may be expressed in changes within the categories themselves, measured, first, by preferences, choices, and practices and, second, by their impact on religious authority.

TABLE 2.1. *Religious and Secular Israelis*

		Ultra-Orthodox (%)	Religious (%)	Traditional (%)	Secular (%)
Education	10 years or less	5.8	22.2	11.6	4.9
	High school	32.4	29.1	47.6	32.5
	Post high school, nonacademic	47	15.3	15	19.4
	Full academic degree (B.A. and above)	14.7	33.3	25.8	43.2
Ethnic origin[a]	Mizrahi	16.2	43.8	54.5	22.3
	Ashkenazi	27.9	32.9	16.2	35.5
	Former USSR	0	5.5	7.7	21.4
	Israeli	55.9	17.8	21.7	20.8
Political affiliation	Right	73.6	56.9	45.1	22.4
	Right of center	17	16.9	16.9	16.7
	Center	9.4	21.5	28.6	26.8
	Left of center	0	1.5	4.2	13.9
	Left	0	3.1	5.2	20.2
Socioeconomic status	Low	17.7	8.6	3.5	3.9
	Medium-low	19.4	12.9	11.7	11.9
	Medium	5.4	50	61.7	52.5
	Medium-high	8.1	21.4	18.3	27.8
	High	0	7.1	4.8	3.9

[a] Ethnic origin, following the Israel Bureau of Statistics, is measured by place of birth or father's place of birth. Individuals born in Israel whose father was also born in Israel are labeled "Israeli."
Source: Author's own survey, 2009.

The attempt to place the categories on a single-dimensional axis of religious belief, based on self-definition, therefore, not only misses out on the uniqueness of the groups and subgroups (Goodman, 2002), but also overlooks the complexity and the multidimensional nature along the different axes of faith, behavior, and values and the changes that occur within those categories as they unfold in the everyday behavior of individuals. Thus, being "secular" or "traditional" might mean different things for different people and, more important, this meaning can change over time or depend upon the context in which identity is defined. Consequently, secularization unfolds not necessarily in identity change (as individuals continue to describe themselves as "traditional" or even "religious") but in actual choices and practices that defy religious authority. Similarly, people who identify themselves as "secular" may, in some instances, choose to obey religious authority and engage in religious practices.

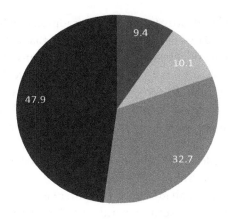

■ Ultra-Orthodox ▨ Religious ▨ Traditional ■ Secular

FIGURE 2.4. Religiosity by self-identity. *Source:* Author's own survey, 2009.

Surveys and studies of Jewish religiosity in Israel depict a complex picture of beliefs, practices, and values. Many Israelis observe religious rites selectively, without being concerned with their theological import or with religious consistency (Liebman and Susser, 1998; Levi, Levinson, and Katz, 2002). Thus, adherence to kashrut laws may be partial or complete, motivated by belief or respect for the environment and accompanied by the observance of various prohibitions and commandments – or

TABLE 2.2. *Secular/Traditional Practices*

	Traditional (%)	Secular (%)
Fast on Yom Kippur		
Always	89.5	43.7
Sometimes	5.5	14
Never	5.0	42.3
Participate in a traditional Passover dinner (seder)		
Always	97.0	84.3
Sometimes	1.3	9.0
Never	1.7	6.7
Believe circumcision is important		
Not important at all	2.2	15.2
Not so important	5.2	16.1
Fairly important	11.3	20.2
Very important	81.4	48.4

Source: Author's own survey, 2009.

not. Conversely, individuals who identify themselves as traditional, when faced with economic or leisure-related decisions, make choices that can be described as "secular" in the sense of defying religious laws or norms. People who shop on the Sabbath often do not regard themselves as secular, provide pragmatic and instrumental reasons for defying religious commandments, and obey other commandments and practices (Ben-Porat and Feniger, 2009). Finally, many of those who identify themselves as secular practice some religious rituals, such as the fast on Yom Kippur and the Passover traditional seder, and believe that circumcision is an important ritual that must be observed.

The societal changes affect almost all groups, but in different ways. On the religious side, openness toward the secular world (or to "modernity") is manifested both in artistic creation (literature, cinema, and art) and consumer culture. Even among *haredim*, some changes are emerging in the patterns of consumption, culture, and leisure, as well as civil and political values and involvement, all of which draw them nearer to the secular world (Elor and Neria, 2003; Stadler, Ben-Ari and Lomski-Feder, 2008) but exert no influence on the essence of their religious identity (Caplan, 2007: 252). Whereas religious Orthodox Jews and committed secularists demonstrate a more or less coherent pattern, the majority of Israelis show different levels of belief and attitudes and a selective choice of practices and rituals (see Table 2.2 and, in detail, Levi, Levinson, and Katz, 2002). The selective and partial fulfillment of religious commandment is neither random nor necessarily the result of "sloppiness." Rather, patterns of religiosity can display a pattern of commitment to "Jewish popular culture" (Liebman, 1997), be a conscious choice of individuals who choose to modernize but not secularize (Yadgar, 2010), or result from an ethnic heritage that provides a more relaxed and flexible model of religiosity (Leon, 2009).

Secularization in Israel, as elsewhere, is a complex and nonlinear process that unfolds in a bricolage of beliefs, values, and choices and is matched by counter-secularization processes. This bricolage is not arbitrary or individual but is mediated by ethnic, class, and religious identities. Measured in the declining authority of religion, secularization is manifested in practical choices of everyday life or in concrete demands for change that require neither a secular identity nor a coherent secular political agenda. Following these choices, the reasons behind them, and their impact reveals what is being secularized and how. The diversity and the seemingly blurred boundaries of the religious and secular categories do not necessarily indicate compromise and moderation. Rather, the

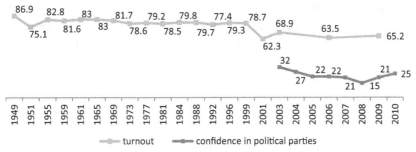

FIGURE 2.5. Decline of confidence. *Source:* Data from Israel Institute for Democracy, Democracy Index, http://www.idi.org.il/sites/english/ResearchAnd Programs/The%20Israeli%20Democracy%20Index/Pages/TheIsraeliDemocracy Index.aspx, and the Knesset website, http://www.knesset.gov.il/elections17/heb/ history/PercentVotes.htm.

demographic, economic, and ideational changes undermine the foundations of the status quo, which is no longer able to provide the answers, and present a major challenge for the political system to provide answers and solutions.

Religion and Politics: From Status Quo to Crisis

The new demographic and economic developments described earlier presented new demands – for shopping on the Sabbath (Chapter 6) or civil marriage (Chapter 3) – that could not be answered by the status quo. However, even though the political system was no longer able to enforce the old rules, it was also incapable of creating new, updated rules that would answer the rising challenges and contain the differences. The political standstill was not unique to questions of religion but was indicative of a deeper and wider political crisis and an unstable political system. This instability included frequent changes of elected governments that failed to complete their terms of office, and a loss of public confidence in the democratic institutions. This depleted confidence was expressed in a significant decline in voter turnout (from 80% in 1999 to 63% in 2006 and 65% in 2009) and a marked drop in the overall satisfaction with the function of Israeli democracy (Arian et al., 2008), confidence in political parties, and the ability of citizens to exert political influence (Figure 2.5) (Arian et al., 2003: 125–144; Arian et al., 2008: 67).

Political apathy was not the only reaction to the political crisis and stagnation. The ossification of political parties and low responsiveness of the Israeli representative government led, first, to a high level of extrapolitics, so that by 1981 Israel held a world record, with 21.5 percent of the adult population reporting participating in at least one protest event (Lehman-Wilzig, 1991). The disappointing results of protest activity and extraparliamentary pressure led to a new approach: the establishment of an alternative social system that existed side by side with official ones (ibid.). Thus, the political stalemate and the inability of the government to produce efficient and stable policy decisions encouraged citizens and political entrepreneurs to seek alternative courses of action – legal, semi-legal, and even illegal – outside the political system.

Like other institutions, formal and informal, the status quo rapidly lost its legitimacy and was no longer able to provide guidelines for religious and secular compromises. The institutional power of the status quo was derived from the political context in which it was created, the ideological consensus, and the dominance of the Labor Party that enabled constructive compromises. The party's dominance, however, gradually eroded until its final collapse in the 1977 elections, when it was defeated for the first time. Labor's partner to the compromise, the National Religious Party (NRP), was no longer satisfied with simply maintaining the religious status quo but also aspired to determine the country's borders. The younger generation, associated with Gush Emunim, that now dominated the party no longer sought the partnership of the secular Labor Party. The right-wing Likud, the successor of the Labor Party, was able to form governing coalitions (with the NRP and other partners) but could not reproduce the dominance of the Labor Party and the stability it fostered. Elections from the 1980s onward ended with the two blocs, hawks and doves, almost tied and in need of bringing the ultra-Orthodox, *haredi*, parties into the coalition.

The political status of the *haredi* parties was bolstered by the fact that they began to hold the balance of power and were a potential and desired partner in every coalition. While several significant political gains were made after 1977 – such as funding of private religious schools – the *haredim*'s image and their relations with other Israelis were hurt, as they were accused of "extortion" and of "religious coercion." SHAS's meteoric rise to prominence meant that it became a major player in Israeli politics, which was further enhanced by the party members' willingness or ambitions to serve as ministers in government, a step that the Ashkenazi *haredi* parties had refused to entertain. The appointment of ministers from the SHAS party often led to it getting embroiled in disputes with secular politicians, whether these involved the Ministry of the Interior, in which the minister responsible had to deal with granting citizenship or implementing the Law of Return, or the Ministry of Labor and Social Welfare, which exercises authority in matters relating to business operation on the Sabbath.

The politics of accommodation that characterized the status quo was replaced by a "politics of crisis" that undermined stability, split the political system (Susser and Cohen, 2000), and eventually rendered it ineffective. Secular resentment against what was perceived an infringement of religion on public lives and the exemption of ultra-Orthodox men from military service was channeled into political action and extra-parliamentary activity. Opposition to "religious coercion" and support for pluralism became major issues for the secular parties and the parties representing immigrants from the FSU, all competing for the "secular vote." Political parties with a pronounced secular agenda demanded curbing the *haredi* parties' powers and promised to protect liberal freedoms. FSU immigrants voted in large numbers for "Russian" parties that combined a hawkish foreign policy with a secular agenda focused on immigrants' needs. Meretz, a left-wing dovish party and home for many secular Israelis, was challenged in 1999 by the new Shinui (Change) party, which presented a more radical and focused secular agenda and, in 2006, became the third largest party in the Knesset. The competition for the secular votes became more radical, but, after its initial success, Shinui all but disappeared and Meretz lost much of its support, shrinking from twelve to three or four parliamentary seats.

This disappearance of secular parties did not indicate a change in the secular frustrations but, rather, similar to the trajectory described earlier, a loss of confidence in the political system and the ability to promote change through formal legislative processes. Frustrations, needs, and desires, consequently, have found the way to alternative arenas.

Secular Entrepreneurs: Agents of Change

The political inertia described previously has disillusioned many Israelis from thinking that change can be achieved through formal political action but has not diminished demands and frustrations of secular or secularizing Israelis and has opened new opportunities for change. The failure of the political system to adapt the status quo to the changed reality encouraged the rise of secular entrepreneurs who acted outside the political system and filled the political vacuum. The entrepreneurs – ideological atheists, advocates of Jewish renewal, FSU immigrants, or business owners – identified the needs, desires, and demands against the restrictions of the status quo and the opportunities to challenge the restrictions by different actions and services. These entrepreneurs, discussed in detail in the following chapters, were the agents of change who challenged religious authority institutionalized in the status quo.

Secular entrepreneurs reacted to the political and economic opportunities they identified. In some cases, the motivations were political-ideological goals (promotion of civil marriage) and, in other cases, they were economic (opening businesses on Sabbath). The choices and strategies, based on different combinations of ideological or economic motives, at times consciously challenged the status quo with a clear political objective (civil marriage or burial). Many other times, however, these were individual choices that took advantage of opportunities (private marriage or burial services) and had no political aspirations. The dividing line between the economic-profitable and ideological-political was often blurred when economic initiatives were legitimized by ideological statements (freedom to choose) and ideological initiatives merged with economic opportunities and used marketing techniques.

Initiatives were supported by different arguments, including individual rights and freedoms, republican citizenship claims, and market rationality. Individual freedom arguments are characteristic of the ideological entrepreneurs and the more established Israeli secularism, but have also been used by more recent secular initiatives. Liberal arguments, somewhat paradoxically, were complemented with republican arguments of good citizenship. This "republican equation" (Levy, 2008) included a reciprocal relationship between the state and its citizens, in which the citizens' contribution to the common good (military service) determined their citizenship status and allowed their claims toward or against the state. Thus, soldiers refused Jewish burial (Chapter 4) or prevented from marriage (Chapter 3) were used in effective campaigns against the Orthodox monopoly, and even the producers of pork meat (Chapter 5) referred to their republican contribution when their businesses came under threat. Since the 1990s, however, the market rationality argument has gained prominence, incorporating the other two, as arguments of efficiency, service, and customer choice have entered the debate and have been used to legitimate and promote secular entrepreneurships.

The "transformative effects" entrepreneurs had on politics, policies, and institutions (Sheingate, 2003) described in the following chapters were the cumulative result of different actions that extended beyond formal political action. This does not exclude formal political action, as secular entrepreneurs included politicians or political activists who attempt to introduce formal change of existing rules. But, when efforts in the formal political channels failed to achieve the desired results and trust in the political system declined, political action shifted elsewhere and new entrepreneurs appeared on stage. The transformative effects of this new secularization have nevertheless remained limited by several constraints. First, the ambivalent attitude of the majority of Israelis toward religion and the general desire for consensus discouraged a direct challenge to the existing rules of the game. Second, the conservatism and the narrow commitment to liberalism of some the entrepreneurs and many of the nonreligious Israelis who took part in the process often led to partial solutions. Third, similarly, the market-based initiatives that dominated the contemporary era were, almost by nature, limited in their transformative motivations and potential, often instrumental in their strategies and satisfied by partial rather than comprehensive solutions.

Taking It to the Courts

The judicial system became an alternative for secular entrepreneurs frustrated with political parties that failed to provide the needed solutions or refrained altogether from making decisions on significant questions regarding the role of religion in public life. Questions such as civil marriage or the draft exemption of Orthodox men were pushed aside by politicians in power who preferred to remain on the sidelines rather than anger religious or secular voters. The weakness of the political system meant that the courts soon became an alternative institution to which the secular public could turn in hope of a clear and binding decision. Individuals and groups appealed to the courts initially requesting a solution to tangible troubles, but later these submissions were expanded to include questions of principle. The Supreme Court was an agent of liberal values (Mautner, 2011) that, beginning in the 1980s, adopted an activist approach. This approach recognized standing for a "public petitioner" who raises an issue directly relevant to the rule of law or a violation of basic civil liberties or who blows the whistle on government corruption. In the same vein, the court extended its jurisdiction from protection of concrete, personal rights to ensuring the realization of general public values and reduced the scope of issues considered non-judicable (Mautner, 2011: 57–8).

For its critics, the Supreme Court has amassed extensive powers and, in its intervention in religious–secular affairs, it became a route bypassing the politics of accommodation (Susser and Cohen, 2000). Conversely, defenders of the Supreme Court argued that its interventions were inevitable owing to the vacuum left by the collapse of the status quo and the inertia of the political system. Irrespective of whether the court aspired to attain power or whether it was drawn against its wishes into the vacuum of religious–secular politics, the Supreme Court became a key player in the religious–secular interactions in Israel. Secular activists who perceived the court as friendly to their liberal demands attempted to generate a change by means of court rulings. To a large extent, the court became the first institution to which to turn for the protection of secular rights and the liberal viewpoint in opposition to the policies of the government, the Knesset, and the rabbinate.

Two basic laws with a constitutional status, passed by the Knesset in 1992, provided the court with greater capacity to intervene in political life. The Law on Human Dignity and Freedom and the Law of Freedom of Occupation were part of what was described as a "constitutional revolution" that supposedly took part in Israel in the 1990s. Although this may not have been the intention of the government and the Knesset, these basic laws granted the court the right of judicial review and the possibility to make decisions in cases in which the basic laws and new legislation seemed to clash. In actual practice, the basic laws had fairly limited power; the rights they promised could be infringed by new laws, as long as these did not contradict the values upheld by Israel as a Jewish and democratic state, were passed for a valid purpose, and did not diverge from what was absolutely necessary to serve this purpose (Shafir and Peled, 2002). However, the fact that the court could apply judicial control together with its actual intervention increased the public criticism of its positions. Particularly harsh criticism was voiced against the rulings that aspired to introduce liberal norms into the way religion was manifested in public (ibid.) and weaken some of the status quo arrangements, as well as reduce the gains achieved by the religious parties in the political sphere.

The courts, as the following chapters will demonstrate, became an important arena for secular groups and individuals who appealed for the right of businesses to operate on the Sabbath, to import nonkosher meat, marry outside the rabbinical jurisdiction, or be buried in a civil burial ceremony. But, in spite of several victories in the courts, the overall result of the legal struggles not only was limited in scope but also turned out to be a two-edged sword. First, the government had the last word, as it could react to court rulings with counter-legislation (see Chapter 5 on pork sales) that annulled the court's ruling. Second, the growing involvement of the Supreme Court in what were previously considered political questions alienated it from important religious groups, which saw the court as a secular, anti-religious entity. This religious discontent exploded in a mass demonstration that took place in 1999 against the Supreme Court and followed in opinion polls that indicated a significant fall in the religious population's confidence in the Supreme Court (Arian et al., 2003: 189). The resentment was also translated into different attempts to restrict the court's power and guarantee the supremacy of the government and the parliament. A decade after the constitutional revolution it seemed that the Supreme Court could no longer be the champion for liberal-secular freedoms and that new arenas had become available for operation.

Subpolitics and Secularization

Neither the formal political arena nor the courts was necessarily the "place" where the new rules of the game were shaped. Rather, as the following chapters illustrate in detail, secularization advanced by actions, small and large, that circumvented the status quo rather than directly challenge it. Frustrations with political systems and declining faith in the prospect of formal political change resulted in growing apathy and withdrawal, but also with different initiatives and alternative courses of actions. These actions, described earlier as "subpolitics," had two important advantages for secular entrepreneurs compared with formal political channels. First, they replicated other initiatives and matched the political culture that developed in Israel, in which informal solutions to problems were found more productive. Second, they were able to take advantage of the neoliberal economic policies and the freedom of choice these policies supposedly offered.

The reaction of secular entrepreneurs replicated those of other individuals and groups frustrated with political stagnation. Independent activities, both legal and illegal, became an integral part of the political culture in Israel as different groups that failed in their efforts to promote change through formal democratic means created a new situation by establishing facts on the ground, ranging from settlements to pirate radio and TV broadcasts to "gray" education and health services (Mizrahi and Meydani, 2003). Similarly, various secular activities reacted to the changes – demographic, economic, and political – and challenged the status quo by measures that can be described as subpolitics. These practices of subpolitics sidestepped the formal political system through various initiatives in which citizens filled the political vacuum and took responsibility for matters in their everyday lives (Holzer and Sorensen, 2001).

These practices, with different motivations and strategies, involved both principled issues that concerned individual values (in our case, marriage and burial) and leisure and lifestyle (in our case, commerce on Sabbath and nonkosher meat).

Conclusions: Between Secularization and Secularism

Secularization was described in the previous chapter as the decline of religious authority that may or may not be paralleled by changes of individual beliefs and identities, is independent from a secular-liberal worldview and a commitment to a political struggle. In Israel, secularization as a process is driven both by secular-liberal ideology and by economic and demographic changes removed from ideology and, particularly, from liberalism. This multifaceted process includes various needs and demands that encounter both a stagnant political system and religious opposition. Consequently, secularization is based on different arguments, unfolding through different strategies used by entrepreneurs in different arenas. Arguments of liberal rights used by secular ideologues were supplemented by republican claims that underscored the secular contribution to the public good and the rights this contribution supposedly entailed. These arguments, however, were overshadowed by a market rationality that became dominant in the 1990s also as a secularization force.

These changes were also reflected in the shift of the focus from the formal political realm to the legal and the civil-economic realms. Secular entrepreneurs who encountered resistance, on one hand, and were engaged with a wider and more diverse nonreligious public, on the other hand, found ways to circumvent rather than directly challenge the existing rules of the game. These alternatives provided an outlet to a public that in general terms can be at best described as "nonreligious," whose response to the new initiatives often created more demand and, eventually, institutional change. The rules of the game were now determined, among other things, by the purchasing power of the secular public and in the civil-economic sphere that became central to matters relating to religion–state relations and to the shaping of the public domain. Secularization advanced, therefore, incrementally and not necessarily via formal changes registered in formal decisions. Changes were often partial and short of answering all needs and demands, the direct result of the loose commitments of many entrepreneurs and the nonreligious public they catered to.

Marriage, burial, and observance of Sabbath and the rules of kashrut in Israel are not only individual choices but also institutions regulated by the state. From a formal viewpoint, neither the status quo arrangements established in early statehood nor the status of religion in political life changed. Rules pertaining to religious monopoly largely remained in place, the privileges and rights of Orthodox Jews were protected, and religious parties' power did not diminish. Focusing, however, on the formal aspects of politics – lobbying, negotiation, and legislation – may miss important developments that take place elsewhere. Changes of preferences, initiatives, and choices, with or without political intent, may bring institutional change incrementally. Looking beyond the formal aspects of politics and political change, therefore, uncovers a dynamic reality.

A general trajectory for secularization in Israel can be drawn from the discussion so far. First, the institutional framework of the status quo established in early statehood could not contain the new secularization forces that emerged in the 1980s: neoliberalism and the consumer society, the mass immigration from the FSU, and various cultural demands for recognition. Second, new religious developments emerged as counter-secularization forces that added pressures on the political system. Third, the political system, in a deep crisis since the 1980s, was unable to craft new arrangements or to efficiently enforce the existing ones. Fourth, the frustrated needs and desires of secular and nonreligious Israelis were answered by secular entrepreneurs and various actions described as "sub-politics" (Beck, 1996:18). These individual choices, ideological and non-ideological, were not registered as "politics" in the formal sense but were "political" in their impact measured in institutional changes.

The following chapters, based on the theoretical framework developed thus far, are an empirical study of secularization measured in institutional change, namely the decline of religious authority over specific domains of public life. In these domains different secular initiatives that shape the public domain, intentionally or not, are mapped and contact points between the economic and ideological planes are studied. Specifically, in the four selected areas, the book exposes the contradictions between formal rules and socioeconomic changes, traces the motivation and strategies of secular entrepreneurs, and demonstrates the cumulative impact of their actions.

3

The State of Marriage

Regulating and De-Regulating Love

Marriage can be secular Israelis' most significant encounter with religious authority. Rabbinical courts hold jurisdiction over matters of marriage and divorce for all Jews in Israel, regardless of their beliefs and preferences, and the rituals are conducted in accordance with Orthodox laws. Demands for reform made by secular Israelis who object to the Orthodox monopoly, and by those prevented from marrying in Israel by that monopoly, have gained in momentum and intensity in the past two decades. Until now, these demands have failed to change the formal rules, but the new needs and desires have been channeled into secular initiatives that have aimed at bypassing the political impasse. In fact, as this chapter shows, by adopting and applying relevant strategies, the various secular entrepreneurs succeeded in creating a range of different alternatives that, to all intents and purposes, ignore the rules of the game dictated by the status quo.

Marriage is not only a private choice of two individuals. Defined and regulated by religious and political authorities, marriage is an institution that guarantees the right to a domain of privacy, but this right is itself defined by public policy (Josephson, 2005). In fact, as the anthropologist Claude Levi-Strauss (1956: 147) stated, "marriage is not, is never, and cannot be a private business." Marriage is a social institution that "relies [on] and reproduces complex accounts of the connections between individual and community; public and private; belief and behavior; and sexuate, social, and political self understanding" and relies on formal public recognition and regulation (Metz, 2010: 86). Thus, the distinction between, on the one hand, the proper or the desired marriage and, on the other hand, the improper or banned marriage has been institutionalized and regulated by various social mechanisms. Regulation of marriage involves questions of religious and political authority and includes limitations of age and gender and boundaries between classes, ethnic, and religious groups. Consequently, the roles played by religious institutions and by the modern state in regulating marriage not only are prime movers for control and legitimization but also, on occasion, become an incentive for political debates and struggles within society and between the state and its citizens (Witte, 1997: 11). Religious authorities held control over marriage in many European and North American jurisdictions until the eighteenth and even the nineteenth centuries when the state took control over marriage (Metz, 2010: 4). Secular authorities were reluctant to leave marriage in the hands of religious establishments and, in many cases, civil marriage was established that enabled the state not only to maintain religious tolerance but also to have the ability to keep track of its subjects or citizens (Gottlieb, 1993: 70).

Marriage in the modern state was no longer solely a religious issue and was integrated into state policies and subjected to state rules. The modern state not only put the seal of approval on marriage, but also regulated it through licensing, distributing benefits, and overseeing duties of the marriage, as well as the process of its dissolution (Eichner, 2006). The regulation of marriage taken over by the state included the right to marry (e.g., legal age for marriage, legitimate partnership), individual sovereignty (arranged marriage or free choice), accepted or prohibited sexual behavior (e.g., same-sex marriage), duties and obligations for the partners (financial and legal), and bans on nuptials between individuals with biological relations and, in some cases, on interracial marriage (Cott, 1998; Haider-Markel and Joslyn, 2005). In practice, state regulation has either granted specific religious institutions the right to conduct marriage, offered civil marriage as an alternative to religious marriage, or turned marriage into a civil-bureaucratic matter in which religious or other ceremonies are a private affair separated from the bureaucratic-legalistic approval.

When the modern state wrested the regulation of marriage from religious authorities, it maintained the basic tenets of marriage as a relationship between a woman and a man, as well as the view that a nuclear family is a normative way of life. The modern state and religion, as in other instances, have struggled over questions of authority but did not diverge much on their treatment of marriage as a social mechanism. The formal recognition by the state views the normative family as desirable and privileges the marital family in designing and dispersing legal benefits aimed at protecting it (Metz, 2010: 3). For the state, marriage has become a foundational institution associated with order and stability, as Justice Stephen J. Field of the U.S. Supreme Court described it in 1888: "[I]n its purity the public is deeply interested, for it is the foundation of family and society, without which there would be neither civilization nor progress.... It partakes more of the character of an institution regulated and controlled by public authority, upon principles of public policy, for the benefit of the community" (quoted in Metz, 2010: 22–3). State power and resources were used not only to prevent marriages defined as "objectionable," but also to initiate and encourage "desirable" marriages. Marriage was perceived as part of the social order and morality and a solution to economic and social distress linked to the disintegration of the traditional family structure (Nock, 2005).

Like other societal institutions, marriage in the Western world has also been affected by changes in recent years, both losing its mandatory status and becoming more flexible. Andrew Cherlin (2004) describes a process of "de-institutionalization" in which the social norms that define people's behavior in the social institution of marriage are weakened. From a stable and permanent institution, often mediated and sanctified by religious authority, marriage has been transformed into an individualistic and flexible framework and a "pure relationship" (Giddens, 1992: 134), intimate and central to self-identity, that lasts only as long as it satisfies both partners. This flexibility pertains not only to the decision to initiate and end marriage, but also to choices of intimacy outside the traditional family framework, enabled by the loosening of the links among marriage, sexual activity, and parenthood (Nock, 2005). Alongside the traditional family institutionalized in marriage between men and women emerged new intimate relationships and arrangements that have been described as "post-modern families" (Fogel-Bijaoui, 1999: 110). These include cohabitation, childbearing outside marriage, and same-sex couples who demand the rights and recognition they regard essential for full, equal citizenship (Kiernan, 2002; Josephson, 2005).

The de-institutionalization of marriage, paradoxically, often implies politicization when demands for recognition and rights challenge existing rules. Liberal countries, with a separation of religion and state, have made the registration of marriage a purely technical and formal matter and resolved (most of) the debates over rituals, which were left to private choices. However, even those countries must engage with questions regarding the definition of which relationships constitute a marriage (and which cannot), and what are the rights and duties of couples who live as families outside the institutionalized system. One alternative, advocated by liberal theorists, is that the state should not privilege one form of affiliation that better comports with the private morality of the majority of citizens and should disestablish marriage altogether (Eichner, 2006; Fineman, 2006; Metz, 2010). However, as many individuals want their marriage recognized and states are unlikely to give up this power, regulation of marriage is likely to remain a politically contested issue.

The preferential status for the institution of marriage over other types of partnerships expresses the state's position that the heterosexual relationship based on marriage embodies the normative family unit deserving of various state benefits (Marin, 2004). Whether they organize politically to demand recognition or not, the actual existence of new kinds of families and relationships forces the state to respond to the ensuing practical questions such as responsibility for children, taxation, and inheritance (Seltzer, 2000) and to engage in normative debates regarding the regulation of marriage. The changes have been recognized by international law. For example, Article 16(1) of the Universal Declaration of Human Rights provides, inter alia: "Men and women of full age, without any limitation due to race, nationality or religion, have the right to marry and to found a family" (Marin, 2004). Within states, however, the right to marry is yet to be resolved and the status of the institution of marriage remains a politicized issue.

Israel: Rules of the Game

Israel is considered the most family-oriented society among the postindustrial societies, a reality that is reflected in its high marriage rate, low divorce rate, and high fertility levels, as well as the small number of children born to unmarried parents (Fogel-Bijaoui, 2005). As elsewhere, conservative attitudes toward family life and questions of marriage are strongly influenced by religiosity reflected in opposition toward abortion, gay marriage, and children out of wedlock, which, in spite of the family-oriented attitude, are not uncommon in contemporary Israel (Table 3.1).

Among Western countries, Israel is alone in not allowing civil marriage and having personal law governed exclusively by religious law. Section 2 of the Rabbinical Courts Jurisdiction (Marriage and Divorce) Law, 1953 provides: "Marriages and divorces of Jews shall be performed in Israel in accordance with Jewish religious law." Critics of the laws of marriage and divorce in Israel argue they are incompatible with the fundamental

TABLE 3.1. *Israelis' Views on Abortion, Same-Sex Marriage, and Out-of-Wedlock Birth*

	Ultra-Orthodox (%)	Religious (%)	Traditional (%)	Secular (%)	
Women should have the right to decide over abortion					
1 (Strongly disagree)	43.3	29.6	6.6	1.5	Cramer's $V = 0.350^*$
2	34.3	19.7	16.7	4.1	
3	11.9	8.5	7.9	5.8	Kendall's tau-c $= 0.399^*$
4	9	33.8	52.6	52.6	
5 (Strongly agree)	1.5	8.5	16.2	36	
Gay and lesbian marriage should be legalized					
1 (Strongly disagree)	53.5	43.8	21.6	11.3	Cramer's $V = 0.287^*$
2	35.4	38.4	31.3	14.9	
3	1.5	5.5	8.8	11.9	Kendall's tau-c $= 0.370^*$
4	4.6	11	28.2	40	
5 (Strongly agree)	0	1.4	10.1	21.8	
It is acceptable to have a child out of wedlock					
1 (Strongly disagree)	39.1	24.6	20.4	9.4	Cramer's $V = 0.268^*$
2	40.6	29.8	30.9	14.8	
3	17.2	22.8	13.8	9.9	Kendall's tau-c $= 0.349^*$
4	3.1	19.3	22.1	40.9	
5 (Strongly agree)	0	3.5	12.7	25.1	

* $P < 0.05$; ** $P < 0.01$.
Source: Author's own survey, 2009.

human right to marry and to establish a family as recognized and accepted in the international sphere (Marin, 2004). Consequently, the laws are also a source of discontent for Israelis who object to the patriarchal character of religious laws, are prevented from choosing the way they wish to marry, or are completely prohibited from marrying because of religious limitations.

Marriage in Israel is a religious arrangement measured by the nature of the ceremony, the religious laws that regulate marriage status, and the body in charge of administering and implementing the laws (Sapir and

Statman, 2009). The authority granted to the rabbinate over marriage and divorce was part of the status quo. For the religious public, marriage according to *halakhah* was perceived as essential to maintain the unity of the people and, consequently, the Orthodox monopoly was considered imperative. As explained by one of the leaders of the religious Mizrahi movement when the status quo policy was formulated:

[Marriage is] a key condition for the unity of the people and its cohesion.... [A]ny breach of the laws pertaining to marital relations could smash the house of Israel into smithereens.... The introduction of civil marriage and the authorization of mixed marriage could lead to the destruction of the sanctity of the Israeli family, to physical intermixing and spiritual assimilation in Israel and the Diaspora, as well as erecting an iron curtain between one Jew and another as a result of a prohibition on marriage between different sections of the nation and the evolvement of a splintered people, separated from each other. (quoted in Elam, 2000: 92)

This fear of a rift and the desire to preserve the unifying "mantle" were shared by large sections of the nonreligious public, who perceived Orthodox marriage as an absolute necessity. The marriage law, it was argued, was instrumental for the protection of national boundaries and Jewish Orthodoxy had the means and capacity to act as the gatekeeper. Apart from the consensus on this issue, the secular leadership also had pragmatic considerations, as Prime Minister David Ben-Gurion explained in the opening session of the first Knesset:

This government is unwilling to introduce a law on civil divorce and marriage. The reason for this position is that non-religious civil divorce could lead to a major fracture in the House of Israel, and at present we believe that we have far more pressing issues with which to deal, such as *Aliyah* (immigration), housing and settlement. This dispute should be left on the back-burner until a later date. (quoted in Elam, 2000: 86)

The Rabbinical Courts Jurisdiction (Marriage and Divorce) Law stipulated that rabbinical courts have sole jurisdiction to rule not only with respect to marriage, but also regarding divorce procedures. Jews, citizens of the state of Israel, are by the power of the law subject to the monopoly of the chief rabbinate and can marry in Israel only by religious marriage in the rabbinical courts. Equally important is that the dissolving of marriages is also subject to the religious law and the authority of the rabbinical court. This arrangement, which constituted an integral part of the status quo, did not find favor with secular groups from the very outset. During a Knesset debate on June 2, 1953, on the proposal for the law on marriage and divorce, Member of Knesset (MK) Beba Idelson (of the Labor Party) voiced her disappointment with the law:

> The fact that there exists a secular public in our country is no secret to the religious people. We should not turn a blind eye to the fact that this secular public does not want to go to the rabbinical court. This is an inescapable fact and so it is incumbent upon us to find a solution beyond the existing arrangement. (Knesset records: 1460, June 2, 1953)

When the law was debated in the government in 1953, Minister of Labor Golda Meir referred to the demand for immersion in the *miqva* (Jewish ritual bath), part of the Orthodox procedure, in harsh words: "Primitive things and I am not aware whether the people abided by them even during the Middle Ages.... [M]any members of the Knesset including myself now face a serious question of conscience: How can we possibly vote for such a law?" Eventually, under pressure from Ben-Gurion, who argued that the law was necessary for the unity of the Jewish people, the ministers voted in favor of the law. Several years later, however, Ben-Gurion expressed his regret over that decision and supported the introduction of civil marriage (Maoz, 2007) .

Opposition from secular groups to the Orthodox monopoly was limited in size and scope. The secular public regards the various prohibitions on marriage that stem from religious norms as discriminatory and, more particularly, irrelevant to their way of life. These include the restrictions on marriage (for example, between a man whose family – Cohen – is supposedly descended from the biblical temple priests, and a divorced woman); the Orthodox ceremony, in which the woman's role is largely passive; and the difficulties with the divorce process (especially for *agunot*, "chained" women bound to their marriage with no way out because their husbands refuse to grant them religious divorces).

The liberals among them could not accept the *halakhic* perception of rights and duties that define a woman's status as a "man's wife" (Shiffman, 2001). Others, from their own experience or in principle, objected to the refusal of the courts to adopt "liberal" reasons for divorce (Lifshitz, 2005: 57–62). However, in the conservative and burdened society characteristic of the country during its early decades, when the state was preoccupied with what was perceived as a struggle for its very survival, the idea of marriage as part of the status quo was accepted as inexorable by the majority of the public. Protest against the Orthodox monopoly was limited and restricted to a small group of ideologist secular individuals who refused to marry within the system run by the rabbinate.

Status Quo: Undermined

Until the 1990s, the number of people prevented from marrying and those opposed in principle to the Orthodox monopoly remained too small to force change. Couples had always been able to make the choice to live by common-law marriage or marry abroad since the status quo was first implemented. Sometimes these couples attracted the public eye, especially when celebrities were involved, but, limited in number, they failed to become a real political force or constitute a significant threat to the position of the status quo. A decisive majority of the Jewish public in Israel during those years chose to marry within the framework of the rabbinate; some did so as a matter of preference, whereas others felt that they had no other option and, in practice, accepted the status quo arrangements.

Immigrants from the FSU were a major factor that began to undermine the status quo. Unlike couples who, for various reasons, are not interested in getting married through the rabbinate, many couples living in Israel *cannot* be married by the rabbinate. If, in the past, this group consisted of only a handful of persons prohibited from marrying – couples of mixed religions, and couples in which the partners were a man considered to be a descendant of the priestly sect) and a divorced woman who were prevented from getting married in Israel – the migration from the FSU created a new reality in which a large number of Israeli citizens not recognized as Jews could not marry in Israel. According to the data of the Central Bureau of Statistics from late 2006, 264,000 citizens could not be defined according to religion (*Ha'aretz*, April 26, 2006). This population is largely the result of the discrepancy between the Law of Return, which grants the right to immigrate to Israel and citizenship to any person who has at least one Jewish grandparent, and the *halakhah*, which recognizes only Jews by matrilineal descent. The Law of Return allowed a large number of non-Jews or those whose Jewish lineage was in doubt according to the *halakhah* to become citizens of Israel. However, as the *halakhah* does not recognize these new citizens as Jews, they cannot marry at the rabbinate unless they undergo an arduous and complex conversion process, which frequently goes against their beliefs and secular way of life.

Changes also occurred among native Israelis that had to do with consumerism and new lifestyles that affected not only traditional weddings but also the demands of some younger Israelis, based on a secular identity or self-expression values, to make their own impact on the ceremony or to dismiss the Orthodox ritual entirely. Until the 1970s, wedding ceremonies were relatively modest and largely similar to one another. By the 1990s, however, weddings had become a display of class and lifestyle, and the choice of venue, music, and food all supposedly testified to good taste and meticulous choice. The annual turnover of the market for weddings in Israel is estimated between $1 billion and $1.5 billion a year, and the cost of a wedding with 300 guests ranges from $18 thousand to $40 thousand (http://walla.co.il/?w=//695635). Weddings have become more sophisticated and expensive, a display of style rooted in the repertoire shared by members of the same economic and social class. Preparations for the wedding include designing the bride's dress, choosing a makeup artist and hair stylist, selecting a photographer and disc jockey or band, lighting, designing the wedding canopy, and choosing the menu as well as the dishes for serving the food, and of course selecting the suitable venue (a garden with an attractive "atmosphere" is preferred). All these are influenced by well-known "trend setters" (Kaplan, 2001).

The new trends and the restrictive religious rules did not always match, presenting dilemmas for both sides. The demand of the rabbinate to hold weddings only in places that hold a kosher certificate forced the couples who wanted what they perceived as a gourmet menu to either find creative caterers who could overcome kashrut's limitation (not using dairy where meat was served, for example), fabricate fictitious kashrut certificates, place the wedding canopy at a distance from the dining area, or conduct the Orthodox wedding ceremony at the rabbinate separate from the party (Shalom, 2003). Practical solutions were also adopted by the rabbinate, including turning a blind eye to issues such as a wedding date not being fixed in accordance with the bride's menstrual days, as required. The material questions, therefore, were solved, allowing the majority of couples to both maintain the style they wanted and remain within the accepted rules of the game. Moreover, at some weddings, the choice of the rabbi officiating at the ceremony was another demonstration of the couple's status. The demand for well-known (Orthodox) rabbis increased, with some couples ready to pay more for a rabbi known for his style that would add a touch of prestige to the wedding.

The nonmaterial demands of secular Israelis to take charge of the ceremony were more difficult for the status quo to accommodate, as they directly challenged the Orthodox hegemony. Secular Israelis – largely middle-class Ashkenazim – became increasingly discontented with the Orthodox ceremony, the rabbinate, and the status quo arrangements in general. Complaints were raised about the rabbis' attitudes toward the secular public, payments demanded by the rabbis for officiating at the wedding ceremony, and the yawning gap between the religious ceremony and the couple's secular way of life. Secular women complained about the obligation imposed on them to hear a lecture from the rabbi's wife about marital relations, arrange the wedding date in accordance with their menstrual days, and undergo mandatory immersion in the *miqva* prior to the ceremony. Secular couples found ways to evade the Orthodox regulations – lying about menstrual days or finding friendlier, more lenient rabbis – but a determined minority was insistent on having wedding ceremonies that matched their worldview and would reflect their identity as secular Jews. This expression of postmaterial values discussed in the previous chapters ultimately involves questions of self-expression, quality of life, identity, and individual authority.

One can have a say about every detail of the ceremony including the time, location, banquet and even the individual performing the ceremony. Should this person be somebody of significance from your community, or a government official? The decision cannot be avoided... culture is a dynamic element; just like fashion. What was fine for your parents during the 1950s will not always seem attractive to us.... Planning a wedding ceremony with which you will feel comfortable, does not require a B.A. degree in anthropology or a M.A. degree in Judaism. It is not necessary to think of absolutely everything as the couple only has to know what is right for them to leave as it is, what they want to forego and what stimulates them to demand.... As building a home within the culture is no easy task, it requires thought and learning, courage and creativity. The individual who succeeds in this effort will find his reward by feeling at home in his culture. (Calderon, 1999: 8)

This process of de-institutionalization of marriage included also the demands of a growing number of alternative families and gay couples to be formally recognized by the state. Until the 1980s, homosexuality generally existed on the margins of society and was kept secret; however, after the successful campaign to annul the law banning homosexual intercourse (1988), the struggle for equal rights was intensified with the emphasis placed on the desire to integrate into Israeli society (Kama, 2000). The gay–lesbian community entered the public dialogue via politics, courts of law, cultural creativity, and the media, and relationships between couples of the same sex became increasingly legitimate, especially among the secular public. The next step, which was deemed virtually essential to facilitate equal rights, was the struggle for the recognition of gay-lesbian marital relationships and family units.

Even among the religious public, questions have arisen with regard to the status quo on matters relating to marriage and divorce. One argument has been put forward stating that conducting a religious wedding ceremony for people who are remote from the Torah (the body of Jewish law) and the holy commandments is improper and requires the rabbinate to relax the strict prohibitions, or that the damage done by enforcing this arrangement on the secular public is greater than any advantage to be gained (Shiffman, 1995a: 6–8). An equally important factor has emerged in recent years following increasing criticism among the religious, and especially the national-religious, public directed at the rabbinate and the way that body functions, in addition to demands that the rabbis need to be more sympathetic to the needs of the secular public and work toward "bringing hearts closer" (Ferziger, 2008).

The combination of these different developments de-institutionalized marriage in general but more importantly have undermined the legitimacy of marriage rules based on the status quo. As an increasing number of Israeli citizens were prevented from marrying and/or refused to accept the existing rules of the game, new opportunities were created for secular marriage initiatives and, consequently, more individual opportunities for marriage alternatives.

Secular Entrepreneurs: Creating Choices

The changes in the 1990s both influenced and were influenced by secular entrepreneurs with different goals and strategies. These included entrepreneurs who promote freedom of choice in marriage with no obvious preference in supporting any particular form of marriage; non-Orthodox Jewish groups that seek recognition of their status and the abolition of the Orthodox monopoly; and secular Jewish entrepreneurs who propose ceremonies of a secular Jewish cultural nature. To this, another group of profit-motivated entrepreneurs can be added: those who offer alternative ceremonies or arrange for marriages to be registered outside Israel. The distinction is analytical to a large extent, owing to the fact that ideological and profit motives are not always distinguished and, consequently, strategies are a mixed bag and depend on the resources available.

In the reality of our situation today it is difficult to point to a winning strategy from the political or public, communications, or legal point of view and we must, in all probability, advance this cause through a combination of strategies; none of them is revolutionary and none is sufficiently powerful to solve the issue. Our task at present is to devise some sort of "cocktail of remedies" in countless ways, such as to increase the number of people getting married abroad and provide information to the public on this subject. (Rabbi Gilad Kariv, interview)

The Forum for Freedom of Choice in Marriage, a coalition of several organizations and movements, was established in 2000 to promote change in the existing legislation on issues of marriage and divorce and to mobilize the secular and non-Orthodox public for a struggle.

The major aim was a change in the legislation in Israel so that any individual will be able to marry according to his or her choice. When we declare according to their choice, this is our aim, a comprehensive and wide objective of recognition of civil marriage and religious marriage for all the streams in Judaism, whether Reform, Conservative, or Orthodox alongside civil marriage, like the accepted norm in the enlightened Western world. (Zemira Segev, interview)

The campaign, however, to the disappointment of the activists, failed to capture popular support and to promote the desired political change.

When we analyzed the problem [why it is so difficult to mobilize support?] we reached the conclusion, among other ideas, that the question of marriage concerns every person at a given moment, for a very limited time during life, and so they failed to protest in the streets [for it]. Something in the Israeli public has been pulverized into a fine powder as the reality wears us down completely, for there are so many appalling issues, whether they are related to corruption or poverty and social gaps that expand continually and the wars and hostilities. (Zemira Segev, interview)

Other organizations and groups, many of them members of the forum, have taken their own initiatives. The Association for Civil Rights has led several initiatives to promote civil marriage in Israel and petitioned the Supreme Court on several occasions on the subject of the rights of same-sex couples. The New Family organization, established in 1999 by a group of lawyers, fights for the legal recognition of families that do not comply with the traditional definition, in which a Jewish man and woman enter the covenant of marriage. The organization provides legal advice on family matters for individuals, raises public awareness for the difficulties unrecognized families face – including gay and mixed marriages – and offers "contract marriages" as a substitute for marriage by the rabbinate.

Secular initiatives are not only concerned with the constitutional and legal status of marriage, but also aim to challenge the Orthodox establishment in presenting content, significance, and interpretations to be expressed in the various life-cycle ceremonies. The Movement for Progressive Judaism (Reform Jews) and the Masorti movement (Conservative Jews) are working to achieve recognition for the marriage ceremonies they arrange and thereby permit them to register marriages. The objective here, as explained by members of the Reform movement, is to allow for pluralism in marriage.

There is a religious aspect to marriage and therefore, as far as we are concerned, the most appropriate solution is for the state to permit a diverse range of marriage options and allow the religious and non-religious establishments to serve as institutions for the registration of marriage.... The principle of pluralism will be expressed in that the state will admit additional entities into the pool, or, in other words, if today there will be Reform, Conservative, and Orthodox marriage in addition to civil marriage, then tomorrow another group of Jews can come forward and request marriage in a different format so that, as long as that group accepts state regulation, the state can empower them to register marriages according to the requirements to be determined. (Rabbi Gilad Kariv, interview)

The wedding ceremony adopted by Reform Judaism integrates traditional components of the Jewish ceremony but, unlike the Orthodox ceremony, equality between the partners is expressed in the exchange of rings and the nature of the *ketubah* (Jewish marriage contract). The couple designs the *ketubah* and the ceremony, selecting the different wordings for the blessings, passages to be read, and songs, which are integrated in the ceremony. The marriage package includes the ceremony under the canopy (*huppah*) and *kiddushin* (sanctification of marriage) that is followed by civil marriage abroad, because the movement demands that the couple formally arrange their relationship in civil marriage. The Masorti (Conservative Jewish) movement also conducts Jewish marriages that combine a commitment to *halakhah* with an open positive approach to the modern world. While some native Israelis choose the Reform and Conservative alternatives, the large majority, to the dismay of the activists, still prefers the Orthodox wedding, possibly unaware of the alternatives.

They are still not aware of our presence to a sufficient degree.... We have not invested enough... and we have to propose a comprehensive alternative. We erred in that we did not continue the move toward a dramatic change to create a comprehensive alternative, for this is where the power of the Orthodox system lies. On this topic of religion and state, prejudice and enormous ignorance, it means that defeating an establishment, which has been in power for a hundred years, is not so simple. To defeat an establishment with unlimited financial resources is not a simple matter and what is more this establishment is very aggressive and problematic by nature. (Rabbi Meir Azari, interview)

Non-Orthodox religious movements are not the only ones creating alternatives for Orthodox marriage. Secular Judaism (see Chapter 2) has been enjoying increased prosperity over the past two decades. What began as studying groups of Jewish texts in an attempt to heal the breach between religious and secular has also turned into a cultural power struggle over the meaning of Jewishness. The strengthening of the trends in the search for spirituality, together with the weakening of the position of the established religion, turns the religious sources and texts into an area open to competing interpretations (Sagiv and Lomsky-Feder, 2007). These interpretations are also expressed in struggles over the right to conduct wedding ceremonies adapted to the secular and Jewish way of life.

The Secular Ceremonies Institute was set up to assist the secular public in holding life-cycle ceremonies in the spirit of secular Judaism, that combine traditional Jewish features with a modern secular interpretation. Guy Oren, a secular rabbi, describes the secular ceremony as one based on vitality and choice: "What choice means here is that the couple accepts responsibility for the ceremony and decides what ideas will be included in the ceremony. Every word or gesture during the ceremony is relevant for you, the bride and groom. Whatever is irrelevant is omitted from the ceremony" (Oren, 2008). Similar initiatives are taken by the Havaya Institute, which proposes a secular alternative while researching Jewish tradition. In addition to the learning process and writing the *ketubah*, which each couple experiences, Havaya also offers marriage workshops to deepen their familiarity with the ceremony's contents, symbols, and customs.

The different secular initiatives pride themselves not only in the choice they provide and the involvement they allow, but also on commitment to friendliness and good service. The latter is a necessity because secular ceremonies, unlike the Orthodox ones, are not financed by the state and their very existence depends on popular demand. The good service theme is also an attempt to distinguish themselves from the Orthodox establishment, which is often blamed for poor service. Those officiating at the ceremonies are described as

holders of advanced academic degrees in social science and the humanities, and with considerable knowledge of contemporary Judaism; charismatic individuals, with a special appearance and a sense of humor. They are committed to the

creation of a comfortable and pleasant atmosphere, without introducing religious features or other effects which the families do not want. (from the Secular
Ceremonies Institute website, http://www.tekes.co.il/)

Secular entrepreneurs' strategies include political struggles to allow marriage outside the rabbinate but also the formation of an alternative authority of "ceremonial experts" responsible for conducting secular ceremonies
(Prashizky, 2011) as a substitute for the Orthodox ceremony. Secular
entrepreneurs, however, face two challenges and a paradox. First, many
secularists still opt for the traditional Orthodox wedding. Second, the
secular demands for marriage reforms have so far failed to force a formal
change. Paradoxically, as will be discussed later, the alternatives created
by secular entrepreneurs may have further delayed the chance for a comprehensive reform.

What Do Israelis Want?

Secular entrepreneurs find a growing number of Israelis who either cannot marry in Israel under the Orthodox monopoly or want to marry
outside the Orthodox rabbinate. The support for civil marriage in Israel
has grown in recent years – about 63 percent of the Jewish population
expresses support for civil marriage and only 25 percent opposes it. The
support, obviously, is very strong among those who describe themselves
as "secular," but even among those who describe themselves as "traditional" there is strong support for civil marriage (Table 3.2).

However, in spite of the support for allowing civil marriage, a majority
of Jewish Israelis still prefer the Orthodox ceremony and would choose
to marry in the rabbinate (68 percent either think they would not or are
sure they would not marry in a civil ceremony). Even among those who
describe themselves as secular, only slightly more than 50 percent would
choose civil marriage, or would have chosen it if it had been available
when they married. This might be either a result of being unfamiliar with
non-Orthodox services, concerns about the consequences of not marrying
in an Orthodox ceremony, or a belief that tradition must be maintained
and that the Orthodox ceremony is an expression of traditions. Thus,
interviewees describe choosing an Orthodox ceremony as a preference, or
even an obligation, to maintain tradition. Others provide more pragmatic,
down-to-earth reasons and concerns that prevent them from considering
alternatives:

This is the way my parents were married and the way their parent were married
and I am part of this chain. I believe the people of Israel are unique...since

TABLE 3.2. *Support for Civil Marriage*

	Ultra-Orthodox (%)	Religious (%)	Traditional (%)	Secular (%)	
Support for civil marriage					
1 (Strongly against)	60	31.5	11.6	2.6	Cramer's $V = 0.416$*
2	26.2	41.1	17.7	2	
3	4.6	12.3	19	6.9	Kendall's tau-c $= 0.505$*
4	9.2	11	36.6	45.7	
5 (Strongly support)	0	4.1	15.1	42.8	
Preference for civil marriage					
1 (Definitely yes)	0	2.8	7	31.4	Cramer's $V = 0.291$*
2	0	4.2	12.6	21.7	
3	7.6	5.6	11.7	15.4	Kendall's tau-c $= -0.372$*
4 (Definitely no)	92.4	87.5	68.7	31.4	

* $P < 0.05$; ** $P < 0.01$.
Source: Author's own survey, 2009.

the time Jacob had 12 children, the Jewish nation was formed and this chain continues since and we must keep it. . . . I will not accept that my children will choose a civil marriage. (Ben-Zion, traditional)

This is how the Bible says Jews should be married, and that is what is accepted in this country that you marry in the rabbinate. This is what ordinary people do, and I am not a special person who would do something different. (Daniel, traditional)

Why did I marry in an Orthodox ceremony? I don't know. . . . I think you choose it because everybody does. . . . Also. I think alternative marriage can create problems later, with children and things like that.(Yossi, secular)

Other secular interviewees had different perspectives, including those who married in an Orthodox ceremony but today would choose something different. Secular Israelis, especially those who were married more than twenty years ago, describe the lack of choice back then and their regret about not marrying in a ceremony that reflects their way of life.

I would never set a foot in the Rabbinate, nor would I bother to marry in Cyprus. Just a contract in a lawyer's office a ring and that is it. . . . In the past I did what

TABLE 3.3. *Ethnicity and Marriage*

	Strongly Oppose (%)	Oppose (%)	Neither Oppose Nor Support (%)	Support (%)	Strongly Support (%)
Do you support the establishment of civil marriage in Israel?					
Mizrachim	14.1	17.3	16.5	35.3	16.1
Ashkenazim	8.0	9.5	8.0	38.8	35.8
FSU immigrants	5.1	6.1	6.1	42.9	30.8
Israelis	23.7	16.2	9.2	29.5	21.4

	I definitely Would	I Think I Would	I Don't Think I Would	I Definitely Would Not
If civil marriage were possible in Israel, would you choose this form of marriage?				
Mizrachim	11.7	12.6	11.3	64.4
Ashkenazim	23.0	17.3	12.0	47.6
FSU immigrants	34.8	19.6	8.7	37.0
Israelis	10.0	12.9	15.9	61.2

	Very Important	Important	Not So Important	Not Important at All
How important is it for you that you and your family members will have an Orthodox marriage ceremony?				
Mizrachim	64.4	14.9	15.8	5.0
Ashkenazim	38.4	28.3	20.0	13.2
FSU immigrants	32.2	15.5	22.2	30.0
Israelis	51.7	22.9	13.6	11.9

Source: Author's own survey, 2009.

was common because I did not know to behave differently, even if I thought differently. Today, I would never marry in the rabbinate. (Amnon, secular)

Who thought of something else? We chose what was available and also did not want to fight the establishment and the family. Today, I would certainly marry in Cyprus.... If I want to express my commitment to the person I love, I have no need for the Orthodoxy to be there. (Idith, secular)

Ethnicity has a strong explanatory value for the support of and preference for civil marriage. Among Mizrahim, the support for civil marriage was lower than that among Ashkenazim and FSU immigrants. A stronger difference was found in the preference for civil marriage, if it would become available, and the importance of the Orthodox ceremony, between Mizrahim, more conservative and traditional, and Ashkenazim and FSU immigrants (see Table 3.3). A difference was also found between the importance of an Orthodox marriage for those without an academic degree (80 percent) and those with an academic degree (41.2 percent). Gender made no difference in the support for or the opposition to civil marriage.

The growing support for civil marriage is, to a large extent, an expression of empathy with the difficulties of FSU immigrants. In addition, in the interviews, secular and traditional Jews expressed tolerance toward others who would prefer a non-Orthodox ceremony, for any reason. Similar tolerance was expressed for having children without marriage (see Table 3.1). Gay marriage, conversely, received relatively limited support even among seculars (see Table 3.1), who remain committed to the traditional family unit. This mixture of beliefs, preferences, and commitments, as we will see later, creates different challenges and opportunities for secular entrepreneurs.

The Political Realm

Proposals for civil marriage legislation were raised as early as the 1950s, as secular Knesset members submitted bills that were rejected out of deference to the status quo. In the 1990s, however, the demographic changes and the renewed energies of secular entrepreneurs indicated a possibility for change. Especially significant was the large number of FSU immigrants not recognized as Jews, who could not be married in Israel and had to travel abroad to get married. This anomaly, along with the growing power of FSU immigrants' political parties, seemed to offer the necessary support to the native Israeli secularists' yearning for change.

The Forum for Freedom of Choice in Marriage (hereinafter referred to as the "Forum") initiated several campaigns for civil marriage that included petitions, advertisements and billboards, wedding fairs, and meetings with politicians. Although their chosen strategy focused on freedom of choice, it highlighted the hardship faced by immigrants unable to marry in Israel. As in many other debates in Israel, rights were presented within a republican equation of contribution and sacrifice that merit rights. In some of the advertisements, a soldier serving in the army appeared underneath the slogan: "The country sends me to fight but refuses to permit me to marry!"

Down through the years we have held many discussions and consulted with a large number of experts about how to raise the subject in the best possible manner so as to capture the public's attention. One of those experts, who, of all people, was American, said, "Avoid the message referring to rights, because such a message is ineffective; instead, concentrate on a message of distress." The truth of the matter is that during the past decade the whole issue has changed direction.... When we talked about distress and hardship, we had to admit that we were discussing those citizens who were not prevented from getting married here, but chose otherwise. Then we spoke about citizens who were prevented from marrying by the state and in practice were fined heavily because they had to pay $1,500 to fly to Cyprus and we often hear about couples who cannot make the journey because they lack the necessary funds. In such cases, the message is indeed one of hardship in the sense that the idea of the state infringing on a basic human right is unthinkable. (Zemira Segev, interview)

FSU immigrants were the target of secular entrepreneurs seeking, on one hand, to help immigrants and, on the other hand, use the cases of immigrants prevented from marriage as a leverage for change. The New Family organization conducted a public wedding ceremony to demonstrate the problem.

Beneath the tent which served as an improvised wedding canopy, Elah who is a 25 year-old high-school teacher and an authentic Jewess held the hand of her charming fiancé, a mechanical engineer by profession, and although "there exists a doubt as to his Jewish status" he has served in the army and continues to do regular reserve duty, and also pays taxes as required by law. (Kempner-Kritz, 2002)

The Forum called on Ehud Olmert, the elected Prime Minister, and Amir Peretz, the leader of the Labor Party, to honor their promises to the electors with respect to civil marriage. At a press conference a couple was introduced – Evgeni Lantzman, an army officer, and Kristin Dan, a student soldier – who were prevented from marrying in Israel because Ms. Dan's mother was not Jewish. The military service performed by the immigrants was used once and again to stress contributions and rights supposedly associated with them.

"It is absolutely absurd that citizens like myself, who have chosen to serve in the army for many years, in professions, which contribute to society, are forced to travel abroad to exercise their elementary right, which every democratic state is bound to grant its citizens, namely, the right to a life of matrimony," declared Lantzman. (*Ha'aretz*, April 24, 2006)

The proposed bill drafted by the Forum stated that any person in entitled to marry on condition that he or she is more than seventeen years old, and the marriage can be either religious or civil in line with the couple's wishes. Religious marriages would be conducted according to the existing procedure, whereas civil marriages would be held according to the power vested in civil marriage registrars to be appointed by the Minister for Justice. Accordingly, there would also be a procedure for civil divorce proceedings for whoever married by civil marriage or by agreement between the spouses. According to Zemira Segev, General Manager of the Forum for Freedom of Marriage, under the proposed bill, the content and character of the wedding and ceremony all would remain at the couple's discretion. Although the right of same-sex couples to marry was not mentioned explicitly, nevertheless, the declaration of the right of "every human being" to enter the covenant of marriage also included marriages of couples from the same sex and the gay-lesbian organizations were partners in the Forum. (Zemira Segev, interview).

Another marriage and divorce bill was submitted in 2002 by the New Family organization. The organization explained that the change in the legislation was designed to reflect the many changes that have occurred in the family framework, nowadays including mixed families in which the spouses have different nationalities, as well as single-parent and same-sex families, all of which are not recognized as such in Israel. The proposed basic law expanded the definition of the family to encompass married couples, unmarried couples who manage their home jointly and are mutually committed to a shared life, and an adult and a minor sharing the same home where the adult is the parent or the legal guardian of that minor. This expansion, it was explained, would cover 40 percent of family units in Israel that are not legally recognized.

Political parties purporting to represent the immigrants from the FSU have made promises to resolve the difficulties of couples not recognized as Jewish, but in practice did little to rectify the situation. The 1999 coalition agreement between the Yisrael B'Aliyah party, representing FSU immigrants, and Ehud Barak, the prime minister at the time, focused mainly on foreign policy questions; on the issue of marriage it stated simply that "the government will continue to work toward a solution, in coordination with the Chief Rabbinate, for registering the marriages of couples who are Jewish" (cited from the Knesset website: http://www.knesset.gov.il/docs/heb/coal_ib.htm). The party's leader, Natan Sharansky, who served as the Interior Minister, announced that he would support the reinstitution of consular marriages as a solution for those couples prevented from marrying, a procedure that had been severely restricted following a request submitted by the Israeli Foreign Ministry to the foreign consulates in Israel asking that they refrain from conducting marriages in Israel. Sharansky also declared his support for a mechanism for registering civil marriages (*Ha'aretz*, March 17, 2000), but in July 2002, the leaders of the party faction absented themselves from the vote on the civil marriage bill, which was tabled by Knesset members representing the Meretz and Labor parties (*Ha'aretz*, July 17, 2002).

The Yisrael B'Aliyah party was replaced by Yisrael Beiteinu as the leading party representing the new immigrant population. After the 2006 elections it seemed that on the marriage issue the party had found a partner in the Kadima ("Forward") party, the major winner in those elections, which promised to enact a "civil covenant" as a substitute for marriage. The Russian-language manifesto of Yisrael Beiteinu emphasized the intolerable situation of young people who serve in the army but cannot marry, so the promise was made to implement a marital relations covenant. In contrast, the party's Hebrew manifesto failed to mention the issue at all, probably due to its effort to attract native Israelis on the political right wing (*Ha'aretz*, March 21, 2006). During the coalition negotiations, the Yisrael Beiteinu party chairman laid down the legislation of a civil marriage bill as one of its conditions for joining the coalition (*Ha'aretz*, April, 8, 2006), but the very next day it was clarified further that this was not a *sine qua non* and that "the [portfolio of the] Ministry of Internal Security was more important" (NRG, April 9, 2006).

Parties representing the immigrants were less concerned with a general reform of marriage that would include all Israelis and more with finding a pragmatic solution for immigrants prevented from marrying. In recent years, a bill promoted by Yisrael Beiteinu suggested that when both partners are not recognized as Jewish, the couple could register for marriage outside the rabbinate. This suggestion seemed feasible and raised little opposition from the religious but could not solve the problems of couples in which only one partner is not recognized as Jewish, or of couples who want a non-Orthodox marriage for different reasons. Secular entrepreneurs have come to realize that these parties are an unlikely partner for their struggle.

The "Russian" politicians have taken no interest in what is happening with the new immigrants concerning marriage and also failed to relate to the difficulties experienced by the immigrants when it came to questions of Jewish identity. In my opinion, the new immigrants demonstrated a failure to convey the issue into the political sphere. There were [only] attempts by several Russian politicians from Yisrael Beiteinu's marginal elements, or from Sharansky's party in its time, to deal with this subject. (Rabbi Meir Azari, interview)

In July 2007 Daniel Friedmann, the Minister for Justice, and Rabbi Shlomo Amar, the Sephardic Chief Rabbi at the time, signed a draft document of a law they formulated that would allow a couple to marry in Israel in a civil procedure, but only if both partners were not recognized as Jews according to *halakhah* (*Ha'aretz*, July 19, 2007). The supporters of this law saw it as an important compromise, and even a precedent, in that it essentially broke the taboo of the rabbinate's opposition to civil marriage. On the other hand, its critics considered the compromise proposal as contemptible, as it provided a response to only a small proportion of the difficulties encountered in this area, ignored the public who wanted non-Orthodox marriage, relegated the secular or non-Orthodox religious alternatives to a secondary status, and left the Orthodox monopoly fundamentally intact.

The Friedmann-Amar initiative is deceptive in that it solves the problem of approximately one hundred fifty couples who lack any religious classification and marry partners who have no religious classification. Therefore all the Friedmann-Amar initiative achieves is to solve the hardship faced by about one hundred fifty couples out of the five thousand or so Israeli couples altogether who marry abroad. (Rabbi Gilad Kariv, interview)

More comprehensive reforms faced strong religious opposition. A bill proposed in 2004 by the liberal Meretz party sought to permit any person to marry according to his or her conscience and allow civil marriage for every individual who wanted it. However, other secular parties who were part of the governing coalition did not support the bill, as Yosef Lapid, the leader of the secular Shinui party, explained:

We are currently holding very serious negotiations with the coalition partners in an effort to find the solution to which we all aspire. . . . At present, the problem for both you and us is that your fine proposals have no chance of being passed because they do not have majority support, and so you should delay this proposed bill until we bring to the Knesset a practical bill, which will help thousands of citizens. (*Ha'aretz*, March 10, 2004)

The Knesset committee was on the verge of submitting a bill that would allow couples to choose between a civil procedure of registration and a religious ceremony at the rabbinate. Whereas secular politicians declared a "revolution," the Ashkenazi Chief Rabbi was quick to warn that "the law endangers the unity of the people, breaks the strand of the generations and will result in the need to start keeping genealogical records." The Sephardi Chief Rabbi joined the fray in warning about the danger of the proposed bill: "Is the plague of assimilation occurring now around the world not enough for us?" (*Yediot Aharonot*, July 26, 2004). The bill, eventually, was not submitted.

Secular entrepreneurs debated whether to struggle for a comprehensive legislative change or settle for a more limited legislation that would solve the distress of those prohibited from marrying. However, in retrospect, initiatives restricted in scope have not fared much better than comprehensive ones, indicating the weakness of the political system and leading some of the entrepreneurs to question the utility of those struggles.

> Currently, my problem is that should, heaven forbid, the struggle for civil marriage succeed then in a given situation where a certain political lineup characterized by a specific government [comes to power] it could legislate a law against such marriages. [Therefore], the struggle could have the reverse effect and then we might not be able to enjoy even the existing freedom to marry by civil marriage abroad or conduct a ceremony [as we see fit]. For the present, the situation in Israel allows for a measure of freedom in which we can work freely. (Nardi Green, interview)

Others regretted the reliance on political forces, especially parties that fostered an anti-*haredi* stance that failed to make the most of the window of opportunity that became available in the 1990s.

> I think that the group I belong to made a major mistake in attempting to play an "anti" role instead of presenting a real alternative and, at the end of the day, this policy cost us dearly. Although you stand to gain a lot of seats in parliament with an "anti" policy, you cannot maintain this position in the long run. . . . These parties did not bother to budget for this alternative, nor even to legislate, fund and facilitate; [one can speak] here of betrayal by the political system on these issues because politicians saw this idea only as a banner to boast about and unfold to its advantage but when the time came to fulfill their promises they were found wanting. (Rabbi Meir Azari, interview)

Public support for civil marriage and the efforts made by the various secular entrepreneurs to change the status quo – the existing law and the Orthodox monopoly in matters pertaining to marriage and divorce – have failed, signaling to groups and individuals not to exert efforts in the political arena. Indeed, struggles for civil marriage have all but disappeared in the past decade. However, parallel to the constitutional struggle in the political arena, and especially when it became evident that this struggle was not producing results, secular entrepreneurs have found other channels for their activities.

Course of Action: The Courts

The courts became an address for secular entrepreneurs and even more for individuals seeking assistance after their request for marriage was denied by the rabbinate and the state. Limited in power, the courts could not directly challenge the Orthodox monopoly, but in a series of rulings they did help create alternative frameworks to Orthodox marriage and equal rights to alternative family structures and, thereby, made it easier for the secular public to get around the Orthodox monopoly.

The first and possibly most significant step taken by the court was the recognition of the validity of marriages performed abroad. In 1962, Henriette Anna Caterina Funk-Schlesinger petitioned the courts against the Minister of the Interior, claiming that it had refused to recognize her marriage conducted abroad and allow her to register under her new surname (Schlesinger) in the civil population registration. In its verdict, the court endorsed the validity of civil marriages conducted abroad in keeping with the laws of a foreign country, and compelled the Ministry of the Interior to register these marriages as all other marriages. This decision, however, was restricted only to marriages conducted and formally registered abroad. When a case was brought to the court of a couple, a *kohen* (member of the priestly sect) and a divorcée, who could not be married by the rabbinate and who demanded that a private ceremony they conducted outside the offices of the rabbinate be recognized by the state, the court could only offer its sympathy:

They [the couple] find themselves facing a prohibition that is entirely related to a religious ritual, which is based on ancient concepts concerning the status of the *kohen*'s birthright in sacred worship. Imposing such a prohibition on a person who does not believe in religion is difficult to resolve with freedom of conscience and the freedom of action that it entails. (HCJ 80/63, *Gurfinkel and Haklai v Ministry of the Interior*; see Shiffman, 1995b: 168)

Careful not to directly challenge the status quo, the court was consistent in its refusal to accept the demands of secular Israelis for civil marriage in Israel, even when they advocated the Declaration of Independence promise for "freedom of religion and conscience." The court's decisions affirmed that Jews in Israel were subject to the authority of the rabbinic courts in matters relating to marriage and divorce, without any consideration for their religious or secular opinions (HC 450/70, *Ilan Rogozinski, Yael Tsahori, Dani Shiponi, Tami Shiponi v. the State of Israel*, Verdict:

26 (1) 129). The court's reasoning was that a couple who married in a private ceremony despite the fact that there was no obstacle to performing the marriage through the rabbinate does not deserve any legal relief (Shiffman, 1995b: 328) and there is no valid reason to sanction a ceremony that arises from an anti-religious standpoint because "the courts are not the suitable stage for conducting a campaign for the revision of the laws relating to personal status of Jews in Israel" (quoted from Justice Landau in HCJ 130–132/66, as cited by Shiffman, 1995b). In a similar vein, the petitions submitted by the Movement for Progressive Judaism (HCJ 47/82, *Segev v. the Rabbinical Court of Zfat*) to authorize its rabbis to register marriage or to compel the Minister for Religious Affairs to appoint a registrar for civil marriage (HCJ 4058/95, *Ben-Menashe v. Minister for Religious Affairs*) were rejected and petitioners were referred to the legislative authority.

The court does not have an unambiguous solution to the problem of those defined as common law spouses as there is no consensus on this problem in Israeli society and therefore the court cannot be expected to rule clearly in this direction or the opposite one. Unambiguous decisions on this sensitive issue may only come from extra-judiciary bodies. Some observers believe that the solution to the problem lies in the introduction of civil marriage.... Whereas others think that the solution to the problem can be found in Jewish civil law itself, but in any case, the court itself cannot and should not solve this problem fundamentally. The court should not be expected to order that civil marriage be upheld, and the court has consistently refused to do so. (Justice Aharon Barak, HCJ 693/91, *Efrat v. Director of Population Register in the Ministry of the Interior*, verdict 47(1) 749, 789)

Although the court refused to discuss the principle and avoided thorny issue of civil marriage, it was willing to confront more "limited" questions of personal distress. The court, explained described Justice Barak, cannot avoid making decisions when those dilemmas are brought up:

[We encounter] cases of a single-parent family, [long-term] relationships between man and the woman who are not married... yet they have set up a family unit, with the status of common-law marriage. Moreover, the homosexual relationship requires our judicial recognition. We are coming across an ever-increasing occurrence of civil marriage. [Consequently] the law faces new issues with which it must cope. The court now confronts a new reality and it must come up with solutions for it. (Rosenblum, 2004)

The courts, through different rulings, granted rights ranging from adoption to inheritance to couples who did not marry at the rabbinate, thereby, to all intents and purposes, recognizing alternative family units.

The legal system gradually sanctioned "common-law marriage," used as a general term for couples involved in a relationship that is similar to the relations existing between married couples (Lifshitz, 2005: 17) and ruled that a married woman could be recognized as the common-law wife of another man in all matters pertaining to inheritance and pension rights (Shiffman, 1995b: 56). The rulings brought the position of common-law spouses closer to that of officially married couples but, legally and status-wise, common-law marriage remained inferior to formal marriage and could not be a comprehensive substitute (ibid.: 250).

The court was called on to make an additional decision in 2005 when five gay couples, aided by the Association for Civil Rights in Israel, petitioned against the director of the population registry in the Ministry of the Interior, who refused to register their marriages, which was held in a civil ceremony in Canada (HCJ 3045/05, *Yossi Bar-Ari and others v. Population Administration*). These couples claimed that the registrar had no authority to turn down a marriage that was legally valid and was duty bound to register the applicants as married. In his response, the director of the population registry argued that the legal format for marriage in Israel refers only to a man and a woman and that the proper place for deciding issues relating to the recognition of a new personal status was the parliament. In this case, the court ordered the registrar of the population to register as married the five couples in the civil register, but made it quite clear that the decision was purely "technical," concerning the authority or powers of the registrar, and that the decision did not constitute any recognition of same-sex marriages. This ruling supplemented a series of rulings according to which the court reinforced the position of same-sex couples, as it ordered that an adopted girl of a couple of lesbian mothers should be registered as such (HCJ 1779/99, *Brenner-Kadish v. the Minister of the Interior*); allowed a lesbian couple to adopt the children of one another (HCJ 10280/01, *Yaros-Hakak v. the Attorney General*); granted rights based on collective labor agreements to a homosexual couple (HCJ 721/94,; *El Al v. Danielowitz*); and granted pension rights to homosexual spouses (HCJ 369/94, *Steiner v. Israel Defense Forces*).

The court's rulings have challenged, but not changed, the Orthodox monopoly. Recognizing the opportunities the rulings created, and the harsh criticism the court suffered for them, entrepreneurs had to realize that, for the present, the legal options to enforce change have been exhausted.

One cannot expect the High Court of Justice to commit suicide on the altar of liberalism. One must choose wisely when the court is effective and when not, and this is especially true where marriage and divorce proceedings are concerned because here the High Court of Justice has expressed its opinion on enough occasions in the past. The very move made by the High Court of Justice in stepping forward to declare that civil marriage abroad is in essence equally valid to rabbinical marriage in Israel, created a basic precedent so that at some point in the future the court will come and say that if in any case this or that couple can travel to Nicosia then why shouldn't they fly to Eilat or for that matter fly 45 minutes to avoid the traffic on their way to the court in Haifa? The court has in fact exposed the religious establishment's embarrassment and slowly but surely it will lead that establishment to the point where the Israeli public, including the dedicated supporters of the religious establishment, will understand that all that is involved here is power and control and not ideology. (Rabbi Gilad Kariv, interview)

Secular Ceremonies: Bottom-Up Changes

For some secular entrepreneurs, the alternatives of marriage abroad and common-law partnerships, discussed later, constitute an end in their own right, as they could gradually weaken the Orthodox monopoly and allow freedom of choice. Other secular entrepreneurs view the legal options as only a means to an end: an organized and attractive non-Orthodox alternative for marriage that would require a cultural revolution and an assertion of a Jewish secular identity. These alternatives for marriage are political, explicitly or implicitly, but at the same time circumvent the formal political arena in favor of bottom-up, grassroots changes.

We try to stay away from two things, politics and the legal issue. We are concerned with the cultural domain although this does not mean that we will not contribute to the political and legal struggles for we side with all the ongoing struggles to introduce laws for civil marriages and the marital relations covenant in certain matters, and so forth. We shall join in all these struggles but we shall not lead them, and I doubt whether they are all that important. (Nardi Green, interview)

The problem, as some of the entrepreneurs explained, was not only the Orthodox monopoly but also the would-be secular public that fails to assert its rights and refrains from engagement with its Jewish identity. This shallowness and lack of debate, according to entrepreneurs, must be tackled first in order for real change to take place.

The public is ignorant, as we are discussing a public which hardly engages in its Jewish identity at any stage in their lives. They unfurl the secular flag in almost every other place, they will loathe the religious groups because this public perceives them as imposing their will with respect to all sorts of things.... I see that there is virtually no religious coercion.... [The problem here is] the identification of the rabbinate with the "right thing."... the establishment reflects the Jewish identity and the perception of the Orthodox groups as the true Jews. (Sagit Mor, interview)

FSU immigrants, a large secular group, many of whom are prevented from marriage, were the "natural" clientele of the secular initiatives. However, as mentioned earlier, this group was reluctant to take part in the struggle for reform painted in liberal colors and preferred particular and practical solutions. Aside from the immigrants' reluctance, entrepreneurs were concerned that if alternative marriage would be associated with the predicaments of FSU immigrants, other Israelis will be turned away.

[I]t is also important that people from the mainstream should come to us and that is precisely where we need to be and not only in the problematic sector.... A certain person came from Russia and it is not clear whether he is a Jew or not, so he is trapped and the Reform group married him. While this development is terrific and the fact that the Reform Jews responded to the challenge is truly an admirable act, it does however pose a question for the average Israeli sitting at home. [However,] if the press reported that I conducted the marriage ceremony for Ehud Barak's daughter, then that will arouse the public interest, because for most Israelis Ehud Barak is hardly a marginal individual. (Rabbi Meir Azari, interview)

The Reform and Conservative movements attempt to attract a wide Israeli audience to a wedding ceremony that includes all the elements of the traditional ceremony but stresses the equality between the sexes and allows the couple to take part in planning the ceremony. In the ceremony under the Reform wedding canopy (*huppah*) there is no reference to property, and the exchange of rings between the partners serves as a symbol of equality and a true partnership. Similarly, the Conservative movement offers a *ketubah* based on equality, in which the bride has a clear statement to make parallel to that of the groom: "You are my husband according to the Law of Moses and Israel, and I shall respect, cherish, and support you as fixed in the law concerning seemly Jewish women who respect, cherish, and support their husbands in faith." The Reform and Conservative ceremonies are well structured but also allow the couple to take part in the planning "of an equal ceremony that will express your aspiration and hopes for the future, together with maintaining all the principal and significant elements of the traditional wedding" (Beit-Daniel, 2007). Marketing the ceremonies to the secular public, not members of their communities, the movements stressed their relevance to Jewish secular life:

Upon what foundations do you wish to build your joint home? Do not compromise! You have the ability to guarantee that your ceremony under the canopy and *Kiddushin* (sanctification of marriage) will reliably express your way and your expectations from your life together. (Beit-Daniel, 2007)

These marriage ceremonies have no official recognition, so the couples cannot register as married after the wedding. The Reform movement insists on making the marriage official in a civil process abroad, gives the couple legal advice as part of the marriage process, and refers the couple to travel agencies that organize weddings in Cyprus. The Center for Jewish Pluralism, the legal and public division of the Movement for Progressive Judaism in Israel, distributes comprehensive information regarding the legal aspects and options for conducting marriage ceremonies abroad. The Conservative movement does not require the couple to marry abroad but asks the couple to sign a statement to the effect that they understand the significance of the Conservative ceremony in that, by itself, it does not allow them to register as a married couple in Israel.

Apart from the regular members of the Reform and Conservative movements, the couples getting married in those communities are generally middle-class Ashkenazi Jews or (in smaller numbers) those who are prohibited from marrying in Israel and are consequently turned down by the rabbinate. The two movements report that in recent years a broader range of couples have approached them. They conduct about 1,000 wedding ceremonies every year, and expect that the numbers will grow as more people will be exposed to the alternatives:

The significance of the fact that an ever increasing number of couples is turning to us is that eventually these people will open the door, and this is the direction in which we are heading. . . . although it may be considerably naïve to suggest that, but after considerable experience in this area I think that in summing up a struggle that has been ongoing for the past fifteen years, the influence of two hundred guests at a wedding who witnessed the Reform ceremony accumulates to become much greater than a news item in the newspaper reporting that the Reform movement had petitioned the High Court of Justice and the judges deferred the proceedings to a later date. This influence will eventually be transformed into a change in the law in the State of Israel owing to the changing situation. . . . And here there is a need for a movement for change that develops from the grassroots upwards and not from high above. (Rabbi Meir Azari, interview)

Additional alternatives for wedding ceremonies have been offered by new entrepreneurs. These "secular weddings" combine, in varying proportions, universalism and spirituality, Jewish-Israeli particularity and individualism, expressed in the couple's ability to fashion the ceremony and choose the person to conduct it. At the Secular Ceremonies Institute, for example, among those conducting weddings are a psychologist and family therapist, a therapist applying the holistic approach, and a coacher. A distinct expression of postmaterial values of self expression can be observed in the ceremonies in which the couples add a personal – universal and/or Israeli – statement to the ceremony, expressing their identity.

A secular ceremony because we are not religious and certainly not *haredi* [ultra-Orthodox]! We have no need for rabbis to tell us what is the right thing to do and what is not or which man or woman is "clean" and which one is "impure." ... We want the secular ceremony because this is the only one spoken in our language and in line with our cultural codes. (retrieved from the website of TEKES, the Institute of Jewish Secular Rites: http://www.tekes.co.il/English-index.html)

The traditional Jewish wedding ceremony serves as the source of inspiration for the ceremony, which we perform. However, we feel duty bound to apply the principles of equality and reciprocity in the Israeli marriage ceremony, and believe that in so doing we are expressing the point of view held by most of the Israeli public.... You are encouraged to update and make additions to the traditional ceremony in keeping with the spirit of the times and your own personal phrasing. (retrieved from the Havaya website: http://www.havaya.info/).

The independent initiatives have considerable significance for the gay-lesbian community, as many of those conducting secular ceremonies see same-sex marriages as a legitimate component in the secular Jewish reality. The gay and lesbian wedding ceremonies, just like the alternative family units, are becoming a more familiar sight and are now accepted by large sections of the secular public as part of the broader emergence of celebrations and ceremonies, from gay pride parades to weddings. Thus, even *Yediot Aharonot*, the popular daily newspaper, provided a story of a lesbian wedding with a positive and humorous note, and the headline, "The bride may now kiss the bride" (February 9, 2003). The connection between universalism, Judaism, and individualism outlined previously is expressed also in gay and lesbian weddings, as one couple, interviewed in a popular newspaper, described their planned wedding.

By my own definitions I am first of all a human being, afterwards a homosexual, and then I am a Jew and later on an Israeli.... We decided that a biblical passage would be appropriate. Although my sexuality is embodied firmly within me and defines who I am, but Judaism does so too. We chose David's lament over

Jonathan for it was amazing that the King of Israel should have declared his love
for men. . . . Rings will also be a feature of our wedding because this also indicates
a certain degree of equality, just like the straight people. (*Tel Aviv Magazine*, May
25, 2007)

Secular ceremonies are sometimes accompanied by a learning process during which the couple, together with the secular counselors who perform
the wedding, study their roots and identities as they plan their wedding.
The counselors, students, and scholars of Jewish tradition meet with the
couple to debate philosophical questions of marital relations and their
relevance for their future. Together, they study the traditional ceremony
and all its elements and significance to discover the suitable ceremony for
them.

From the Jewish religious and personal knowledge which I acquired, and by
paying attention to the thread of love connecting the couple. We shall get together
for two meetings before the *Chuppah* (Jewish wedding ceremony) and talk things
over; together we shall learn traditional and revitalized sources. We shall also
listen to the tune from your hearts and weave it into the ceremony. You should
design the *Ketubah* and a personal declaration, while I contribute my experience
and knowledge in moderating the ceremony. It is the spirit shining from your
faces which is the decisive factor. (from the website of Yair Rothkovitch: http:
//www.tkasim.org.il/49949)

The secular entrepreneurs describe this process as "taking responsibility,"
individually and as a collective, for Jewish identity rather than accepting
it as a given (Orthodox weddings) or avoiding it altogether (opting out
of a ceremony or settling for a civil ceremony abroad). The ceremony,
a joint effort of the couple getting married and the person officiating
at the wedding, should express the couple's worldview and lifestyle and
stimulate them to study what being Jewish means to them as a starting
point.

As a *midrasha* (college), it is important for us to influence and change the nature
of Israeli society and what is currently our Jewish identity and culture. . . . We
at the college see ourselves as the agents for generational change. We have the
commitment and the perception that this is our identity and culture and we want
to reclaim it for the secular public and make it accessible. . . . I am a Zionist, I
define myself as a Jew, a Zionist. I live in the State of Israel and so I think that the
society [is not allowed] to give up its cultural involvement, also where ceremonies
and festivals are concerned. (Sagit Mor, interview)

The objective here is to give the secular people the means to become aware of
their culture, take possession of their Jewish culture in the domain of life-cycle

ceremonies. . . . I don't want to fight the religious establishment, and I have no pretensions, not as far as the law or the [marriage] act itself are concerned. My intention here is to make a positive suggestion and contribute to the cultural life of the secular Jews in Israel. (Nardi Green, interview)

An increase in the number of couples marrying outside the rabbinate and the creation of a value-based alternative that would allow and encourage more people to take this responsibility could, in the longer run, entrepreneurs believe, bring a wider, societal, cultural change and constitute a Jewish-secular identity.

We see ourselves as agents of a generational change. Others will state that the client is the primary consideration, and I am going to provide him or her with what they want and there is indeed a great deal of space within the boundaries of this area with respect to what I offer culturally. . . . We have the commitment and the understanding that this is our identity and it is our culture and so, as secular individuals, we wish to claim it as our own. (Sagit Mor, interview) .

Not all secular ceremonies involve an in-depth study and identity search. Some couples are less committed to the process of learning or prefer media celebrities who perform marriage ceremonies, adding their touch of humor, romance, and probably fame. Secular institutions, therefore, offer a variety of services from which couples could choose and some cater more than others to the preferences of the couples. This businesslike attitude combines a secular ideology with a professional stance and, at times, a belief in the power of markets as forces of change.

One of the most important things for us is to offer the full range available, from secular rabbis like myself to celebrities. . . . Unlike the Chief Rabbinate we do not dictate to anybody what the ceremony should be like but rather we say initially to the couple that you should think about what you want and choose what suits you best. . . . We try to create a market but not in the sense of distasteful competition but rather in the sense of "when scholars vie, wisdom mounts," for we want that those performing the ceremonies will make every effort for the benefit of the consumers of ceremonies. (Nardi Green, interview)

The businesslike attitude is also reflected in the commitment the entrepreneurs declare to service, decency, and honesty, explicitly or implicitly, referring to the negative image of the rabbinate among many secular people. Stories of Orthodox rabbis asking for payments (Orthodox weddings are funded by the state, so no payment is required), hardships at the rabbinate before the wedding, and the general bad service were mentioned in interviews, in comparison with the good service the secular entrepreneurs provide:

When I say "service" I am thinking in economic terms, for I am aware that this is one of the most significant decisions in the couple's lives up to that moment. They pay a lot for whatever they do in connection with that special moment [in their lives] and they also have to pay something to us... although less that what they pay the D.J. but more than what they pay to other service providers. [As far as we are concerned], there exists a promise that we shall perform this process, and at the end of it you will arrive at your *huppah* (wedding canopy) with all the things that are important to you and your families... that this will be an event and a moment establishing relationships, building up connections for the future, to be remembered with joy. (Yiftach HaShiloni, interview)

The quality of service and the freedom of choice are part of the marketing strategy of secular marriage providers that, not funded by the state like the Orthodox, depend on popular demand. For some of those conducting weddings the ceremonies constitute an important source of income. Accordingly, many of them advertise on Internet sites featuring not only pictures, short films, and texts from the weddings they have performed, but also letters received from couples, or "satisfied customers," stating that the ceremony did indeed express their aspirations. Secular ceremonies, unrecognized by the state, rely not only on popular demand but also on the availability of alternatives that allow these marriages either to register or, in practice, maintain a household.

Marriage Abroad

Marriage abroad is a popular and relatively easy way for couples to avoid the rabbinate and register their marriages. In the past it was possible to get married through an emissary ("Paraguay marriage") or at a foreign consulate in Israel if one of the partners was a citizen of that country. Currently, after both these options were curtailed by the Israeli government, couples are required to travel abroad. Cyprus, due to its geographical proximity and bureaucratic straightforwardness, has become the preferred destination for marriage abroad. In 1990, 270 Israeli women and men registered for marriage in Cyprus; by 2000, their number had increased to almost 6,000 Israelis, who changed their official family status to married on returning to Israel. (Figure 3.1). In 2010, according to the Israeli Bureau of Statistics, 47,855 couples married in the established courts (Jewish, Christian, and Muslim), 35,887 in the Jewish courts, and 9,262 couples registered their marriages conducted abroad.

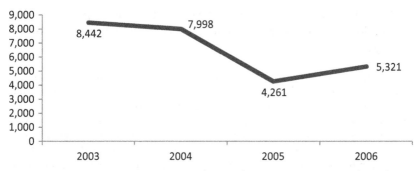

FIGURE 3.1. Marriage in Cyprus (in thousands). *Source:* New Family website, http://www.newfamily.org.il/rec/116-.

Headlines in the newspapers reported that 20 percent of Israelis marry abroad, an indication of the declining legitimacy of the rabbinate and the Orthodox monopoly (*Ha'aretz*, August 3, 2012; *Ynet*, August 2, 2012; http://www.ynet.co.il/articles/0,7340,L-4263745,00.html).

Data on the number of those who married overseas and registered with the Interior Ministry are available from the Central Bureau of Statistics only since 2000, and there is no information on the type of marriage they conducted in Israel (Jewish or civil), if any. Dobrin (2006) found that the age of those tying the knot abroad was higher than those getting married in Israel, apparently because of the greater tendency of divorcées to marry abroad and also due to the secular liberal views held by those getting married that are linked to the tendency to marry later in life. Additional findings show that those getting married abroad are generally Ashkenazi Jews, who are economically well off and relatively highly educated. About half the couples marrying abroad in recent years are immigrants from the FSU or the children of such immigrants.

The decision to marry abroad can be the result of being prevented from marriage in Israel, a secular ideology, lifestyle, or some combination of the three. Internet sites advertise a variety of "holiday packages" abroad where the package includes different kinds of marriage ceremonies. Here, a different type of secular entrepreneur, motivated largely by economic and commercial interests, markets alternative programs for weddings and vacations. An article in the Hebrew daily *Ha'aretz* reported, "They travel to Cyprus in droves, pay 1,000 dollars for a three-day holiday in a five-star deluxe hotel with a sauna, swimming pool, gymnasium, English breakfasts, and, in addition, by the way, they also get married... without breaking the glass, no talk with the rabbi's wife, and no note from the *miqva* (ritual bath)" (Lori, 2008). David Keinan, one of the first entrepreneurs to market marriage packages to Cyprus, describes the development of this phenomenon as a combination of business and ideology:

We began working on this project completely independently; at first we had four to six couples per month, mostly those who were prohibited from marrying and mixed marriages. There were also several couples who were anti-[religious] but these were few and far between. By 1991 we had already reached more than 200 to 300 couples a year, and in good times the number even increased to 550 couples a year.... It all began as a business that simply interested me, but then, as so often happens in such circumstances, I must admit that one identifies with what one does.... You can see that you are performing a good deed and these good deeds accumulate all the time. (interview)

For many years, Cyprus has been marketed as a romantic getaway perfectly suited also for weddings. Glossy travel catalogues distributed by the Cyprus tourist office explain that "conducting a civil wedding in Cyprus is simple and many couples take advantage of the opportunity to get married on the island and have a pleasant holiday in the bargain." For the municipalities in Cyprus, especially for the smaller ones among them, foreigners' weddings constitute a significant source of revenue; one of the town mayors even finds the time to visit Israel every year to market his town to travel companies. A member of the Larnaca city council in Cyprus explained the interest in the phenomenon: "For us, these weddings are part of our livelihood and provide a good income for the city and state. We are prepared to consider special requests, which may even require working on Saturday" (Lori, 2008).

Of the 5,000 weddings of foreigners performed in Cyprus every year, about 1,500 involve Israelis, who pay $2,000 or more for the wedding–vacation combination. Marriages in Cyprus may comprise a short trip for one day to register the marriage or a longer vacation, including a unique ceremony and a holiday for the couple or family. In recent years, more destinations for Israeli couples who wish to marry have been discovered: Italy, Bulgaria, the Czech Republic, and even exotic destinations such as the Seychelles and the Bahamas. The long-established travel agencies were joined by new entrepreneurs catering to FSU immigrants and more upscale exclusive entrepreneurs that promise a more special and "memorable" wedding. Unlike the bureaucratic-like wedding performed in city halls for the purpose of registration, the more exclusive weddings, to cite one example, promise "an enchanting location in a village near Limassol" and a memorable ceremony, designed with class.

A white canopy bed covered with rose leaves awaited us. A different treat filled every corner of the room and these included a bouquet of red roses and heart-shaped butter cookies so believe me, it was worthwhile getting married just for this treat. We suppose that we are the only couple in the world who went to their wedding in a coach together with all the guests but this too was part of the charm, its beauty, and part of the atmosphere which was so relaxed and augmented by the joy that characterized our entire Cypriot wedding. We were surrounded by green lawns, a small amphitheater, fountains and ancient stone buildings against a background of mountains, which rose up on all sides and served as the most perfect scenery we could have wished for. (Naor, 2005)

Marriage abroad is promoted largely by profit-seeking business entrepreneurs but is used also by other entrepreneurs that rely on these business initiatives. For Reform, Conservative, and secular activists that provide and promote alternative marriage services, the travel agencies solve the legal aspects of marriage. Often, these secular entrepreneurs would refer their clientele to travel agents in order for them to supplement the marriage ceremony with formal registration. The Forum published an information booklet about the different possibilities for marriage abroad, including different agencies and the prices they charge (Zemira Segev, interview). In the Reform movement, there are those who believe that the ideological and economic processes should be integrated into their work.

I am referring here to initiatives where regrettably the Reform Movement failed to grasp that it should take up the position of an ideological initiator and an entrepreneur; we needed to start up a travel agency now to make things easier for couples traveling abroad. We should have established a legal mechanism to provide not only prenuptial agreements but also well-prepared comprehensive financial agreements for couples living together without formal marriage ties. (Rabbi Meir Azari, interview)

Marriage abroad provides a relatively easy outlet for Israelis prevented from marriage or those who desire a non-Orthodox wedding. Some secular entrepreneurs believe that an increasing number of marriages abroad will boost the awareness of the marriage issue and eventually lead to a change. "The more Israelis I manage to send abroad to marry – whether because they object as a matter of conscience or otherwise – so the Israeli public, thanks to articles in the press and items appearing on television, in addition to hearsay, see and become aware of the problem" (Rabbi Gilad Kariv, interview). Others question the political effect of registering marriages conducted abroad and argue that this reduces the pressure on the rabbinic establishment by creating a solution for those prevented from marrying and providing an alternative for ideological secular individuals. Moreover, instead of a wedding ceremony reflecting the couple's worldview, they conduct a formal and alienated procedure to have their marriage registered.

I think that this is a waste of good money; the entry in the identity card is insignificant and the main importance associated with registering the marriage in the identity card by civil marriage is primarily for psychological needs, i.e., first of all let us be calm about it; and for the parents.... The problem nowadays is that couples come to me and say that the real wedding is in Cyprus or somebody goes off to get married in the Seychelles Islands or some other place. A person who knows no Hebrew and hardly speaks a little English puts on a tape or disc for them and marries them. (Nardi Green, interview)

Cohabitation and Common-Law Marriage

An increasing number of Israeli couples live together as a family without getting married; they are best defined as "common-law partners" or "cohabitants." According to data from the Central Bureau of Statistics, about 3.1 percent of the couples in Israel (45,000 couples) live together and share a household without marriage, and a quarter of those couples raise children together. These numbers are relatively low compared with Western countries but the legitimacy of marital relations of this type has grown among the general public; whereas in 1994, a poll found that 74 percent of the Jewish population thought that people who wish to have children should marry first, by 2002, this percentage had declined to 65 percent. Among the Jewish public it was also found that the majority (58%) agree with the point of view that there is nothing improper about a couple living together without intending to marry (Glickman, Oren, and Levine-Epstein, 2003). Most of those living as cohabitants in Israel are young couples who wish to live together without making a definite commitment or older people in the second stage of their lives who do not want to remarry. Many of the cohabitants will marry in the future, but for others this is a chosen lifestyle and they will avoid marriage in the rabbinate or elsewhere.

Cohabitation was made an easier choice by several decisions of the court that included formal aspects such as the right of a common-law wife to receive the surname of the man with whom she was living (HCJ 693/91, *Dr. Michal Efrat v. Ministry of the Interior*), as well as more substantive issues. Common-law partners have been recognized as spouses for all intents and purposes, and specifically in cases where property and inheritance rights are concerned. Secular couples who chose cohabitation also have the advantage that in the event of a separation, in contrast to those who married abroad and registered their marriage, they will not have to seek a divorce from the rabbinate. Another advantage from the liberal point of view is that cohabitation is available also to same-sex couples. The rights of common-law partners, however, are still not fully equal to those of married couples, among other things in issues related to adoption and separation of the partners, due, to a large extent, to the lack of formal recognition.

Cohabitants use different legal contracts to formalize financial and other aspects of their relationships. The New Family organization conducts contract marriages that include a letter of undertaking in which the parties declare their love; an agreement on matters pertaining to property, children, and alimony; a secular civil ceremony; and confirmation of the agreement in the court. The price of a legal agreement varies and depends on the attorney chosen, but it normally ranges from $4,000 to $10,000. In 2007, New Family began to issue a "certificate of marital relations" signed by an attorney; it constitutes convenient proof that the two people are a couple who are committed to one another and manage a joint household. This certificate, it was explained, should serve its holders in their dealings with the various institutions in cases in which marital relations grant different rights.

The Orthodox Reaction – Change from within?

For many secular and nonreligious Israelis, marriage is their first significant encounter with the Orthodox rabbinate, and is often not a pleasant encounter. The rabbinate's low popularity among secular Israelis is a result not only of the imposition of Orthodox procedures, but also of its alleged failure to provide adequate service. Accounts of insensitivity and of illegal charges for marriage service have contaminated the image of the rabbinate and increased secular resentment toward it. The majority of Israelis still prefer the rabbinate, but it seems that more and more opt out of marriage altogether. As Table 3.4 demonstrates, the growth of marriage services conducted in the rabbinate does not match the general population growth. Although these changes may not be directly related to the rabbinate's deteriorating image, they may add to a growing perception among Orthodox rabbis that change is required.

Although the rabbinate itself, as in the case of burial (Chapter 4), has initiated reforms to improve its service, an important alternative has

TABLE 3.4. *Marriage in the Rabbinate*

Year	Couples Married in the Rabbinate	Jewish Population
1970	23,983	2,561,400
2005	31,284	5,313,800
Number added	7,301	2,752,400
Percentage growth	30.44%	107.46%

Source: CBS Yearbook, 1971 (p. 25), 2006 (p. 86), 2007 (p. 70).

arisen within Jewish Orthodoxy, but outside the rabbinate. Tzohar, an association established in the mid-1990s by a group of young rabbis from the National Religious movement, has taken upon itself to provide a service for nonreligious Israelis. Rabbi Yuval Sherlo, one of the organization's founders, defined its objective in the following words: "to change the image and the status of the rabbi in Israeli society" (*Ha'aretz*, July 19, 2004). A survey that Tzohar conducted in 2004 found that Jewish Israelis who did not marry in the rabbinate explained their decision by what they described as negative attitudes of the rabbinate and/or a desire for a more liberal attitude or for a ceremony that holds the man and women as equal (News1, August 2, 2004). Tzohar promises a "friendlier" Orthodox marriage, conducted by younger rabbis familiar with secular culture and committed to good service. As one of the Tzohar rabbis explained:

The organization decided to separate the process of registering the marriage, where the presiding official could be more pleasant or less so, from the rabbi performing the marriage, who is the principal personality in the ceremony under the canopy and in *kiddushin* (sanctification of marriage). We said that we should gather together rabbis who have been ordained to serve with the rabbinate, rabbis who are pleasant and competent in establishing a positive rapport with the couple, and in that way we shall increase the number of couples marrying according to the Law of Moses and Israel. In taking this action, we actually work in the best interests of the rabbinate, because we are convincing more people to register for marriage at its offices. (http://www.inn.co.il/Besheva/Article.aspx/6779)

Tzohar's marriage initiative has come in for much criticism among the more *haredi* public; attempts have been made by several rabbis to restrict Tzohar's activities and prevent its rabbis from marrying couples. The Tzohar rabbis did not flinch from voicing their criticism of the rabbinate and how it managed its affairs, as Rabbi David Stav wrote after the rabbinate tried to restrict the organization's activities:

We shall spare no effort in ensuring that the *huppah* will be respectable and appropriate, the preparation for this important day will be carried out seriously, with respect for the couple and not patronizing, for in any event this experience will become a founding element in all matters relating to the affinity for Judaism. There will be no more payments other than the fees legally charged by the Rabbinate, we shall put an end to the delays at the wedding ceremonies, and no longer will the same rabbi perform more than one wedding in a single evening, and no more tasteless talks under the wedding canopy. From now on the *huppah* will be a founding ceremony and the encounter with the rabbi, who will be similar to one with whom we would like to identify. (Stav, 2007)

The popularity of Tzohar, marrying about 3,000 couples every year, has much to do with the strategies it adopted, reminding one of those of the secular entrepreneurs outlined earlier, namely good service and ambition to reach out to wider audiences. Beyond their commitment to service and courtesy, Tzohar rabbis offer an alternative that is more attentive to the secular public's needs but also adheres strictly to the *halakhah*. The popularity of Tzohar can be also attributed to the fact that these rabbis are Zionists and have served in the military, often alongside secular Israelis. Unlike the ultra-Orthodox of the rabbinate, the Tzohar rabbis are on the "right side" of the republican equation that justified wide support when threatened by the rabbinate.

The rabbis of Tzohar are religious, Zionist rabbis who served in the military. They speak contemporary and updated Hebrew secular Israelis understand. They are familiar with Israeli culture, are involved in public life, and show responsibility for all Jewish people. (MK Zvulun Orlev; NRG, November 15, 2011)

The attempt to be open, cooperative, and understanding is coupled with a search for pragmatic solutions that would satisfy secular demands without compromising religious rules – for example, allowing the woman to give the man a ring at the end of the official part of the ceremony and providing guidance on Jewish family life with an effort to bridge the gap between the religious and secular worlds and so draw the couples closer to the Jewish tradition on matters concerning marital relations. Consequently, this Orthodox alternative poses a challenge both for the rabbinate and for secular alternatives, competing with the latter over the secular public. Unlike the secular entrepreneurs, Tzohar does not aim to abolish the Orthodox monopoly, but rather wants to gradually modify it and make it more acceptable to the secular public too – "evolution and not revolution," as one of the leading rabbis put it (*Ha'aretz*, July 19, 2004).

■ not important at all ■ not so important

■ fairly important   ■ very important

FIGURE 3.2. Is it important to have an Orthodox wedding ceremony? *Source:* Author's own survey, 2009.

Conclusions: Marriage and the Decline of Religious Authority

Compared with Western countries, Israel is still a "family-oriented state," where the traditional family structure of marriage and having children in a "normative" framework continues to exist. The institutionalization of family life in Israel makes it more of a public and political matter than a private and personal one (Fogel-Bijaoui, 1999: 114). For the majority of Jewish Israelis the Orthodox wedding remains the preferred option, whether because of the fact that the alternatives come at a cost (economic or other) or owing to the perception that Orthodox marriage defines the boundaries of the collective and breaking the framework will inflict damage on the collective's unity. Thus, about 70 percent of Israelis believe it is important to have an Orthodox ceremony (Figure 3.2).

In spite of this preference, however, changes since the 1990s indicate a de-institutionalization of marriage and a declining authority of the rabbinate. De-institutionalization can be observed in the growing number of "nontraditional" families and families formed outside the rabbinate that may or may not bother to register their marriage through the state. Overall, despite the increase in the Jewish population in Israel, which more than doubled from 1970 to 2005 (from 2.5 million to 5.3 million), the number of people getting married at the rabbinate increased only marginally (see Table 3.4). The National Insurance Institute (2009) reported that in 2007, 13 percent of families in Israel were single-parent families, the result mainly of the growing divorce rates (65 percent of single-parent families) and of single mothers (20 percent).

Cohabitation and common-law marriage offer a substitute for about 4 percent of Israeli families, and registration of marriage abroad provides another way to avoid the rabbinate. All in all, whereas the Orthodox monopoly remains the default option for the majority, others find alternatives that do not require direct confrontation. The authority of the Orthodox rabbinate is challenged directly by Jewish Israelis who criticize the monopoly and demand change, but also by alternative services offered that are based on different readings of Jewish tradition. This challenge is waged not only secularists but also by a small number of religious Orthodox who have decided to avoid the rabbinate and hold private Orthodox services (Ettinger, 2011). The ceremonial alternatives add a "positive" aspect to the process, as entrepreneurs and individuals take control over questions of identity and belonging and defy the authority of religious Orthodoxy.

Non-Orthodox marriage or cohabitation is found largely among two groups – FSU immigrants and secular Israelis. For the former, this is often not a choice but a result of the rabbinate's refusal to recognize them as Jews and marry them. Their preference is for pragmatic solutions rather than a struggle for change. For the latter, this is either a conscious political decision or a cultural preference that expresses dissent toward the limitations imposed by the status quo. This group, because of its small size, presents a minor threat to the status quo. Even though the majority of Israelis express support for civil marriage, in principle, they prefer the Orthodox marriage, in practice, so a change of the status quo is not a major priority.

Consequently, attempts to formally change the status quo through legislation have run up against the conservative views held by the majority of the Israeli public; the weakness of the political system but also the alternatives that allow secular Israelis to marry outside the rabbinate. The political vacuum, the judicial activism, and especially the economic and demographic changes have produced a convenient base for the initiatives of secular entrepreneurs. The de-institutionalization these initiatives introduced has largely avoided confrontation and circumvented not only religious authority but also, in some cases, that of the state itself, seemingly turning marriage into a private affair beyond the jurisdiction of political authority. These alternatives took the edge out of the secular political commitment, deferred the potential confrontation, and, paradoxically, secured the formal status of the rabbinate.

4

Burial

A Matter of Lifestyle

When the legendary pioneer Yaacov Mirkin passed away, his grandson Baruch Mirkin, the protagonist of Meir Shalev's best-selling novel *The Blue Mountain*, buried him on his own land and turned his family estate into the "Pioneer Home," a cemetery for the valley's pioneers, a booming (and controversial) business. In this cemetery, ex-pioneers who have left Israel are offered, for a hefty price, to be buried next to the real pioneers, a status bought with money. The booming business of the cemetery, unheard of before, stands in contrast to the decaying village and attests to the changes society undergone:

Neglect was everywhere, but the money kept pouring in. sacks of it piled up in the old cowshed while my field of graves flowered. *Pioneer Home* made time stop like a great wedge thrust in the earth, shattering by-laws and ways of life, breaking the vegetative cycle, flouting the seasons of the year. (Shalev, 2001: 120)

Private cemeteries, profit oriented, could hardly be imagined until recently, but now provide a way for secular Israelis to avoid the Orthodox rabbinate and assume control over their departure from the world. Death rituals and burial were not officially part of the status quo but became another part of the Orthodox monopoly in Israel, largely uninterrupted until the 1990s. The social, economic, and demographic changes described earlier also had influence on burials when, on one hand, FSU immigrants not recognized as Jews had nowhere to be buried and, on the other hand, secular Israelis demanded services compatible with their worldviews and rejected the uniform Orthodox service. Burial and funeral alternatives began to emerge as an answer to the immediate needs of immigrants and secular demands for new rituals and services and the freedom to choose the way they depart from their loved ones. The new alternatives created by secular entrepreneurs – motivated by ideology, profit, or a combination of both – provided a variety of burial and funeral services that would reflect the worldview of the deceased and the family, their aesthetic preferences, or, in some cases, their status.

Death presents individuals, families, societies, and states with questions and dilemmas regarding the management and authority of funeral rituals and burial arrangements. Cemeteries are often not simply a place where the dead are buried but also a symbol of the living's love and respect for the dead, of society's perception of death and commemoration, and, at times, a political statement of and for the living. The dead, especially the famous, may continue to have a political life when their funeral and burial become accepted political symbols or sites of political struggle. Dead bodies, as the anthropologist Katherine Verdery argues, have properties that make them effective political symbols, and as a site of political conflict they relate to "the process of reordering the meaningful universe" (Verdery, 1999: 36). Consequently, funerals and burials involve questions of identity, religion, economy, status, and lifestyle and, therefore, can become a site of struggle between ideologies and interests involving the deceased, those wishing to honor them, and political and religious authorities.

The modern state, as part of the nation-building process, became a party to the design of the rituals of funeral and burial. Funerals combined a powerful public ritual with the "discipline" of bureaucracy as the ceremonies of leaders and soldiers were designed to generate sentiments of solidarity and loyalty to the state, symbolized by the life and death of the deceased (Ben-Amos and Ben-Ari, 1995). The funeral in the French Republic of the nation's great was constructed as a founding event and a mechanism for solidarity and loyalty through the dead, who represented the republic's values, and the event as representing the order of the modern nation-state (ibid.). In the military cemeteries, it was the uniformity and simplicity that represented the brotherhood and solidarity of the fallen warriors (Mosse, 1979). Death rituals in Israel, like elsewhere, were also a symbolic act in the process of nation-building. Military funerals for the fallen soldiers, bringing coffins of religious and political leaders from abroad for reburial in the land of Israel, or a ceremonial reburial of the remains of Bar Kokhba's ancient warriors were all symbols of the state's ideological system (Weingrod, 1995).

Death and burial presented also more mundane responsibilities for the state in its conduct of public policy. Industrialization and urbanization in the nineteenth century turned burial from a private matter handled by local parishes to a social and sanitary issue in the growing and crowded cities. The small, and at times improvised, cemeteries run by churches and communities were insufficient for the growing needs and turned into a health hazard. "The coffins were only thinly covered with earth as a result of the overcrowding of the churchyards.... There was said to be an offensive smell of decaying bodies in the houses and shops" (Foster, 1984: 73). Thus, new burial arrangements had to provide a solution to the health risks that the decomposing bodies could present as well as meet the aesthetic needs of the public (Walter, 1996). Burial was gradually wrested away from the church, placed under the authority of the municipality and the state, and subjected to rational policies and new professional specialties: pathologists, managers, and privatized entrepreneurship of funeral homes. State regulation, through officers of public health, restricted burial inside the cities and encouraged the municipalities to set up new cemeteries on the outskirts of towns (Walter, 1996: 99). The new cemeteries of Europe and North America were built on principles of public health and hygiene, aesthetics, and rational management (Walter, 2005), and the church was increasingly left in charge only of the funeral service itself.

The secular cemeteries wrested control of burial from the church and redefined the provision of burial space as a civic rather than a spiritual responsibility (Rugg, 2006). In some cases, such as in France, burial reform had less to do with overcrowding and more with that attempt of the secular state to disempower the church (Walter, 1996: 100). Secularization and secular ideologies were reflected also in the funeral arrangements that turned their back to the church. Secular funerals such as that of the writer Victor Hugo became a symbol for the republic's anticlerical ethos. Mayors took the place of the clergy as the directors of funeral ceremonies, and crosses on the graves were replaced by flowers or other nonreligious symbols (McLeod, 2000: 263). In other cases, the market economy was a significant force in the commodification and secularization of burial, providing answers to new problems and demands. The new "death care industry" included funeral homes, crematories, and cemeteries, influenced by technology, consumer preferences, commitment to service, and competition (Kopp and Kemp, 2007). In some cases conflict emerged between the funeral directors and the clergy over questions of authority and roles, as clergymen saw with disdain different professionals taking charge of services previously reserved for the church (Fulton, 1961).

Private business, the church, and the state (or the municipalities) have played different roles in different Western countries in burial and funeral organization. Although all modernizing states responded to the burial crisis caused by urbanization and industrialization, they chose different courses of action that involved state officials, religious institutions, and business entrepreneurs. Competition and cooperation between the different parties resulted in three ideal-type models. In the *commercial model*, the funeral director or cemetery manager, driven by a profit motive, casts the family in the role of customer able to choose among services offered. In the municipal/state or *political model*, the public official, concerned more with efficient management than with profit, casts the family as members of the community or citizens who deserve a public service. In the third, the *religious model*, the clergy provides the family, members of the religious community, with a religious service according to religious requirements (Walter, 2005). These models, first, are embedded in wider institutional settings of state, religion, and the economy. Second, they are ideal types and, therefore, a variety can be found in different countries. Third, they are influenced by social and economic changes as well as by struggles among religious, state, and business entrepreneurs. Thus, religious institutions may continue to perform services for a secular public, states may play a significant role in regulating private or religious institutions or allocating resources for burial services, and private enterprises may choose, for economic reasons, to provide religious services and cooperate with religious institutions.

Funeral reforms since the middle of twentieth century have had to respond to new demands on the religious model and also the political model – either for secular funerals or for different religious services. The changes in burial arrangements, in which markets have a larger stake, are part of a wider globalization process, in which illusions of nation-state homogeneity fade against growing individuality, de facto multiculturalism, and postmaterialist values. *Forbes* magazine attributed the change in the United States to the baby boomers who, on one hand, are consumer-conscious, and, on the other hand, also likely to choose to plan their funerals according to their beliefs and needs (Ein, 2004), encouraging the development of a market for a variety of services (Kopp and Kemp, 2007). Greater life expectancy, a longer period of old age, and improved medical prognoses, providing patients with information on their expected death, have allowed individuals to plan their departure from this world and their own funerals. Personalized "life-centered funerals," celebrating the life of the individual, provided the answer for the desires of either the deceased or the family to take control of the process and personalize the ceremony so it would reflect his or her life, lifestyle, and worldview. The standardized funeral arrangements, provided by the state or the dominant religion, were also rejected by immigrants and minorities who demanded different types of services in line with their tradition.

The ordinary rituals of death and bereavement, like other collective rituals, were replaced by more personalized and creative rituals and a commercial model that could accommodate these demands. These changes expressed postmaterial values and the individual right to take charge over the end of his or her life. However, these changes also had strong material elements, as business entrepreneurs began to create new alternatives, answering to aesthetic and cultural demands. Private businesses, operating according to the commercial model adopted a pragmatic view toward religion or other ideologies, and a flexibility that enabled them to cater to the demands of different group and individual customers. Religious institutions and the state, however, motivated by political or economic concerns, have at times struggled to maintain their control over funerals and burials that, in those cases, remained a politically contested issue.

In Israel, along the lines of the status quo agreement, the state granted Jewish Orthodoxy the monopoly over cemeteries that included both the funeral processions and the burial. This model, combining the religious and the political models described previously, was challenged by the changes in the 1990s – immigration, religious pluralism, and individualization – that translated into, first, concrete needs of non-Jewish immigrants and second, demands for freedom of choice and aesthetic preferences of secular Israelis. These needs and demands were answered only partially by a political decision to establish civil cemeteries and more by private initiatives. Thus, alongside the dominant state–religious model, a commercial model emerged ready to answer a variety of ritual and aesthetic preferences.

Israel – Rules of the Game

After its establishment, the state in Israel assumed the responsibility for burial and the provision of modern solutions to rising needs. State laws (adopting the 1940 regulations of the British Mandate) focused mainly on the technical and managerial issues of building and maintaining cemeteries to ensure that they would not turn into health hazards. The management of the cemeteries themselves – funeral and burial processions – was left to religious authorities. The Law of Religious Services (1971) formalized previous arrangements and granted religious councils, under the supervision of the Ministry for Religious Affairs, the authority over burial of Jews, including the funeral processions. Burial of Jews in Israel is usually handled by Orthodox burial societies known as *hevra kadisha* (hereafter, HK; literally, holy society). About 130 large HKs operate in Israel and there are another 450 smaller burial companies in kibbutzim and other small settlements, all paid by the state for every burial they conduct. HKs are allowed to charge money for specific plots or for plots bought for future use by people who want to be buried, when their time comes, next to their loved ones. Burial is invested in the hands of religious authorities, but the state remains involved in funding and regulation through several institutions that ensure citizens' rights to burial. The religious model, therefore, is combined with and supported by a political model. The National Insurance Institute provides the money for burial (sponsored by the state for all citizens). The land administration allocates land for cemeteries. The ministries of the interior and religious affairs license cemeteries and the burial companies and oversee their operation.

The Jewish Orthodox ritual, the standard in Israel, requires that the burial should take place soon after death. There is no public display of the body, embalming is not allowed, and cremation is strictly forbidden. In Israel, the body, except in military funerals, is not placed in a coffin but is wrapped in shrouds, carried to the grave on a stretcher, and placed in the grave. Before the funeral, the shirts of the close family are torn and the funeral procession begins from the gate of the cemetery to the gravesite, with the mourners following the stretcher with the body (the Hebrew word for funeral, *levayah*, means "accompanying"). Prayers for the dead are said over the grave, including the Kaddish, written in Aramaic and traditionally read by the deceased's son. After the prayers, the grave is filled by the mourners and the HK workers. A headstone will be placed over the grave about a month after the funeral, and family and friends commemorate the death annually by a visit to the gravesite and prayer recitation.

The Orthodox monopoly and the HKs have come under criticism for several reasons. First, investigative reporting has revealed many cases in which families of the deceased were illegally charged large sums of money for plots and for different services (Ilan, 1998). Reports of high salaries in some of the HKs, mismanagement of funds, and great inefficiencies (Winter, 1999) added to the negative image of the HKs among the public. Second, the HKs were charged with insensitivity after in several cases made public that they refused to bury FSU immigrants suspected of not being Jewish inside the cemeteries. Third, the run-down and unkempt physical state of several cemeteries has raised questions on the ability of the HKs to provide adequate services. The Ministry of Religion initiated a survey in the late 1990s and found that only half the respondents were satisfied with the HK services (*Ha'aretz*, April 4, 2006). Another report in April 2002 found cemeteries in a state of neglect that included broken gravestones, trash, and a lack of facilities (ibid.). Fourth, secular Israelis' personal demands to allow them to make changes in the funeral and burial services were rejected by the HKs, raising more complaints on the rigidity of the service providers and their unwillingness to acknowledge personal needs. Demands of secular Israelis to improve and personalize the funeral service were framed in terms of "secular" funerals and burials but, in many other cases, the preferred term was "civil," referring to a service not controlled by the Orthodox establishment, allowing a choice between different options for the funeral and the burial.

The Orthodox monopoly, in spite of complaints, was hardly challenged at first, and Jewish Israelis accepted the standard funeral and burial rituals as a given. In the 1990s, however, the political-religious model was challenged by demographic needs, aesthetic preferences, and secular-cultural demands that introduced a new commercial model and new alternatives previously unavailable.

Immigration as a Force for Change

Theresa Angelovitch immigrated to Israel from Romania; after her death in 1983 she was buried in a cemetery in Rishon Lezion, a city south of Tel Aviv. Shortly after the funeral, the HK suspected that Angelovitch was not Jewish and decided to move the body from the grave, but the family appealed to the court to prevent the removal. While the court was still debating the body was removed from the grave by unknown individuals and was later found dumped in a Muslim cemetery. The court ordered that the body be returned to the grave, against the protests of Orthodox rabbis and the HK that demanded she be buried elsewhere. The Angelovitch case triggered a heated debate over the Orthodox monopoly and, maybe for the first time, a loud and clear secular demand for civil cemeteries, free from Orthodox control. Shulamit Aloni, a member of the Knesset and a long-time liberal activist, acutely observed what would happen if and when a large immigration from the Soviet Union would arrive, many of them likely not to be recognized by the Orthodox establishment as Jews:

Coming here as a Jew, will he be labeled a "non-Jew"?... All these people would require a solution – and a respectable solution. We cannot bring here people according to the Law of Return and we cannot treat Jewish citizens who live here – just because they do not match some religious criteria – as pariahs who must be buried outside the fences of the cemetery or near the dumpster as if, by their presence, they render impure those who lie next to them. (Knesset Protocol, November 30, 1983)

The immigration from the former Soviet Union, a few years later, has proven Aloni right. The presence of a large number of non-Jewish citizens intensified the debate and presented new dilemmas for the state and the HKs. For many immigrants, unlike secular Israelis, this was not a matter of aesthetic or ritual preference but a practical problem. The state cemeteries, managed by the HKs, either refused to accept immigrants not recognized as Jews or buried them in separate plots outside or in the far corner of the cemetery. These practices caused a public uproar, especially when soldiers killed in military action received the same humiliating treatment. In the summer of 1993 a soldier named Lev Pesachov, an FSU immigrant, was killed in action and was buried near the fence of the cemetery because his mother was not Jewish. The HK and religious politicians justified the decision and explained that, in spite of Pesachov's patriotism, Jewish people would not want to be buried next to non-Jews (*Ha'aretz*, August 10, 1993). Secular politicians, conversely, described the decision as a disgrace. Raphael Eitan, member of the Knesset and a former army chief of staff, exclaimed that "a soldier who has given his life for the state is buried near the fence because of narrow political considerations and capitulation to the Orthodox, who live by conducts of the Middle Ages and have never served in the army" (*Yediot Aharonot*, August 10, 1993).

The reactions to Pesachov's ill treatment underscored again the republican equation and a breach of the commitment of the state to its soldiers rather than a universal commitment to civil rights. The younger brother of the fallen soldier did not mince words when saying, "I would not want to even think what would happen if he was not a soldier, because then no one would have fought for him" (*Yediot Aharonot*, August 9, 1993). The funeral itself became a political event when many came to support the family and express their disgust with the treatment Pesachov received, highlighting, as the artist Yair Garbuz declared over his grave, the link between Jewish identity and Israeli patriotism as he addressed the HK:

You have insulted him and not incidentally! You have insulted us and not by a good intention that went wrong! You insulted the army and the soldiers who fought with Lev Pesachov! And you damaged your own dignity, if you have some dignity left at all. Lev Pesachov was Jewish not because of any religious rule or regulation, but because he decided to immigrate to Israel, live as a Jew, serve in the army and defend his country. (*Yediot Aharonot*, August 15, 1993)

Following the public uproar Pesachov was buried again, in the military section of the cemetery and in a full military ceremony. In 2002, after another soldier was buried separately from his comrades, the army estimated that between 6,000 and 6,500 soldiers who are not recognized as Jewish serve among its ranks (*Ha'aretz*, March 14, 2002).

Other cases that involved civilians have also raised criticism, though of lower intensity and limited public outcry. In the northern town of Afula, four FSU immigrants were buried in a field, two hundred meters beyond the cemetery. "I am hurt that my husband was treated this way. Just before his death he asked that we bury him in Russia, but I do not have the money for this," explained one of the widows (*Ha'aretz*, June 16, 1996). Things were different when, after a terrorist suicide bomber took the lives of eighteen young people in a club popular with FSU immigrants, the HK was accused of refusing to bury three of the dead whom they suspected of not being Jewish. Yosef Lapid, chair of the secular Shinui Party, attacked the HK policies (the HK denied the allegations) and demanded to end the Orthodox monopoly immediately: "The Islamic Jihad and the HK cooperate in hurting FSU immigrants. The Jihad does it to living young people and the HK to dead ones.... It has been proven that stupid and heartless rabbis abuse the authority they have" (*Ynet*, June 3, 2001).

The FSU immigration, as in the case of marriage, has turned burial into a critical problem that, unlike marriage, could not be delayed or solved outside the country. Rather, it required an immediate and respectable solution and, as described previously, often placed the Orthodox establishment under criticism for insensitivity. Under these pressures some of the rabbis, such as the former Chief Sephardic Rabbi Eliyahu Bakshi-Doron, agreed that reforms must take place.

We expressed our opinion that in every city, near the Jewish plot must be a plot for non-Jews and those suspected of not being Jewish. We should not force a Jewish burial on those who insist not to have one.... [T]he fundamental error was that this problem of burial was brought to the rabbinate. The HKs belong to the Jewish community and were formed to provide service for Jews. There is a problem of a large percentage of non-Jewish immigrants but it is not a problem for the religious establishment. It is the state responsibility to find an acceptable solution. (*Ha'aretz*, May 3, 1995)

The immigrants' needs, therefore, could be met with practical solutions that would prevent the humiliations that happened in the cases described here. Thus, the military was quick to create burial plots for non-Jewish immigrants near the regular plots. Solutions for civilians took longer to be established and were combined with a more general debate over the Orthodox monopoly and secular/civil burial.

Secular Funerals: Aesthetic Preference and Postmaterialist Values

Secular discontent can be explained by new perceptions among the elites in which burial and funerals became also a matter of aesthetics, tastes, and worldviews. Contrary to Orthodox Jews, who perceive the funeral as a collective ritual focused on the afterlife, secular Jews see the funeral as an event of departing from a loved one, in which the preferences of the deceased or the family must be present (Abramovitz, 2000). Consequently, some secular Jews find the Orthodox funeral ritual itself alien, devoid of any personal attributes and lacking in aesthetics. Because the use of a coffin is prohibited, the body of the deceased is wrapped in shrouds and carried on a stretcher to the grave, a sight some find problematic. In addition, the poor state of many cemeteries added to the dissatisfaction of seculars who wanted their funeral, or that of their loved ones, to reflect something different. Neri Livneh, a journalist in the liberal *Ha'aretz* newspaper, gave voice to the secular desire for an aesthetic, European-style funeral:

Cemeteries in other countries, like the Père Lachaise cemetery in Paris, for instance, are sometimes beautiful tourist sites as well, or sometimes just a peaceful corner of a tree-filled churchyard. The cemeteries in Israel are another story altogether, except for the cemeteries of kibbutzim and moshavim. The religious funerals in Israel also bear no resemblance to those that are held abroad and which are often seen in movies. There, the mourning is always well designed: a small group of elegant people, men in suits, women in wide-brim hats, the widow in a black hat and black dress, the fine wood coffin, even the deceased looks his best. By comparison, funerals in Israel are not very aesthetic. Delicacy isn't always the strong suit of the *hevra kadisha* burial society workers. Frequently, they rush and don't speak clearly, and, afterward, there is the sight of the bodies in sacks tossed into the graves, and, with the cemeteries being so crowded, often several funerals are taking place at once, so it is quite noisy. In certain places, the mourners have to step over other graves and crowd amid the headstones to get near the open grave. (Livneh, 2005).

Unlike marriage, described in the previous chapter, a well-planned event in which couples and their families invest time and money, the death of loved ones often finds the family unprepared and lacking the energies to take responsibility for the funeral arrangements beyond what is necessary.

The majority of Israelis, including secular ones, therefore, tended to accept the HK standard services and avoid the need to plan the funeral. For some secular Israelis, however, alternative funerals were not only about aesthetics but also about meaning and content. These individuals wanted to wrest control of the funeral from religious authority and leave their own mark on their departure, or that of their loved ones. In some instances, they left behind detailed instructions for their funeral processions, including the texts they wanted read. In other instances, it was the families of the deceased who wanted the ceremony to reflect the life of their loved ones, a secular life remote from the Orthodox funeral service. Engagement with funerals could be found in the writings of religious feminist women or secular individuals who confronted the restrictions placed by the ordinary religious ceremony.

I want to ask for a grace of truth. It is a request from my female friends, neighbors, and family members, and maybe more. When I die, and there will be a funeral and eulogies and my daughters will say the Kaddish. But I want also for you to carry the stretcher when my body is wrapped in shrouds. Don't be afraid. Come and carry me together to my place of rest. After the first ones, I hope more women will dare to come close to me for the last time and depart... when the body will be lowered to the grave I want women to cover the pit... one near another, a woman to her sister. (Pinchasi, 2009)

Don't say Kaddish on me. When my time comes I would want my funeral to be held in a civic cemetery when my family members will determine the funeral processions.... I personally would disqualify this prayer not only because of its religious content, its dubious literary value, its foreign language, incomprehensible and irrelevant, its hypocrisy and insensitivity, but also for another reason: the fact that religious orthodoxy forbids women, even in families without sons, to say Kaddish over their loved ones.... We, the free people should nurture a culture: free, authentic, original, sensitive, and relevant to our beliefs and feelings. (Gal, 2007)

Burial in a coffin, women taking an active part in the funeral, or a text substituting for the Kaddish were not part of the Orthodox service and were restricted in the cemeteries run by the HK. Combined with the needs of FSU immigrants described earlier, these new demands challenged religious authority and required an alternative.

Secular Burial – Conservatism, Needs, and Demands

A survey conducted in 1995 found that 34 percent of secular and traditional Israeli Jews were in favor of allowing non-Orthodox funerals

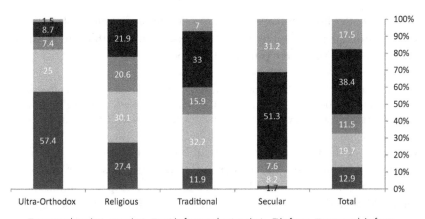

FIGURE 4.1. Support for allowing civil burial. *Source:* Author's own survey, 2009.

(*Ha'aretz*, April 13, 1995). Our survey shows similar trends – a small majority supports the allowance of civil burial (Figure 4.1) but a large majority would prefer the Orthodox ceremony (Figure 4.2).

The conservative approach can be explained by the attitude of many nonreligious and secular Israelis, many of whom think that the traditional aspect of the funeral and its common ritual must be preserved, even at the expense of individual desires. Some of the interviewees were ambivalent or never gave too much thought to the subject ("I was told Jews are not buried in a coffin; I really don't care"; "I leave the choice of where to

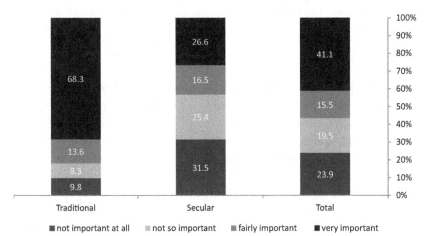

FIGURE 4.2. Importance of an Orthodox service. *Source:* Author's own survey, 2009.

bury me to my children; they should do what they are comfortable with").
Others brought up examples of compromises found within the existing
system to argue that there is no need to rebel:

In a funeral of a friend they brought musicians that played music she loved. It
depends on the local HK manager. Sometimes, you wait for him to finish the
official ceremony and leave, and then you do what you want. (Aaron, interview).

For many of the interviewees, the traditional burial to which they have
become accustomed should be kept as the standard, possibly with some
minor additions. "I don't mind a coffin but we must keep the foundations,
the Kaddish and others must stay. The basic traditions must be kept; if
someone wants to add to it, it is fine" (Etti, interview). People who
described themselves as traditional saw the funeral service as part of
tradition they wanted to keep. "I would not change the basic structure or
do anything not ordinary, like playing music. Maybe minimal changes are
acceptable but I think the ceremony must be short and simple" (Ben-Zion,
interview).

Secular Israelis, as mentioned previously, often have little concern with
funeral and burial issues and at most would like to allow some flexibility
so that personal requests ("something minor") could be added to the
traditional ritual. Some secular Israelis, however, were more critical and
adamant, referring both to the aesthetic and to the ritual aspects of funeral
and burial.

I find the traditional burial humiliating . . . the filthy stretcher on which the body
is placed is repulsive. . . . I think it is important to be placed in a coffin so that
people don't see how the body is thrown into the grave. I wrote in my will that I
will be buried in a coffin and in a civil service. (Aya, interview)

Other interviewees also referred in negative terms to the HK services ("dis-
respectful," "humiliating," or "terrible") and believed that civil burial
would make things easier and allow more choice (e.g., coffin burial or
music playing) alongside the traditional rituals. "I would definitely prefer
a civil service; it is available today for those who can afford it but it
should be available to everyone" (Zvia, interview).

As in marriage, differences were found between ethnic groups in regard
to perceptions and preferences regarding burial. Ashkenazim and FSU
immigrants were more supportive than Mizrahim of establishing civil
burial in Israel, and Mizrahim attributed greater importance to the Orthodox burial ceremony (see Table 4.1). Only 50 percent of people with a

TABLE 4.1. *Ethnicity and Civil Burial*

	Strongly Oppose (%)	Oppose (%)	Neither Oppose nor Support (%)	Support (%)	Strongly Support (%)
Do you support the establishment of civil burial in Israel?					
Mizrachim	14.8	25.8	15.6	34.8	9
Ashkenazim	9.9	13.9	9.4	44.6	22.3
FSU Immigrants	4.3	9.7	7.5	45.2	33.3
Israelis	18.8	23.3	10.2	33	14.8

	Not Important at All (%)	Not Important (%)	Somewhat Important (%)	Very Important (%)
How important is it for you that you, or your family members, will be buried in an Orthodox ceremony?				
Mizrachim	14.7	10.3	14.7	63
Ashkenazim	29.2	25.7	15.1	29.2
FSU immigrants	37.9	25.8	13.6	22.7
Israelis	18.8	18.8	18.8	43.5

Source: Author's own survey, 2009.

college education attributed importance to Orthodox burial, in comparison to 63 percent of people with a high school degree and 89 percent of people with less than a high school degree. Similarly, the support for civil burial was higher among those with college education (72 percent) than among those with a high school degree (56 percent) and below (22 percent).

A majority of Israelis seem to accept or allow civil burial, but would prefer a traditional Orthodox ceremony for themselves and their loved ones. Aesthetic preferences, ritual choices, and immigrants refused burial were not enough to upset the Orthodox monopoly, but were large enough to encourage secular entrepreneurs – politically and economically motivated – to provide new alternatives.

Secular Entrepreneurs

The alternatives for Orthodox burial responded to the needs and preferences described earlier and emphasized not only the freedom of choice but also aesthetics and a commitment to a service of high quality, professionalism, and integrity. Entrepreneurs often describe their own negative experiences in Orthodox funerals that motivated them to instigate change. After he participated in a funeral he found especially unpleasant, Avraham Gal, the founder of Menuha Nekhona (MN; "Rest in Peace"), wrote his will and ordered that when his time came he would be buried without any religious rituals and in a coffin. He then asked one of his employees to send a letter to all HKs, explaining the demands in the will and asking to reserve a place for burial. When his request was refused, the ground was set for an appeal to the Supreme Court.

In the appeal it was said that on one hand, burial in state cemeteries is mandatory but, on the other hand, they will not allow me to be buried according to my will. This is pure religious coercion. I turned this personal matter into a principled issue and initiated Menuha Nekhona, a name taken out of a Jewish prayer. (Avraham Gal, interview).

MN was formed in 1986 by secular, Conservative, and Reform Jewish movements with a goal to allow "every person in Israel to be buried and have a funeral service according to his worldview, belief, and desire, and nearby his place of residence." The association turned down offers to integrate into one of the existing HKs or to operate within existing cemeteries and demanded an independent stance in a civil cemetery that would be run by different principles. In a letter to the council of Jewish cemeteries in Jerusalem, MN explained that it has no desire to compromise secular desires for religious restrictions:

Many of our members are interested in a funeral devoid of any religious ritual or prayer and to be buried not according to the custom (for example, in a coffin). We respect the customs of the HK and have no intention to impose upon them the will of our members just like we refuse that their manners will be imposed upon our members. Therefore, there is no way but to allow the operation of the new association [MN] so that all people could live (and die) according to their beliefs. (letter, December 27, 1987)

In its application for a license in Tel Aviv, MN stated that it will target two main populations, FSU immigrants not recognized as Jewish and citizens who prefer a civil funeral. The latter, explained the chair of MN, extends beyond those who define themselves as "secular" to different people who want an alternative to the existing burial services – including, if they want, an Orthodox ritual. "They don't want to deal with the HK . . . they are looking for something different, to be together, men and women [sometimes separated in HK funerals], to play music, read a poem, or to be buried in a coffin. These are things you cannot get from the HK" (Maurice Halfon, interview). The association estimated an annual demand for 1,500 civil funerals in Tel Aviv and about 600 non-Jewish immigrants who would require their services. Surveys conducted in the 1980s, according to MN, demonstrated an economic rationality for a civil cemetery. Beyond the material aspects, the MN realized, cultural content was also lacking.

Regarding funerals, there was a cultural vacuum and this vacuum had to be filled with a new cultural creativity and new rituals. When a man dies, the family usually does not take the time to plan the funeral. To a large extent, this preserved the Orthodox monopoly, as they provided the solution, sparing the family the need to worry. We began to study the subject and make different suggestions to fill the vacuum. (Avraham Gal, interview).

The Reform movement also took part in the struggle, as active member of MN and independently against what it described as the inadequate – and, at times, illegal – conduct of the HKs, especially fees charged by the HKs for different services. "Our goal is to have adequate and fair religious services for Israeli citizens. When a monopoly like the HK in practice imposes itself and when citizens and families have no choice but to use these services... they often do not receive what they are entitled to. We are working to ensure that this state-subsidized service will be provided adequately" (Yonit Shlain, interview). The legal campaign served three purposes for the Reform movement. The first, and declared, purpose is to improve religious services and fight the alleged corruption of the HKs. The second, long-term, purpose is to turn the criticism of existing funeral services to a critique of the Orthodox monopoly against the Reform alternative. The third purpose is to strengthen the public image of the Reform movement and familiarize the public with the alternatives it provides for different rituals. Here, again, the complaints against the Orthodox monopoly and the accusations of inefficiency and corruption were used as a leverage to demand that the monopoly be brought to an end.

Economic initiatives began to make their mark in the 1990s, often combining with the more ideological ones. In 2004, a new commercial company was formed to offer different kinds of burial and funeral services, including cremation forbidden by Jewish law. The company, Aley Shalechet (Autumn Leaves), conducted a survey and found that a demand for cremation does exist. The company described itself as profit-motivated, but it also stresses its social goals – to pave the way for a cultural and social revolution that would improve burial and funeral services and allow every individual to decide on the rituals with which he or she would depart from this world.

Another important development was the decision of several kibbutzim, formerly collective agricultural settlements, to open their cemeteries to the public. Initially, kibbutzim responded to requests of FSU immigrant families that found themselves without a place to bury their loved ones. "In one case there was a young woman who died and was left for two weeks in the hospital because no one would bury her. We helped and she was buried in the kibbutz, she was the first one... we don't charge money from these people, we are doing this for humanitarian reasons" (Shalom Naim, interview). The opening of the cemeteries to people outside the kibbutz soon turned into a business, catering to a secular population interested in different rituals (provided by different agents) and/or in burial in a coffin – and also willing to pay for the aesthetics these cemeteries provide.

For secular entrepreneurs, the changes brought about by FSU immigrants, on the one hand, provided a powerful rationale for civil cemeteries that became a necessity, not just a preference. On the other hand, however, entrepreneurs were concerned that solutions would be limited to FSU immigrants and would not include secular Israelis who desire a non-Orthodox funeral, or that the rabbinate would "dump" on the secular entrepreneurs the non-Jewish immigrants they would rather not deal with. In an internal document circulated among the members of MN, Avraham Gal, the founder warned of the possibilities:

We must be careful that the MN cemetery will not become the "back yard" to which the Ministry of Religion sends all "problematic" dead people. As in many other social issues, the making of such an image can in the future turn into a reality. For example: the dominance of non-Jews will give the cemetery a foreign character and an image of low social status. The unavoidable result will be that the number of Israeli Jews willing or wishing to be buried in the cemetery will fall... after all, it is not MN's role to become a contractor for the Ministry of Religion... but to pave the way for civil burial in Israel. Whether we like it or not, burial also involves a social status and, at least at this early stage, we should not take this lightly. Taking into account the systematic efforts of the religious establishment to label MN as bizarre and to outcast us, there is no escape of being selective and presenting criteria in the operation of the cemetery... if what will come out is that the local Jewish community refrains, in word and deeds, from using the funeral services of MN and, instead, in the cemetery only "problematic cases" are buried, MN vision will lose its ground, namely: the cultivation of a new, civil burial culture, pluralist and free, and the shattering of the corrupt and repulsive monopoly of the Orthodox establishment over burial. (Gal, 2001)

FSU immigrants themselves were reluctant to take part in the ideological struggles and, as in the case of marriage, preferred practical solutions that would not require political engagement. As such, even though the hardship of immigrants who could not be buried – especially fallen soldiers, whose treatment violated the republican pact – were used by secular entrepreneurs in the political realm, the immigrants themselves have by and large remained outside the debate.

The Political Realm

Burials and funerals, except in specific instances, were hardly a political issue until the 1990s. For the majority of Israelis, the Orthodox ceremony was acceptable, the resentment toward the HKs seemed minimal, and even more minimal was the desire for alternative rituals and burial arrangements. The Theresa Angelovitch case, described earlier, was a hint to the future and raised secular demands to end the Orthodox monopoly. Yair Tzaban, a member of the Knesset and a long-time secular advocate, thought that this was an event that marked the need for change:

We must take action, public and legislative that would wrest the [burial] monopoly away from the Orthodox establishment that many of its people, though not all, represent an archaic, fanatic and close-minded version of Judaism. The time has come that free (secular) Jews would have their own cemeteries... sometimes peaceful co-existence requires separation. (Knesset Protocols, March 5, 1984)

This, however, was an ideological and minority position that could hardly shake the institutional foundations of the status quo and the Orthodox monopoly remained intact despite the criticism.

In the 1990s, as a result of the mass immigration from the FSU, politicians – secular and those representing FSU immigrants – became more interested in the subject. Secular entrepreneurs, such as MN, began to lobby for new legislation that would provide for civil burial. MN presented data it had collected that demonstrated a high demand for secular burial. In Haifa, a northern city with a large secular population, for example, 50 percent of the entire population expressed an interest in civil burial, and it was estimated that 30 percent might prefer the civil option if offered. Moreover, the support for civil cemeteries, regardless of the actual desire to be buried in one, was even higher (Halfon, interview), as many sympathized with the immigrants' difficulties. Incidents in which burials of immigrants were delayed or they were buried outside the cemeteries increased the pressures on politicians, including religious ones who could not deny the need for civil burial.

It was under these pressures that in 1996 the Law for Alternative Civil Burial was passed by the Knesset that granted every citizen the right to be buried in a civil cemetery according to his or her wishes, and ordered the establishment of civil cemeteries across the country. Shortly afterwards the government decided to build four civil cemeteries in Israel's major cities: Haifa, Tel Aviv, Jerusalem, and Beersheba. The implementation of the decision, however, was slow. A decade after the decision, only one public civil cemetery was operating, in Beersheba; by 2011, another one (not one of the four planned) was operating in Kfar Saba, and other local-municipal initiatives had also been formed to provide civil burial.

In Beersheba, a peripheral town with a large immigrant population and where the cost of land was relatively low, the cemetery was established quickly, without opposition. In other parts of the country, where land was scarce and the opposition of the HKs was stronger, however, civil cemeteries existed on paper only. Government offices and bureaucrats in charge of implementing the law, but principally opposed to its spirit, dragged their feet so that land was not allocated (Mei-Amy, 2007). Another decision, in February 2000, to allot a space for civil burial in every new or extended cemetery was also not implemented. Charges by MN and others that bureaucrats and politicians deliberately delayed the implementation were reported in the media; a decade after the legislation, one paper, tongue in cheek, reported that "the law was buried" (*Yediot Aharonot*, March 17, 2006). Secular entrepreneurs, however, have found little public interest in the struggle and, as a result, have received limited political support to press their case.

People do not want to deal with death in general and burial in particular. Even among the devoted seculars, many say that they don't care what will happen after they die and what would be done with their body. It is a very difficult struggle to wage. (Yifat Solel, interview)

Secular burial raised limited public interest, in part owing to the existence of private alternatives described later, and, consequently, was not on top of the agenda of most secular politicians and parties, including those representing the FSU immigrants. For the immigrants, burial (like marriage) was often a practical problem rather than an ideological–secular issue and, consequently, the immigrants were often ready to settle for the solutions the state and its institutions were able to offer. Secular entrepreneurs who hoped that parties representing the immigrants would be partners in the struggle for reform were quickly disappointed, as the latter usually opted for practical solutions and avoided principled struggles – for example, burial of immigrants suspected as non-Jewish in separate plots within existing cemeteries, a compromise negotiated between the minister of absorption (a member of the Yisrael B'Aliyah party, representing FSU immigrants) and the Orthodox rabbinate. Minister of Absorption Yuli Edelstein, an FSU immigrant himself, explained that

> our guiding line was to find solutions for people and families that were hurt by the bureaucratic difficulties.... We said, from day one, that demonstrations in front of the rabbinate with picket signs will not be constructive. We chose the path of negotiation and I hope we will continue to succeed in finding solutions. Between the two options, burial in a separate cemetery or in a regular cemetery like we agreed with the rabbis, when it is clear that it is a respectable burial plot and not in the margins of the cemetery, the latter solution is more respectable, for the deceased and for their families. (Knesset session, July 3, 1996).

The army, after several incidents, was quick to find solutions so it would not be embarrassed again with humiliating funerals of non-Jewish soldiers. The army's chief rabbi reported to a Knesset committee on the different solutions found: burial in separate sections in the cemetery, a funeral without religious rituals, and even a military funeral held by a priest in the non-Jewish section of the cemetery (*Ynet*, May 1, 2002). These solutions, however, fell short of the reform that secular entrepreneurs wished for that would end the Orthodox monopoly and would provide all Israelis with the freedom to choose.

The political struggle for civil burial, unlike other secular struggles, achieved a formal change with the Law for Alternative Civil Burial of 1996. This achievement, however, was at most partial owing to another aspect of the governance crisis, discussed in Chapter 2: the difficulty in implementation of political decisions. Limited resources, bureaucratic and political reluctance, and tepid public support have combined to thwart implementation. The partial solutions were sufficient to prevent more embarrassing incidents of immigrants refused burial by the HKs and, consequently, mainstream politicians lost interest and allowed the procrastination to continue. As with the issue of marriage, the framing of civil burial as a problem of non-Jewish immigrants underscored limited solutions that politicians were quick to support and left the Orthodox monopoly almost intact and secular entrepreneurs frustrated. The struggle for civil burial, consequently, has shifted to other spheres.

The Courts

The debate over burial found its way to the courts, first, by individuals who challenged the restrictions of the uniform religious-political model and, later, by secular entrepreneurs frustrated with the government's refusal to implement its own decisions. In both cases, liberal arguments of freedom of choice were used to contest the existing funeral and burial arrangements in the hope that the courts would fill the political vacuum.

Rules of the HK mandated that dates of birth and death carved on the headstone would be according to the Jewish calendar, not the Gregorian calendar used by the majority of secular Jews in their daily lives. In 1971, a family appealed to the Supreme Court (HCJ 280/71, *Gideon v. Hevra Kadisha*) in a demand to allow it to carve the Gregorian date. The court ruled in favor of the family, explaining that the choice is an "elementary right" of an individual to choose the inscription on his grave. Wrote the judge:

I believe that it would have been better had the respondent [the HK] accepted the request and would have given up willingly on this restriction that is totally unjustified. . . . These [culture] wars come up often in the court and are a result of opposing views regarding the desired structure of our national life. These wars should, of course, not be entirely banned as long as they are about major issues, but not over minor ones that are of secondary importance.

The court addressed a similar problem when it ordered the HK to allow a widower to inscribe his wife's name in English and the date she died according to the Gregorian calendar (HCJ 294/91, *Hevra Kadisha Jerusalem v. Kastenboum*). "I wonder," wrote Supreme Court Judge Mishael Heshin, when another appeal to the court was brought, "if there is any other nation so occupied, with such relentless intensity, with the writing on headstones" (HCJ 6024/97, *Shavit v. Hevra Kadisha*). The court, again, has ruled that in the clash between the HK concern for uniformity and the individual right to choose the latter should have the upper hand so that individual freedoms apply also in the cemeteries.

The court, in a liberal manner, has also defended individual equality when it ruled in favor of women's rights when an appeal against a decision of the rabbi of the city of Petah Tikvah that prevented women from taking an active part in funerals was presented. The petitioner, Rivkah Luvitch, a religious woman and the daughter of Charles Liebman, one of Israel's leading sociologists, wanted to deliver her father's eulogy, but the funeral home representative blocked her way, claiming that women could not eulogize. This so-called Jerusalem practice, separating men and women in funerals, adopted in Petah Tikvah, was not used in most cemeteries in Israel. Another petitioner, a religious man, joined the petition after his mother's female friends were not allowed to speak at her funeral. The two petitioners explained that they had no problem that strict separation was kept in ultra-Orthodox funerals, but there was no reason that this separation should be enforced in other funerals, especially in a city where the ultra-Orthodox were a minority and the HK was funded by the state (*Ha'aretz*, August 17, 2005). The practice of the Petah Tikvah HK, the plaintiffs argued, violated human liberty, freedom of speech, and religious freedom. The court in this case ruled in favor of individual liberties and ordered the Petah Tikvah HK to allow women to speak at funerals.

The court was also used by secular entrepreneurs as a stage to criticize the public conduct of the HKs and the government. Reports of corruption, unjustified high salaries, and financial mishandling at the HKs were often brought up by the media, and complaints of citizens being overcharged for services were common. In 2010, the court ordered the dismantling of the HK in Rishon Lezion after its managers were found guilty of corruption. Another report on misconduct in the HK in Tel Aviv was brought to the court with a demand to dismantle the HK (Globes, December 12, 1999). In the same vein, the Reform movement appealed to the court in 2007, requesting that the HK of Tel Aviv be prevented from transferring funds (public money) to charity, mostly for yeshiva students. Before the court's ruling, anticipating the results, the government announced that HKs could give only 5 percent of their earnings to charity and, according to fair and equal criteria, that only HKs not in deficit could give money to charity and that the charity would be supervised. The Reform movement has also taken upon itself to represent individuals against the HKs on matters such as overcharging families for services, demanding proper civil service, and exposing, again, the malfunction of the HKs.

After the Civil Burial Law (1996) was passed but its implementation was delayed, secular entrepreneurs also turned to the court with their frustrations over the government's foot-dragging in implementing the decision to provide for more civil cemeteries across the country. These entrepreneurs were also concerned that civil burial be undertaken by private entrepreneurs (discussed later) will replace state-funded civil cemeteries. The court, it was hoped, would force the government to move forward and remove all the bureaucratic obstacles for civil cemeteries. In 2006, the Supreme Court, in answer to five different appeals on the subject, ruled that the state had taken too long to implement and allocate the funding for civil cemeteries, and granted the state six more months to provide clear guidelines for funding that would allow the entrepreneurs to operate. In August 2011, the state announced it will allocate 5 million shekels for the development of the existing and new civil cemeteries.

The court, in summary, has served three main roles in the struggle against the Orthodox monopoly. First, and most commonly, it provided an answer for individual pleas for some flexibility in the rules of the HKs. Second, it was used by secular entrepreneurs to point out the misconduct of the HKs and force some reform of the latter. Third, appeals to the court were used to urge the implementation of the 1996 Law for Alternative Civil Burial and the government's decisions. The struggle in the courts brought limited results, mostly at the individual level, and the establishment of civil cemeteries continued to be very slow, as only two cemeteries, in Kfar Saba and Kiryat Tivon, were added by 2011. Consequently, it was the market that began to provide new, economically led, solutions.

Civil Cemeteries – The Public Alternative

In 1999, three years after the passage of the civil burial law, the first public civil cemetery was opened by Menuha Nekhona in Beersheba. The question whether the cemetery would be a "secular" cemetery that would answer to the desires of secular Israelis or be one catering to the needs of the FSU immigrants was a matter of perspective as well as a political question. The ministers, from the secular Meretz party, announced at the inauguration ceremony that the new cemetery would be followed by other alternatives to Orthodox rituals and that it was a "step toward ending the Orthodox monopoly." The mayor of the city, conversely, at the same ceremony, toned down the political message and urged his listeners not to see the cemetery as a political attempt to undermine the status quo but rather as a pragmatic solution to the needs of immigrants in the city (*Ha'aretz*, April 30, 1999).

The cemetery, adjacent to the HK cemetery, serves the Russian immigrants as well as secular Israelis and members of the non-Orthodox Jewish communities, whom the cemetery allows to conduct their own rituals. Funeral and burial services held in the cemetery are conducted according to the choice of the deceased or the family in the Jewish plot or in the common civil plot for all religions. The cemetery advertises its services to reach a wider audience that may have not heard of its existence and that an alternative to the Orthodox cemetery is available for everyone.

Secular is not the right word to describe the cemetery; it is an alternative service that offers also regular Orthodox ceremonies.... If we were located in Tel Aviv I believe the majority of people would come to us, but here in Beersheba, which is a more traditional town, our potential is limited. (Maurice Halfon, interview).

In a visit to the cemetery, the dominance of FSU immigrant culture can hardly be missed – not only is the writing in Russian on many headstones, and the engraved pictures of the deceased, uncommon among veteran Israelis, but also a large number of headstones with crosses indicating the religious identity of many of the buried. The culture of immigrants also influences the daily life of the cemetery, different from the ordinary cemeteries Israelis are familiar with.

When Russian immigrants come to the cemetery they are well-dressed, young children come too, it is a statement that death is part of life and they have a different way to depart. If you come here on the Sabbath you will see them having a picnic with the children... people near the graves and children playing soccer, it is surreal... but I don't see a problem with it. (Maurice Halfon, interview).

According to critics of the cemetery, including one of the founders of MN who has left the association, its un-Israeli character drives away veteran Israelis, as it fails to provide an image of high status that would attract them.

A cemetery is to a large extent a matter of status... the cemetery is of the lowest status. This is exactly what the Orthodoxy wanted to do, turn us into the junk-yard of cemeteries. You come to the place and see a Provoslavie cemetery and culture... we were there on a Monday and the whole place was littered with food leftovers; it turned out they picnic on Sundays. I have nothing against Christians, but this stigmatizes the place and turns it into the backyard of burial. If I was living in Beersheba I am not sure I would have wanted to be buried there, because this really is not my culture. (Avraham Gal, interview)

The dominance of Russian culture, alongside a relatively small number of veteran secular Israelis buried in the cemetery, was all but expected considering the demographics of Beersheba – a large traditional Mizrahi veteran population and many immigrants. The weakness, in other words, was not in the alleged failure to design the cemetery in Beersheba to cater to the liking of secular Israelis, but it was in the political realm, which failed to force the implementation of the civil burial law. For the large secular population of native-born Israelis residing in the central Tel Aviv area, a civil cemetery in Beersheba was hardly an option. Consequently, it was the commercial model introduced – private-based, market-driven initiatives – that provided the answers for the growing demand in the center of the country.

Planning Funerals: Taking Charge

The religious-political model eventually accommodated to provide answers to immigrants not recognized as Jews, but challenges from non-religious Israelis determined to take charge of their funeral and burial arrangements were more difficult to contain. The interest in end-of-life rituals defied the uniformity of the religious-political model in favor of individual statements reflected in both style and content. Commemoration, for many Israelis, could no longer be satisfied with standard headstones with the name of the deceased and the days of his or her birth and death. Instead, headstones created by new professional designers had to demonstrate personal tastes, memories, or lifestyle catered to.

It was important for me to put basalt in the headstone. I also wanted to give it splendor and elegance. I chose red ruby and polished black granite and brown pebbles. Near the headstone a guitar was chiseled from a large basalt stone and from its sound box lines of musical notes from the song "What shall I bless" rise to the sky.

I wanted to create a headstone with something sophisticated, like the things he loved... a headstone with a waterfall that works once a day, at dusk, operated by a solar panel charged during the day.

After her death I began to think how I can create something special for her.... I wanted something that would reflect her and realized I want something with water, representing her beauty. I wanted the gravesite to be a dynamic place, not alienated and cold... we decided to create a wound inside the natural Galilee rock. (Limor Gal, 2007)

The private cemeteries allowed more freedom in creating headstones but, no less important, also in the planning of the funeral ceremonies. For some secular Israelis, the standard Orthodox service seemed no longer to fit their cultural world. The longer life expectancy, secular worldviews, spirituality, and postmaterial values all contributed to the desires, especially among the educated middle class, to plan funeral rituals to reflect their lives. Some left behind them exact plans for the funeral; in other cases it was the families that wanted to commemorate their loved ones, but did not necessarily have the capacity at these difficult moments to plan an alternative ceremony. This void has opened another space for secular entrepreneurs who attempt to provide an alternative to Orthodox rituals. As in the marriage case discussed in the previous chapter, entrepreneurs use words such as "taking responsibility" and "meaning" to explain and justify the challenge to religious authority.

The secular funerals conducted for a long time in the kibbutzim provided an inspiration for some of the secular entrepreneurs who trained themselves to lead funeral rituals and to provide an alternative that would appeal to the secular public, emphasizing gender equality and individuality, embedded in a Jewish tradition and a communal spirit:

Burial and memorial services in a Jewish-secular spirit, ensuring that the ceremony would have a personal seal, a significant content and respect for the memory of the deceased and his family. The ceremony leaders of Havaya will guide you in the design of the ceremony and its themes combining traditional mourning rituals and Jewish texts with contemporary Hebrew texts, music and readings of family and friends ... [T]he women, marginalized from the traditional ceremony and prevented from expressing their grief and pain, are invited to take an equal and active part in the ceremony. (from the website of Havaya: http://www.havaya. info/)

The "individual choice," claimed to be missing in the Orthodox ceremony, was presented to the secular public alongside a flexible model for a funeral with a new role of ceremony leaders. The leaders, an emerging profession but still of small numbers, replicate the processes that secular marriage has undergone. Assisted by secular organizations, they become familiar with Jewish and Israeli traditions to help families plan the funeral ceremony with readings, traditional and modern, and thus are able to adapt the ceremony to the family's desires and needs.

In meeting with a family I try to gather as many resources as possible so that I become familiar with the deceased... once I have the story of his life I want to know who will eulogize, what will be read at the funeral, if anything.... I bring texts with me, Jewish and others, poetry and music that I can suggest to the family. (Doron Keinar, interview).

Many eulogies were written that can be adapted to family needs and we help some families write their eulogies. We decide with them if there is a need for music or poetry, some want to read texts the deceased has written or loved. There are many ways that can make the family feel they departed from their loved one in the best way. We have nothing against religious rituals, we support the use of everything that is a part of Israeli-Jewish rituals and those who want can read the

Kaddish. The idea is not to enforce a new kind of ritual but to provide people with rituals they can identify with. (Yiftach haShiloni, in Livneh, 2005)

Suddenly people saw there is an alternative that is more respectable and pleasant than the religious ritual that two-thirds of Israelis cannot relate to. You follow someone who mumbles religious verses and then the Kaddish, people cannot relate to this.... I personally support the Kaddish, there is something right about it, warm. But it must be done in a respectable way, not in a meaningless way.... A person must take responsibility for his last voyage, while he is still alive. (Doron Keinar, interview)

The cultural alternatives provided by secular entrepreneurs attempt to fill a void. In a difficult time in their lives, unable to cope with the need to plan a ceremony, secular families often choose to rely on the familiar Orthodox structured ceremony. The secular alternative, it is hoped, would provide an available and ready option that could compete with the Orthodox once the secular public becomes aware of its existence and its relevance.

Private Services: Ideology and Lifestyle

The political and legal struggles resulted in a disappointing number of public civil cemeteries, small in size or in the periphery (see Figure 4.3). Secular Israelis in Tel Aviv and other areas, especially those of a higher socioeconomic status, however, have not waited for the state to provide them with civil burial, or for secular entrepreneurs to force the state to implement the law. Rather, private alternatives have emerged to satisfy the cultural aesthetic desires of secular Israelis. Thus, alongside the bureaucratic political-religious model, in which the state authorized religious orthodoxy to administer burials or (later) provided a limited opportunity for civil burial, an economic model emerged, independent and more flexible than the other two. This model evolved not through a formal decision, but rather in a gradual process in which demand and supply met, circumventing both the ideological debate and the political battle. The fact that civil burial had stronger support among the upper-middle class, more secular in their identity, more ready to be involved in planning their departure or that of their loved ones, able and willing to pay for good service, may have added to the relative popularity of the preference of private solutions.

Ironically, it was the kibbutzim – originally collective settlements with a socialist ideology – that became the pioneers of private burial and were quick to adopt the economic discourse of service and customers. What began as a humanitarian gesture when kibbutzim opened their cemeteries to FSU immigrants whom the HKs refused to bury has turned into

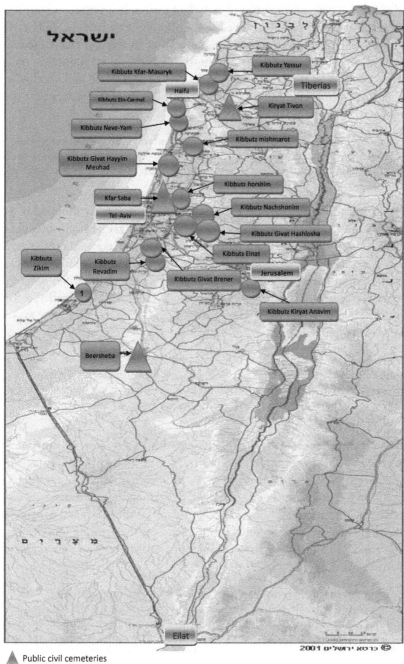

Public civil cemeteries

Private civil cemeteries

FIGURE 4.3. Civil cemeteries.

a business. These kibbutzim not only had available land they could use but also for years, due to their relative autonomy, conducted civil burials with secular rituals in their own communities. In search of new income sources, after the financial crisis in the 1980s and 1990s, kibbutzim could offer secular and non-religious Israelis not only the freedom to choose the services they wish but also the aesthetics of their cemeteries that the state cemeteries could never match.

"Some people say we have turned from pioneers into corpse merchants," explained the manager of one kibbutz cemetery, "but most people understand that all we do is link an existing infrastructure with an existing demand." (Heruti-Sover, 2007)

The businesslike explanation reflects the model chosen by kibbutzim, as well as the changes these collective settlements have gone through. In Einat, one of the popular kibbutz cemeteries, burial costs about $5,000 to $6,000. The price includes twelve years of maintenance of the gravesite and an overall service described as "high quality" (Shalom Naim, interview). Kibbutz Horashim, ten kilometers north of Einat, had land allotted for burial much larger than what it needed, and a similar economic rationale was employed.

Even after the second generation of kibbutz members will die, we will not be able to fill this space, yet this land can only be used for a cemetery. We know that there is a demand for burial in the kibbutz style, which is a form of secular burial. So it [private burial] made perfect sense, and we were not the first to do so, to maximize profits. (Shlomi Cohen, interview).

In the commercial model, the family is cast in the role of the customer, offered and able to make choices (Walter, 2005). These practically private cemeteries take pride in what they describe as high-quality service and attention to personal needs and desires, something that the state cemeteries run by the HK do not provide. They advertise themselves as providers of comprehensive services that take the load off the grieving families but also enable them to make choices on matters of importance such as the planning of the ceremony.

No company in Israel knows how to provide the basket of services that the family needs when a loved one dies. We created one. It begins with a 1–800 number that operates 24 hours a day, 365 days of the year. There is a person on that end of the line so that the family knows there are no administrative details for them to be occupied with. . . . We created a computer system that sends a reminder of the memorial day, this way the family can ask for anything they need . . . it creates a positive energy to this place. (Shlomi Cohen, interview)

We are always at your service. Unlike others, we work 24 hours a day, 7 days a week. There always a person on call... for the families it is important, they feel that they did not pay for nothing but that you are always on call for them, whenever that happens. (Alon Nativ, interview).

The more established cemetery in Einat has become familiar through funerals of well-known Israelis who chose to be buried in this cemetery. Other cemeteries have had to advertise themselves to convince would-be clients to pay for a burial offering aesthetics, freedom of choice, and good service not offered by the HK cemeteries.

Our motto is that the place is first and foremost for the living. We believe that a cemetery with ample space, gardening, and blooms creates a peaceful atmosphere for the visitors... we take upon ourselves the commitment to tend to all arrangements with a personal touch and do our best to respond to all special requests. (from the brochure of Garden of Eden, the cemetery of Ein Carmel)

The private cemeteries stress the ample space between the graves (unlike the crowded state cemeteries described earlier), the landscaping, and the surrounding views ("Is this what heaven looks like?" wrote one enthusiastic journalist after visiting a kibbutz cemetery; Yahav, 2003). This combination of aesthetics and good service aims not at non-Jewish immigrants and even not at ideological secularists who are likely to prefer civil burial anyway. Rather, it is the upper-middle class that has made those cemeteries a symbol of status and a preferred commodity, not necessarily for ideological or political reasons. As one cemetery manager explained to a journalist, "We provide a different class of a cemetery. A private, groomed and well-kept place. It is pleasant here" (Mazori, 2005).

Not only the general aesthetics of the cemetery but also the more particular aesthetic of burial in a coffin they offer brings nonreligious people to the private cemeteries. Overall, the flexibility of the commercial model that allows the customers to design their own service enables the cemeteries to cater to a public beyond the secular minority. In some cases, for example, a regular Orthodox service is offered, for those whose only desire is the aesthetics of the private cemetery, similar to any other request that does not offend other families or clients.

We fax the family a list of service providers, Orthodox or Reform.... If they want to take something out of the ordinary texts or not, service providers adjust themselves to family needs... we do not intervene. (Shalom Naim, interview)

It is possible to have a regular rabbi. If they want a rabbi, I will bring them a rabbi. (Shlomi Cohen, interview)

Some wanted to plant a tree, others asked for spices, because that is what the deceased loved. In another case a whisky bottle was brought for everyone to drink, as their dead father has asked them to. (Mazori, 2005)

This professional attitude and commitment to a good service receive positive feedback from families that have paid for a private funeral, a feedback used to promote the cemeteries. "Good things cost money," explained one satisfied customer (Yahav, 2004). Another described the service:

> My brother died suddenly; we were under immense pressure but nevertheless we chose not to use the ordinary service. We called Kibbutz Einat. Everything worked perfectly: the ambulance with the coffin arrived on time and the procession followed it for several yards. After the coffin was placed in the grave the ceremony began. Every person can pick his choice, you can bring a rabbi, play music or sing.... We played the songs my brother loved so much and people spoke to him and about him.... The kibbutz provided water to drink, a sound system and chairs for those who wanted to sit. (Yahav, 2003)

The funerals are not necessarily "secular," as some customer-clients may prefer to combine Orthodox services with the aesthetics of the cemetery and many others choose to include some religious rituals. Interestingly, privatization imposes also some limitations – for example, separating Jews from non-Jews, catering to the wishes of would-be customers, and also, implicitly, indicating the boundaries of Israeli secularism. In the Horashim cemetery, only Jews can be buried; although the formal reason is that the license is for a Jewish cemetery, it also fits the agenda of the cemetery. "It might not bother you or me, but others may care. We are not dealing with political opinions, we respect all Jewish groups, but he or she must be Jewish [to be buried here]" (Shlomi Cohen, interview). In Einat, non-Jews are buried, but in a separate plot. The division is hardly noticed, but those who need to know will receive the information.

> Among the Jewish public that uses our services for some the Jewish character of the cemetery is of importance. Among the non-Jewish graves you can find crosses and if an Orthodox service is conducted, it is a problem.... I have to respect the feelings of the Jewish public that can be offended by non-Jewish symbols... the majority may not care but we are not putting this to the test. (Shalom Naim, interview).

Secular cemeteries have raised little debate and, as in many cases like that of non-Jewish immigrants, they have solved a problem that the Orthodox HKs could not handle. Cremation, however, strictly forbidden by Jewish religion, has elicited a strong, and at times violent, opposition. Unlike the kibbutzim that somewhat accidentally found themselves in the funerary business and stress the social aspect of their service, Aley Shalechet (Leaves of Fall) was formed as a commercial enterprise designed to provide civil burial services, including cremation. The economic approach was the raison d'être of the company that demanded to be treated as a legitimate business.

Our output in the last two years is the result of our economic motives and capabilities. . . . I am not asking for charity or state support, I don't want any favors. On the contrary, I pay taxes, me and everyone else who works here. . . . I am a legitimate business that does not take money from the state . . . the religious have accused us that we are doing all this for profit, that we make our living off the dead. But we don't, we don't kill people. I have no problem to state what we do: we are a company that has a funeral home, we bury, we help people, we create content, and we charge money for our services from those interested in them. (Alon Nativ, interview).

In 2007 the company reported that 450 people, most of them still alive, had approached the company, and about half intend to be cremated (Heruti-Sover, 2007). The company indicated to its would-be clients the advantages to cremation – personal and familial ones regarding the ritual, the burial place, or the scattering of the ashes, and social and ecological ones regarding the saving of burial spaces that cremation allows. The company has also alluded in its brochures to the common use of cremation in the United States, where 15,000 Jews are cremated every year (Livneh, 2005). The reference to American lifestyle, often a winning argument, however, had a limited appeal in this case that tested the limits of tolerance of a secular enterprise that challenged not only religious monopoly but also its authority. The Orthodox strongly opposed the idea, among other things referring to the Holocaust, when Jews were burned in the extermination camps as a reason that cremation should be banned. The Rabbinate Council has ruled that a person whose body will be cremated will not be buried in a Jewish cemetery and will not be mourned according to Jewish tradition (*Ynet*, January 30, 2006). A government minister from the Shas religious party declared that he would initiate a law that will ban cremation and prevent the execution of a "final solution" (referring to the Nazi regime) in Israel (*Ha'aretz*, August 24, 2007). Finally, the crematory, located in a secret location, was burned down by religious activists in July 2007. Religious leaders denied any connection to the act but did not hide their satisfaction.

As with other secular entrepreneurs discussed here, the economic motive does not stand alone. Rather, even in the case of a profit-oriented company, it has a social agenda and is backed by social-political arguments. Aley Shalechet's vision, as its website declares, is to open the way and revolutionize the concept of funeral, burial, and mourning in Israel. Accomplishing this business vision, the company explains, cannot be done without an ideological commitment. Thus, as in other struggles, economic and ideological motives were used together. Religious freedom, freedom of choice, and the need to end the Orthodox monopoly were all evoked to support commercialized burial: "a free Judaism, of free people, free thinkers... we have invested a lot of thought in this, researched the history and tradition to create a professional service to escort a person in his last voyage" (Nativ, interview).

Civil Burial – Public vs. Private

For secular entrepreneurs such as MN, the privatized cemeteries in the kibbutzim were viewed with suspicion, possibly because they undermined MN's campaign by providing outlets on the gray side of the law. MN has turned to the government and demanded that it revoke the license from the kibbutzim that it claimed illegally charge money for burial (*Ha'aretz*, April 4, 2006). Two years before MN's demand, the Israel Land Administration examined the issue and announced it would prevent the kibbutzim from turning their cemeteries into businesses (press release, May 23, 2004); a government decision banned the sale of grave plots for people who were not members of the kibbutz. The decision was intended to prevent using agricultural land for cemeteries and from allowing private enterprises to charge money for what should be a public service (Mey-Ami, 2007). The kibbutzim attempted to find a way around the decision by, first, claiming that they charge money not for the burial itself, but for the maintenance of the cemetery. Second, and more important, they claimed that they provide an answer to a problem the state has so far ignored and, therefore, must be allowed to continue operating (Yahav, 2003).

Other voices among secular and non-Orthodox groups supported the economic channels that seemed more productive than the political ones.

If several serious businesspeople would be brought in to this... Israelis are willing to pay 10,000 [shekels] for burial, the government pays part of this. Let's build a serious business like Kibutz Einat did all over the country with land allocated by the government.... The entrepreneurs have not succeeded in bringing private money into this system. I have come to the conclusion that we cannot rely on public budgets because the way the system works, under the influence of the religious... we must create our own economic alternative. (Rabbi Meir Azari, interview).

Private cemeteries prided themselves on providing better services, but their continued operation was legally problematic. The State Comptroller's report in 2009 criticized the government for not implementing the civil burial law and its failure to prevent the illegal use of agricultural land and illegal charges for private burials. In addition, the comptroller warned that many of the companies that provided burial services did not have the required licenses. On one hand, said the report, the authorities in charge of burial must expand and advance civil burial according to the law so that civil cemeteries serving the public will be made available to every citizen. On the other hand, the authorities must act to prevent the illegal use of agricultural lands for commercial purposes and to ensure that the rights of the families of the deceased will not be compromised in those difficult times and their distress will not be exploited for unfair and possibly illegal profits (State Comptroller, 2009).

Private burials and the solutions found to bury non-Jewish immigrants in non-Jewish plots in existing HK cemeteries took the edge off the political campaigns and allowed the government to drag its feet in implementing the civil burial law. Civil private burial among Jews in Israel remains minor and consists of only 2 percent of the total burials. In 2009, for example, 858 burials out of 38,000 were civil burials, a number that includes also people identified "without religion" (Itim, 2011) who, by definition, could not be buried in the HK cemeteries.

Orthodox Reactions

Jewish Orthodoxy has had in this case, as in marriage, to fight to preserve its monopoly against secular demands and initiatives. The HKs' mistreatment of FSU immigrants has tarnished their image and brought harsh criticism of its practices. However, although solutions for immigrants were found, the general image of the HK cemeteries remained negative for other reasons as well. Charges of inefficiency, corruption, poor service, and neglect in the HKs, on one hand, and the positive image of the private cemeteries, on the other hand, have made the latter a new status symbol. The majority of Israelis continued to use the HK services, but as funerals, and especially celebrity funerals covered in the media, expanded, more Israelis were exposed to the alternatives. The aesthetic qualities, the service provided, and the ability to plan the ceremony worked in favor of the private cemeteries that became a target for the educated upper class.

The secularists for whom the standard Orthodox ritual of the funeral no longer seemed to represent their way of life and their culture, however, could be convinced to use improved and more flexible Orthodox services. Even Orthodox rabbis were aware of the new needs and the possibility to be more flexible:

> Like in weddings, if the rabbinical establishment was attentive enough for the needs and wants of people, with their personal style, the privatization of religious services would not be necessary. If we would only be ready to provide worthwhile services for our clientele, if we, as rabbis, were service oriented, we would not be required to consider privatization... there is no problem with playing music or singing, it is only about the good will of the HK. (quoted in Ettinger, 2011b)

A new policy adopted by the HKs in the early 2000s is described on the HK Tel Aviv website as "revolutionizing" attempt to achieve higher standards (http://www.kadisha.biz/). The change includes a 24/7 hotline, improved services, renovation of cemeteries, and even online broadcast of funerals. More important is the business-like attitude that turned into a surprising flexibility for secular requests. In Tel Aviv, the HK manager explained that "we provide services according to the *halakhah* but nobody is forced to have a religious ritual. Those who don't want a rabbi or the reading of the Kaddish can read poetry or any other texts. We don't have a problem with this" (Yahav, 2003). In Haifa, the HK manager explained that he has no objection to civil cemeteries, but they are not needed, as everything can be solved in the existing cemeteries. "Music is allowed and burial in a coffin is possible, maybe with holes at the bottom. If someone does not want a rabbi, it is also OK" (Sinai, 1997) .

Conclusions

As in the case of marriage, described in the previous chapter, new needs and demands that encountered a stagnated political system created new alternatives, driven by a secular ideology, demographic necessities, and economic interests. In Walter's (2005) terms, burial in Israel can be described as a combination of a state-led religious bureaucracy and an economic model in which private entrepreneurs offer a variety of services. This combination is less a formal division of authority and more the result of the limited success of the principled struggle for civil burial. The attempt of secular entrepreneurs to establish civil burial through formal political channels and the courts, aided by the new demand created by non-Jewish immigrants, has led to the establishment of one large civil cemetery in the periphery and several small ones near the center. These cemeteries, together with some flexibility in the Orthodox cemeteries, have solved the majority of the problems of immigrants but have not answered the demands of veteran secular Israelis.

The gap between government decisions that were not implemented and the growing demand for civil burial was filled by private entrepreneurs who have turned the burial issue into a business. For secular Israelis seeking to depart from their loved ones in a personal rather than the standard Orthodox ritual and for those who wish, while they are still alive, to plan their departure from the world, private cemeteries provide an alternative. The business approach translates into flexibility, personal service, and aesthetics that appeal to secular Israelis able and willing to pay for their burial. The business attitude sometimes blurs the lines between religious and secular when private and secular cemeteries provide religious services and even adhere to religious restrictions and state-religious cemeteries become more flexible and accommodate secular demands. At the moment, the new alternatives provide a way to express a worldview and social and economic status and offer a solution that, for the time being, does not require a political or legal struggle.

5

Pig on the Plate

From "White Steak" to Pork

In the early years of statehood, the majority of Jewish Israelis, including nonreligious ones, refrained from eating pork. The evolving status of nonkosher food in general, and of pork in particular, symbolizes – probably more than anything else – the new reality, according to which such meat, which had been sold in the past mostly under the counter and given the vague name "white steak," has now established a presence on the menu of many restaurants and is sold openly in new delicatessens and food chain stores throughout the country. Although the religious public, and most of the traditional population in Israel, regard pork as a symbol of impurity, and for them eating it is a serious transgression, for many Israelis it is now a commodity judged by taste and price. The increasing legitimization and expansion of the nonkosher meat industry and the eating of pork constitute a fundamental change of lifestyle and the decline of religious authority, both underscored by demographic and economic transformations.

The Jewish *halakhic* prohibition on eating pork and raising pigs is an ancient and blanket ban. The pig is a forbidden food not only because it is identified as a repulsive animal but also because it signifies the persecution and humiliation of the Jews for many generations. The story of Hannah and her seven sons, who were put to death during the Maccabean revolt for refusing to eat pork, has become a symbol of firm resistance or martyrdom and the abomination of the pig for both religious and national mythologies. Berl Katznelson, the secular Zionist thinker, called, before statehood, for the ban on pork for national reasons:

Therefore, I can understand that a nation whose war for freedom in Hasmonean times was linked to the resistance to eating pork, and those people suffered significantly during two thousand years of history because of their refusal to submit to those who tried to feed them pork, so this ancient custom should be treated with respect, and the Hebrew or Jewish city should ban the sale of pork within its boundaries. (cited in Barak-Erez, 2003)

The reservations about the pig, shared by many nonreligious people, were reflected in various legal and political arrangements that did not completely ban pork, but pushed it to the margins and kept its consumption minimal. The demographic, social, and economic changes in the 1990s, however, have also changed the status of pork, reflected in the growing number of supermarkets, delicatessen stores, and restaurants that sell pork. Pork and other nonkosher foods became part of the diet of many Israelis and a business for secular entrepreneurs. Reports in mainstream media are indicative of the transformation of the pork from an agreed-upon symbol of disgust to an object of consumption, at times even associated with class. Thus, for example, *Yediot Aharonot*, the newspaper with the largest circulation in Israel, described the opening of a nonkosher supermarket in the following words:

A major commotion erupted with scores of cars and hundreds of people crowding the entrance to the new branch of Tiv-Ta'am, which opened there. The words "Tiv-Ta'am (a culinary celebration)" appeared on the advertising boards directing the customers to the new store, and the brackets that formed part of the slogan featured two chubby shrimps, thereby hinting at the fact that Tiv-Ta'am is not just an ordinary supermarket but a nonkosher supermarket. This branch, which has a floor space of 3,000 m², sells in addition to the regular products items such as shrimps and mollusks, eels from New Zealand, fresh meat products ranging from pork to rabbit, different types of bread and other delicacies imported from all over the globe, including ice cream from Russia and fruit berries from Hungary. In the cafeteria at the entrance to the store one can buy pizza with shrimps as well as sandwiches with salami and hard cheese. (Zomer, 2002)

Unlike the struggles for the freedom of marriage and the right for civil burial that combine a secular worldview and ideology with economic entrepreneurship, the initiative concerning nonkosher meat is, first and foremost, economic. However, ideological elements of individual liberty and freedom of religion are also interwoven in this struggle, and even the republican question emerged whenever an attempt was made to restrict the sale of pork.

Food: Beyond Eating

Food is a basic need, but its production, trade, and consumption involve cultural preferences, restrictions, and regulation. What people eat, what they refrain from eating, and the reasoning they apply for their choices reflect identities, lifestyle, and social boundaries and limitations (Belasco, 2002: 2). Eating habits delineate the boundaries that impart a sense of consistency and stability that people use to define their group and distinguish it from others. Foods common in one culture may be perceived as "repulsive" or even forbidden in another, and the infringement on prohibition may result in punishment or even expulsion from the group (Simoons, 1967: 108). Frequently, religion sets the boundaries and restrictions as it defines traditional foods connected with rituals, as well as prohibitions and taboos with respect to other dishes. The existence of these customs and prohibitions constitutes an expression of faith in the deity and a commitment that distinguishes the faithful from the "others" (Fieldhouse, 1995: 147–8). Boundaries, however, are not always fixed, so that foods previously prohibited or considered repulsive may turn into desired luxuries and, later, common dishes. Young American soldiers during World War II, for example, described the Japanese as "not human beings" because they ate their fish raw; fifty years later, Americans of various classes and with different ethnic origins were eating sushi throughout the United States (Mintz, 2002).

The dynamism of food consumption seems to challenge the relationships between food, space, culture, and identity. In the seventeenth century, the British East India Company proudly claimed that in its products "we can taste the Arabian spices but never feel the scorching sun that brought them to us" (Belasco, 2002: 9). National food itself, associated with a place, often concealed a complex history of trade links and cultural exchanges that would later become an integral part of national culture (Bell and Valentine, 1997: 169). The globalization of the food industry at the end of the twentieth century further undermined the connection between the place/locality, myths associated with the local food cultures (Tomlinson, 1999: 123), and the restrictions on food consumption.

Local food habits that demarcated cultures were transgressed by global mass-production commodities and by the unique and the exotic products that globalization made available. Consumption of food in developed countries of the contemporary era is no longer curbed by scarcity or by a Puritan ideology. Rather, food has become abundant and eating a cultural event or an "experience" embedded in consumer culture and shared by many people. If, in the nineteenth century, it was mostly the British aristocracy that broke local diets in favor of French cuisine, by the end of the twentieth century not only French but many other "ethnic" foods became available and familiar to all classes (James, 1996). The "concentration of time and place" facilitated the placing of a wide range of ethnic restaurants and food stores in a relatively small area, evident in any Western city of a medium size or greater (Harvey, 1989: 300). This change allows or encourages people to experience new tastes, even those previously considered strange, forbidden, or repulsive.

Eating has turned from a necessity to an experience, a leisure activity, and an expression of status and lifestyle for an expanding middle class that eats in restaurants, cooks at home, and/or travels abroad to satisfy an interest in food. This change seems completely disconnected from politics, as there is no hint to the origin of the food consumed, the production processes involved, and the production interactions existing in those processes (Harvey, 1989: 300; Tomlinson, 1999). Changes relating to food have taken place in different societies over many years and are rarely characterized by major dramas or significant tensions. Rather, they are usually perceived as a mundane experience that neither threatens nor undermines identities and social order (Tomlinson, 1999: 128). In some instances, however, when changes seem to threaten the existing order or are perceived as part of a wider threat to identity and culture and a transgression of existing norms, they will evoke resistance.

The politics involved in production, marketing, and consumption of food cannot be ignored entirely when existing culture and social (or religious) order are directly challenged. McDonald's and Coca-Cola, two products symbolizing globalization, are marketed in a similar format worldwide as symbols of freedom, modernity, globalization, and "America" (Howes, 1996), exported and emulated in other countries (Fantasia, 1995; Ritzer, 1996; Stephenson, 1989). However, these products may also become symbols of "cultural imperialism" that provoke resistance. Changes in local food cultures – brought by immigrants, local entrepreneurs, or global commodity chains – can present more vague challenges to local cultures but can also, even unintentionally, defy religious restrictions and offend feelings of believers. Food consumption, therefore, can be politicized when moral debates, identity questions, and challenges to the status of the existing limits and restrictions are involved. On the personal level, changes unfold in moral dilemmas concerning the food production process (e.g., cruelty to animals or fair trade), health concerns (e.g., genetically engineered food, diseases spread by food), and doubts related to adherence to existing religious prohibitions. On the collective-institutional level, these issues are manifested in questions over the fate of existing regulations, demands for new regulations, and clashes of principles between opposing groups and ideologies. In these struggles over the public and private domains, the rules of the game – what is permitted and what is prohibited – are decided.

Rules of the Game: Politics of Pork

Debates over the regulation and restriction of pork production and sale began in pre-statehood times, during the British mandate. Despite religious prohibitions and the pig's problematic image, pork was available and consumed by secular Jews. However, because the Jewish community had virtually no power to enforce rules and because the practice of eating pork was not very widespread, no major political struggle took place. Things changed in the early years of statehood, when regulation was in the hands of the Jewish state. Massive immigration and a consequent shortage of basic food products encouraged some, especially the kibbutzim belonging to the HaShomer HaTza'ir socialist movement, to rear pigs alongside the dairies and chicken coops as a relatively cheap source of meat. As some kibbutz members had certain reservations about this practice the rearing of pigs was conducted far from the members' homes (Rinat, interview). The practice also became widespread in urban areas after the War of Independence when cow sheds and stables were converted into pigsties and slaughter houses (Barak-Erez, 2003). The Chief Rabbinate rallied its supporters to fight this development and in 1951 published a sternly worded pamphlet condemning the pig farmers:

As part of the effort to put a stop to this curse and banish this shame and disgrace, the Chief Rabbinate of Israel has convened at a special meeting and seen fit to condemn this abomination which the pig farmers are doing and in so doing offend God and Israel, His people. In the name of all the Rabbinical offices in Israel we call on these farmers to repent for this shame and depart from the way of this accursed deity which has brought this revolting sin to enwrap his people. Let any person who raises pigs be damned! Then on the contrary, let anyone who can object and protests be blessed. God is blessed, so is the moral public and its spokespersons, in addition to those local council leaders, council members and the committees of the *Moshavot* and other settlements who take action. Those who have already agreed and those who will decide in the future to recognize the facts and take a stand in this campaign, and also use all the power of legal force and exercise strongly their proper influence to destroy the obscenity within their boundaries, uproot the affliction by its very roots, and eradicate it from underneath the Lord's heavens and from the surface of the great country, the land of the fathers.

The religious political parties concentrated their efforts on a complete ban of pork rearing, production, and sale. But, because the government was concerned with sweeping laws that would pertain also to non-Jews, only administrative steps were taken to curtail the practice, such as reducing the supply of fodder to the pig farmers, limiting the pigs to specific areas, or having local authorities take action. The effect of these actions was rather negligible, as these initiatives, mostly bylaws instigated against businesspeople, were either ineffective or rejected by the High Court, which ruled that the authorities had exceeded their powers and noted that a fundamental prohibition must be resolved on a national level (Barak-Erez, 2003).

The debate in Israel on the raising of pigs and the sale of pork proceeded in the historical context that was repeatedly introduced into the political and social discussion, marking the ban of pork as a national rather than a religious issue and attempting to de-politicize the debate. "Generations may come and go," wrote Zerach Warhaftig, one of the leaders of the national religious movement during the 1950s, "and the pig has always been the symbol and characteristic mark of Israel's adversaries. When those who hated us have always sought to express their malicious loathing towards us, then they would force the people of Israel to eat pig, as they knew there is no comparable torture to distress them, terrify, depress and humiliate them into the dust" (Warhaftig, 1988: 297).

In 1956, religious Knesset members, using the national argument, initiated a decision that authorized local authorities to legislate a bylaw to limit or prohibit the raising of pigs or the sale of pork. The law's opponents rejected the national arguments and claimed that this was "religious coercion," but the coalition's considerations and a relatively broad consensus with respect to the status of the pig paved the way for the Local Authorities (Special Enablement) Law of 1956. Local authorities had to decide whether pork could be sold and to balance between religious and national demands, on one hand, and individual liberties, on the other hand. The Tel Aviv municipality and others that followed their example passed laws limiting the raising of pigs and the sale of pork within their boundaries. The head supervisor in charge of enforcing this bylaw reported that more than forty pigsties operated in the Tel Aviv area, in addition to pork factories that were opened around the time of the War of Independence and immediately afterward. In 1957, municipal inspectors carried out 13,689 inspections at butcher shops, restaurants, stores, and factories and confiscated 500 tons of pork.

> At that time we reached the conclusion that we should have no illusions about our success rate and achieving the complete and total eradication of the meat from this unclean animal in the city.... However, we are convinced that persistent inspections will substantially reduce the distribution of this abominable meat in public and the criminal activity will be conducted only underground. (Broide, 1977: 199–200)

Several local councils passed bylaws prohibiting the sale of pork within their boundaries, but most of them did little, if anything, to enforce them; even in Tel Aviv, the inspections did not last for long. Zerach Warhaftig, who served as Deputy Minister for Religious Affairs, expressed his disappointment with the law that led to some reduction in pig farming in Israel but failed to solve the problem in the manner that the religious public would have liked to see (Warhaftig, 1988: 299).

In addition to political-legislative means, economic sanctions were also used to restrict or ban the production and sale of pork. The chief rabbinate threatened Tnuva, the principal marketing organization of agricultural produce, that its *hekhsher* (religious permit) for milk would be revoked if it continued to purchase milk from farms where pigsties were kept. In response, Tnuva undertook to liquidate the pigsties in the kibbutz farms and promptly notified the kibbutzim that they had to comply with that decision. In a letter to Kibbutz Mizra sent in November 1958, Tnuva stated that it is bound

> to prevent any conflict whatsoever with an important group of its consumers, and to take into consideration the position of the Chief Rabbinate on the issue of the milk's kashrut and Kibbutz Mizra is therefore required to liquidate the pigsties no later than December 9, 1958. Should you fail to close down the pigsties by that date then Tnuva's creameries will be unable to accept milk from you. (archive of Kibbutz Mizra)

Although other kibbutzim yielded to the pressure and closed down their pigsties, Mizra postponed the decision until legislation by the Knesset made pig farming impossible.

Religious politicians, not satisfied with the results achieved by the bylaws and economic pressures, demanded wider restrictions and stronger enforcement. These parties were determined not only to take advantage of their political power but also to use the broad (national, rather than religious) consensus against pork that also had support among nonreligious

MKs. The Pig-Raising Prohibition Law, passed in 1962, was described by its religious proponents, again, as a national law based on national-historical sentiments and arguments of collective identity rather than on religious grounds (Warhaftig, 1988: 302). MK Moshe Unna, who presented the law, emphasized its national significance:

This law expresses to some extent the special character of the State of Israel as it keeps alive the nation's unique tradition and upholds the need for continuing the way of life to which the people of Israel have grown accustomed throughout its entire history. (cited in Barak-Erez, 2003)

The Pig-Raising Prohibition Law stated explicitly that in the state of Israel the raising, keeping, or slaughter of pigs was prohibited, with the exception of non-Jewish towns and villages, in addition to scientific and research institutes, which were entitled to receive a special permit. In compliance with this law, pig farmers closed down their businesses located in areas where pig farming was prohibited, but some of them transferred the raising of pigs to areas where these activities were permitted, mainly in Arab villages in northern Israel. The religious Knesset members protested at a meeting against the concessions made in the law; MK Yitzchak Rafael pointed out that the law "is defective in two principal areas: (a) It leaves the pig with an impure foothold in our country; (b) it leaves open the possibility for its distribution all over the country" (Knesset meeting, February 19, 1962).

The impact of the new rules of the game was largely symbolic. Loopholes in the law and limited enforcement allowed farmers and producers to continue to work with relatively few disturbances and meet the existing, and rather small, demand for pork. At Kibbutz Lahav, a research institute was established to facilitate the continued raising of pigs, and whatever meat was left over after the research needs were met was sent to the meat factory constructed at the kibbutz. Kibbutz Mizra, which transferred its pigsties to the Christian-Arab village of A'eblin, became the largest producer and gradually also developed its business to become an exporter of pork. In addition to the kibbutzim there were also smaller family-run factories; two of them expanded during the 1990s and are now known to the public as Tiv-Ta'am and Ma'adanei Manya, discussed later.

The target population for the pork factories was a small-sized secular public – urban, Ashkenazi, and particularly Eastern Europeans who immigrated prior to the 1970s, Romanians, Poles, and Russians. Pork was available in some restaurants that served "white steak" or at

delicatessens and butchers that sold nonkosher salami. The low-key strategy of entrepreneurs was reflective of their delicate position: "We tried to
avoid publicity, used no promotion campaigns, the stores were located in
areas inhabited by a mostly secular population and our promotion was
indeed minimal... all this industry developed from 1990 onward, until
then it was all quite minor" (Yaakov Manya, interview).

Ma'adanei Mizra adopted a similar strategy and continued to develop
the factory and the delicatessens selling its produce while maintaining
a low profile, taking care to avoid enraging the religious groups. Thus,
for example, the trucks marketing the product went about their business
bearing no advertisements at all to avoid attracting attention (Micah
Rinat, interview). The loopholes in the law that enabled the entrepreneurs
to continue working, the limited production and trade, and the low profile
of the businesses involved kept the pig off the political agenda until the
struggle was renewed during the 1980s.

Politicized Pigs: An Age of Strife

In the 1980s, the question of pork production and sale was re-politicized
when the religious parties attempted to close the loopholes and restrict the
marketing, sale, and distribution of pork. In the debate on the proposed
law, which was tabled in 1981, MK Shlomo-Yisrael Ben-Meir of the NRP
explained that the existing law failed to stand up to the test of reality, so
new legislation was required.

Some twenty years have passed in the meantime and the results are plain for all
to see. This loophole in the law is really an open door and opportunity makes a
thief. We are well aware of the fact that this loophole in the law has led to pig
farming on a massive scale and the widespread sale of pork is evident in almost
every city in Israel.

The people of Israel can get along without having pork on open sale, for this
trade constitutes a mark of disgrace for us, the state and the nation, as we witness
the sale of pork publicly in the independent State of Israel. This is not simply
a religious matter, but a national issue, a Jewish matter, a question of national
honor, an issue of respect for one's heritage and culture. (Knesset meeting, March
11, 1981)

The resumption of the struggle may be linked not only to the expansion of the trade in pork, but also to changes in the political map of
Israel that occurred around that time. The struggle this time was led
not by the NRP but by the empowered *haredi* (ultra-Orthodox) political parties. As the parliamentary strength of the two major parties,

Labor and the Likud, was evenly balanced, the *haredi* (ultra-Orthodox) political parties became sought-after partners in the coalition government (see Chapter 2). These parties, which held the balance of power in Israeli politics, took full advantage of this status for both material gains for their constituency and attempted broader legislative changes. The "Pig Law" became one of the principal issues in the coalition negotiations as the *haredi* parties sought to change the rules of the game and curtail the trade in pork by closing the loopholes in the existing law.

The charged political atmosphere had made it difficult for religious parties to present the new law (again), as underscored by national rather than religious interests. MK Mordechai Virshuvski, in a debate in the Knesset, explained that times had changed, and that the national argument was no longer accepted by secular Israelis:

In the State of Israel nowadays the eating of the so-called white meat.... and it's sale is almost everywhere, at least that is the situation in my city of Tel Aviv, with pleasure and enthusiasm. Everyone is eating it and this provides an excellent income... a large proportion of the people want to eat it and actually do so. (Knesset meeting, July 30, 1985)

Secular opposition to the law maintained that it was a blatant case of "religious coercion" and "political blackmail" by the *haredi* parties. The producers and marketers of pork were joined by the Association for Civil Rights and by the Tel Aviv municipality, the first one to introduce municipal bylaws restricting the pig trade, which now disbanded the unit charged with enforcing the bylaw (Barak-Erez, 2003). Thomas Friedman, the *New York Times* correspondent, described the million people who ate pork in Israel as being "under siege." Eyal Sar-Shalom, the manager of the Mizra factory, in an interview with Friedman, linked the obvious economic interest with the liberal ideology, a link that would be repeated many times during the coming years:

I think that there are only three countries in the world which have such laws. The first one is Libya, the second is Saudi Arabia, and Iran has not yet succeeded in passing such a law.... Israel is proceeding at a quicker pace than Iran here, for we have our own Khomeinis. (Friedman, 1985)

Kibbutz Mizra was especially concerned about the proposed law, a private bill tabled not by the coalition but by an individual MK, Avraham Shapira of the ultra-Orthodox Agudat Israel Party. The meat factory had developed rapidly over the preceding years and became the principal source of income for the kibbutz, with an annual turnover of $7 million, about a quarter of that for export (internal document dated June 24,

1985, from the archives of Kibbutz Mizra). MK Shapira, chairman of the Knesset Finance Committee, promised to assist in converting the factory at Mizra to a different production line (*Al Hamishmar*, January 22, 1986). The kibbutz, in response, emphasized the strict veterinary supervision and the quality of its products, estimated the number of consumers at about one million people, and warned that the prohibition of trade in pigs would push the trade underground and hit the law-abiding organized factories hard at the entire public's expense. Its representatives, speaking for the entire industry, reported that it included some thirty producers, 13,000 to 15,000 workers, and an annual sales estimated at $120 million (*Al Hamishmar*, December 26, 1985).

The producers were to learn that in the new balance of power ("their") political parties could no longer be relied on for support. The Labor Party (with its leader, Shimon Peres, serving as prime minister) was expected to support the kibbutz – the kibbutzim being an integral part of the party – but many of the party MKs abstained from the vote. The kibbutz expressed its disappointment in a letter:

You ... who championed the cause of protecting individual freedom and the prevention of religious coercion ... abandoned the principle of freedom of conscience and thereby allowed those who seek to impose the *halakhah* on our way of life, to throw political mud at our fine factory and use an archaic abomination in the process ... yet we, your partners, you have sold us for a questionable broth of lentils associated with a political stamp of approval from a gang of blackmailing rabbis. You have handed over the common values that were shared by both us and you in the past and opted to favor those who crave religious coercion. You have done all this for a mere handful of scant hopes for political support. (letter to the prime minister's office, April 11, 1985, archives of Kibbutz Mizra)

Although the law was passed at its first reading and was then referred to the Knesset Economic Affairs Committee, the discussion there made no progress and the law never reached its second reading. The struggle, however was renewed a few years later when, in 1990, the coalition agreement between the Likud and the ultra-Orthodox Agudat Israel included "the legislation of the law prohibiting the marketing of pigs, which is still on the agenda of the Knesset Internal Affairs Committee, to be concluded in a final version to be agreed" (Barak-Erez, 2003). Threatened again by legislation, producers expressed their anger at the government and *haredi* public, at times using harsh language and the republican equation, highlighting their contribution against the exemption of *haredim* from military service, and even using severe words of threat:

[T]he [butcher] knives that will be brought to rest could easily take on a new lease of life and be used to shave off the side locks and beards of the *yeshiva* students.... For every butcher shop closed, a special army recruiting office for enrolling full-time *yeshiva* students will be opened, and after this clash they will never touch us again. (*Kol-Bo*, January 11, 1991)

The new reality, in which the pig law seemed to be almost an accomplished fact, forced the secular entrepreneurs to change strategy. As they could no longer rely on a low-profile policy to guarantee their continued existence, the entrepreneurs had to set up a political campaign that would merge their economic interest with the secular ideology of individual rights in opposition to the *haredi* initiative – "The economic struggle combined well with human rights and Mizra became a symbol" (Micah Rinot, interview). Kibbutz Mizra, the owner of the largest factory, led the struggle against the pig law. An internal document distributed among the kibbutz members explained the new strategy:

For many years now Kibbutz Mizra has served as an outstanding example in its political and public non-belligerency... [but] when danger lurks at our gates it becomes apparent that we cannot succeed without full and practical mobilization... we do so with the feeling that one is fighting for one's home, for our living and the image that this state is adapting. (archives of Kibbutz Mizra)

An action team formed at the kibbutz defined its objectives as follows: mobilizing public opinion in the country, applying pressure on the politicians and policy makers, as well as mobilizing all the law's opponents for a massive protest. The struggle against the "Pig Law" was framed as a struggle for liberal rights that extended beyond meat and as a liberal cause for secularists to rally behind. The fact that religious parties prepared additional legislation on issues such as abortions or stopping all public transport on the Sabbath, it was believed in the kibbutz, would, in the long run, turn out to be an advantage in their struggle and be part of their strategy:

As responsible citizens of the state we cannot launch a campaign against this law purely on the grounds that it damages our interests directly or that we have only a limited economic interest and we are fighting only for fair compensation. We must lead and initiate a broad public struggle for citizens' rights, freedom of conscience aimed at protecting the state from descending into an age of Khomeinism. (internal document, June 19, 1990, archives of Kibbutz Mizra)

The struggle was therefore defined as a secular fight against what was termed "religious coercion" that threatened to spread into additional spheres of daily life. It combined an economic rationale with a liberal ethos of freedom of choice but, no less significant, a republican discourse stressed the societal contribution of the kibbutzim in contrast to the ultra-Orthodox.

"Religious coercion" in general, not to mention imposing minority will on the majority whereby a marginal and noncontributing minority dictates to the majority how to behave. A minority that forces its will on others belongs to a bygone age, particularly as it is mostly non-Zionist and refrains from sharing in the responsibility for the state. This planned legislation constitutes an infringement of individual rights and interferes in everyone's personal choice, acts that even totalitarian regimes have ceased in recent times. There is no room for compromise with religious fanatics because secular people will always have to concede. There is also a danger that legislation may be enacted with respect to the Sabbath laws and in general a move could be made to transform the state into a Khomeini mode characterized by fanaticism, extremism, as well as feeble and archaic leaders who decided everything for all. (ibid.)

An advertisement in the form of a military callup notice called on all young men and women to report for duty to fight a "war against religious coercion" and explained: "This order serves to stop the *haredim* shirking from enlisting in the army. This order was issued to get the *haredim* to join the army – and not engage in coercion." Members of the kibbutz even threatened to hand back their army reserve duty cards if the legislation passed, stressing again their contribution and sacrifice and linking the material interest and the Zionist ethos into which the pork industry was woven.

I never came across Rabbi [Menachem] Porush in the military posts during the War of Independence, neither he was there in the Sinai Campaign and not even during the Six-Day War on a troop carrier, like the one in which my son was killed... neither did I see any wounded from among Rabbi Porush's followers in the hospital. A whole platoon of kibbutz sons have been laid to rest in Kibbutz Mizra's cemetery because they gave their lives for this country! And now that very same state for which they fought comes and seeks to deprive us of our living, our life insurance, everything we have and cynically cast us aside straight out into the street, without even paying some compensation... we shall block roads. We shall march on the Knesset and bring with us the Kibbutz founders who are now in their eighties, the ones who drained the swamps. These older members will also rally to demonstrate against the law. (quoted in Zamir, 1990)

This division between I, who put my life on the line, pay taxes, and those who continue to behave like parasites and play no part in the creative activities or security but continue to live their ghetto-style lives as though they were still in the nineteenth century. This will simply not work any longer! (ibid.)

During the latter stages of the struggle, when almost everything seemed lost, Kibbutz Mizra began to think about converting the factory to one producing kosher products and hiring attorneys to demand compensation (Micah Rinat, interview). The minister for religious affairs who met with the kibbutz members promised to assist the kibbutz's economy, in the hope that this would ease the tensions between the sides (*Al Hamishmar*, December 27, 1990). Additional Knesset members from the religious parties also expressed their willingness to compensate the farmers and producers (*Al Hamishmar*, December 18, 1990). However, the Pig Law was eventually delayed and put on the back burner for, among other reasons, the more pressing matter of the Desert Storm campaign in the Persian Gulf that diverted attention from the issue. The window of opportunity afforded to the *haredi* politicians during the mid-1980s to change the rules of the game or, as they understood it, to enforce the existing regulations, was shut tight immediately after the Gulf War, when the immigration from the FSU changed the social and political reality. In 1991, while the proposed bill was still on the table of the Internal Affairs Committee of the Knesset, the manager of the Mizra factory reported on the factory's preparations to cater for the market: "here with us it is business as usual" (*Al Hamishmar*, October 31, 1991).

De-Politicized Pigs – Demography and Economics

In the 1990s the pork debate moved from the national political realm to the legal, economic, and local arenas. During the 1980s, Israelis, as the *New York Times* reported, developed, in spite of religious laws, a taste for pork products and consumed them in increasing quantities (Friedman, 1985). In addition to the change in the culinary tastes of the Israel middle class, the immigration from the FSU lent real momentum to the expansion of the production and sale of pork. Entrepreneurs were more than ready to respond to the growing demand. By 2000, the Mizra factory owned 42 delicatessen stores throughout the country and had 1,500 outlets, 1,300 of them owned by FSU immigrants; the total sales turnover was $13 million. It added a new production line, turning out prestigious Italian products, and began advertizing its meat products, including pork. According to estimates made by the factory's director, the annual consumption of pork in Israel had reached about 9,000 tons (Gross, 2000).

The demographic reality and the ensuing demand for pork weakened the bylaws, which were in any case virtually ineffective, as small delicatessen stores and large supermarkets selling pork had sprung up in every area with a significant concentration of new immigrants, sometimes thanks to the initiative of the immigrants themselves or because veteran Israelis identified an economic opportunity. Religious leaders had to face a new reality in which the window of opportunity for a comprehensive pig law, which had opened several years earlier, no longer existed. MK Porush of the Agudat Israel party expressed his frustrations:

It is to our disgrace that we have before us here a list of some 130 stores selling pig. It is quite shocking but how come not all of us are disgusted nor feel ashamed? I ask the secular people: Are your feelings so dulled that you do not realize the extent of the shame as you see this other thing spreading? Not only are some 130 stores marketing this revolting pig but Ma'adanei Mizra even exports pig. . . . Who could ever have imagined that pig produce would be supplied from the Land of Israel not only within the country but also to the wide world? (Knesset meeting, May 19, 1993)

Apparently aware of the new reality, MK Porush did not propose a new law but rather was satisfied with referring the discussion to the Internal Affairs Committee. The chair of the committee, however, rejected the discussion, attesting again to the change and the de-politicization of the issue:

We would waste three hours, summon all the interested parties, we would make an announcement to the press – will that satisfy you? Holding such a futile debate will be a waste of the Internal Affairs Committee's time. Are you serious about this idea? Table a private members' bill. (ibid.)

The new demographic reality was clear, as were its implications. A survey conducted by the Manufacturers Association of Israel found that the immigrants, while integrating in some measures, maintained cultural detachment, including in eating habits. The survey also found that since a previous survey, conducted four years earlier, the potential of the "Russian" delicatessen stores and supermarkets increased, probably due to the immigrants' improved economic position, enabling them to buy more than before (Degani and Degani, 2004). A journalist's report of a visit to a branch of Tiv-Ta'am, a nonkosher chain established in the 1990s, described the change that had occurred over the preceding decade due to the immigration from the FSU and much to the delight of the Israeli gourmet secular public:

The clear influence of the Christmas season at the Tiv-Ta'am supermarket in Rishon LeZion only indicated part of the story. Here the atmosphere was reminiscent of foreign lands – a free market, democracy, and normality – even without any connection to the Christian festival. What captures the eye here in this spacious store, which caters mainly to the Russian community in Israel, is everything that is missing from the Israel kosher chain stores . . . i.e., everything that is prohibited to sell there, all that is restricted and withdrawn from the shelves. Here, alongside the regular brand names, there is a tremendous abundance of products from Russia and the other countries of Eastern Europe, as well as food supplies from Asia, or more simply stated, a wide range of dishes that are not kosher by definition, or those which were not passed by kashrut supervisors. The Russians in Israel immigrated as a community... they were not assimilated as new immigrants – they established here culinary centers with distinct consumption, thereby enriching the local market. (Coussin, 2001)

The republican argument of the kibbutzim and the liberal discourse of freedom of choice were overshadowed by a new reality, in which consumer's choice and the demand for pork set the rules. From the immigrants' perception this was an inevitable change, as one explained to a reporter: "the *haredim* do not want us to buy pork, but we buy it.... There is demand and consequently there is also a supply. That is how life goes on and the *haredim* are not going to stop it" (*Yediot Aharonot*, June 15, 2004). For secular entrepreneurs, however, the changes signaled an opportunity to transform the rules of the game.

Israelis and the Pig: New Perceptions?

The change in perceptions toward pork and other nonkosher foods is part of a wider cultural change and the emergence of a consumer society. The puritan attitude of the pioneering society, the scarcity, and the limited resources were replaced in the 1980s with affluence, choice, and a gourmet food culture. Ethnic and local restaurants, cooking utensils, imported foods sold at specialty stores and supermarkets, best-selling cookbooks, prime-time television shows devoted to cooking and culinary travels, and celebrity chefs all attested to the new food culture. For many Israelis, food was now part of leisure and lifestyle, and shopping for food, cooking, and eating became an "experience." These new culinary adventures, in some instances, transgressed different religious restrictions and presented dilemmas for Israelis still committed to religious tradition.

The majority of Israelis, in spite of the changes, still refrain from eating pork. In another survey that focused on observance of kashrut, only 24 percent of Israelis describe themselves "completely nonobservant" in regard to the purchase of meat (Figure 5.1). However, establishments that sell pork will not necessarily be completely shunned by those who keep some degree of kashrut. More than 40 percent of Israelis stated they will eat in a restaurant that serves also nonkosher food (some would not eat meat) and 43 percent will shop in a supermarket that sells nonkosher meet (but some will not purchase meat).

Differences were found between the ethnic groups in regard to the observance of kashrut and the question whether the sale of pork should

TABLE 5.1. *Ethnicity and Kashrut*

	I Do Not Observe Kashrut (%)	Only at Home (%)	Always (%)
Do you observe the rules of kashrut?			
Mizrachim	19.0	13.4	67.6
Ashkenazim	47.1	11.8	41.2
FSU immigrants	66.3	8.2	25.5

	1 Certainly Not (%)	2 (%)	3 (%)	4 Certainly Yes (%)
Do you think that the sale of nonkosher meat should be allowed in Israel?				
Mizrachim	34.2	14.2	39.2	12.5
Ashkenazim	19.4	9.0	35.3	36.3
FSU immigrants	7.2	7.3	40.6	44.8

Source: Author's own survey, 2009.

be allowed or restricted (Table 5.1). Mizrachim are far more observant of kashrut than other ethnic groups and tend more to support restrictions of the sale of pork. FSU immigrants, conversely, tend not to observe kashrut and strongly support the sale of pork in Israel.

In interviews of Israelis professing a secular identity, the issue of pork seemed one of minor political concern. Those who eat pork felt no restrictions that prevented them from doing so, but agreed that some rules should be observed in public institutions shared by religious and secular

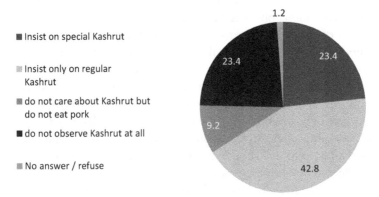

FIGURE 5.1. Level of kashrut observance. *Source:* Author's own survey, 2009.

Israelis. Kashrut, interestingly, was perceived by secular Israelis as an important and unifying symbol, even if they did not personally observe it. The rules of kashrut, they felt accordingly, should be observed, but should not interfere with personal freedoms.

I think that Ben-Gurion was right when he agreed that kashrut laws be observed in the army and other public institutions. It is also important for Jews abroad that observe Kashrut and look up to Israel . . . but people who want to buy and consume pork should be allowed to do so. It is a personal decision. (Elinor, interview)

I don't keep kosher at all. . . . People who think it is important can observe kashrut. I believe in live and let live. . . . I think that it is important that there will be kosher places because it is part of our values, our religion, because otherwise we lose our identity. I personally don't believe in kashrut but it is part of our symbols. It is important that there will be kosher places for those who want and also important that everyone can choose what to do. (Amnon, interview)

The rules of kashrut have become for many Israelis a personal matter that should be left to individual choices rather than to state laws and regulation. Most traditional Israelis interviewed refrain from eating nonkosher meat, but seemed to accept the relaxation of the rules. Attempts to forbid the sale of pork, they explained, were unlikely to succeed and therefore should not be attempted. Most of them seemed to agree with secular Israelis on the separation between the public institutions that must remain kosher and private businesses that should be allowed to operate as long as the demand exists.

It is important to maintain kashrut for those who observe but also allow those who don't to have a choice. There are non-Jews and immigrants who want to eat pork, why prevent them? We are a democratic country and religious coercion should be avoided – do we want to be Iran? (Etti, interview)

I don't mind it. I just want stores that sell pork to make it explicit so that people would know and mistakes be prevented. There are people who are not religious who eat pork, their parents ate it, why forbid? I just want to make sure it will not reach our stores. (Moshe, interview).

For some Israelis, pork retained its symbolic value and was detested, and many others avoided pork for different reasons. However, for a growing minority, immigrants and connoisseurs, pork was part of their menu or an object of desire. The "normalization" of pork could be observed in popular newspapers, and websites openly recommend nonkosher restaurants or pork products.

I ordered what was called "white steak" on the menu; it was pork steak on the bone, thick and juicy, enhanced with an adequate quantity of fat. It was cooked medium, as I requested, so that when I cut it an inner pinkish shade was revealed. (*Ha'aretz*, July 24, 2008).

The opening platter was brilliantly simple, also thanks to its price . . . on a wooden board diverse slices of salami are served daily (in our case, homemade Damshenia in Russian, a warm and pleasant combination of beef and pig, with a full taste, properly fatty) . . . garlic-flavored butter, beef liver paté, and a small loaf of bread . . . typical of the Russian farmers who know what is good. (*Ynet*, March 26, 2008).

Indeed, a portion of pork fillet, sliced into rings of the precise right thickness and grilled superbly, it was far from being disappointing: It was excellent – juicy and very tasty, meat that you cannot only bite into but also chew and its high quality simply glowed after every red mouthful, dripping with juice. (NRG, October 27, 2007)

The descriptions found in these food sections in popular media leave no room for doubt about the way in which nonkosher meat has become established as an accepted item on the menu of many Israelis and an integral part of the "food experience" they seek. More important, for the majority of Israelis, regardless of whether they eat pork or not, pork has ceased to be a political issue, national or religious. Thus, 60 percent of Israelis believe (or strongly believe) that the sale of pork should not be restricted.

The Legal Sphere

Secular entrepreneurs were interested in change that would allow more freedom to import, produce, and sell nonkosher meat but had limited, if any, hope that politicians would be prepared to undertake a campaign of this nature. The legal sphere, conversely, offered better opportunities, thanks to the liberal position of the Supreme Court and because of two new basic laws that could serve as a stimulus for the entrepreneurs. The Basic Law: Freedom of Occupation and the Basic Law: Human Dignity and Liberty, which were passed in 1992, are sometimes described as a "constitutional revolution" in the liberal spirit of individual rights. Even though these two laws did not obviously relate specifically to the pig issue, the entrepreneurs did believe that they could put them to use – especially the first one, concerning freedom of occupation – to permit an increase in their activities. This law clearly stated: "Every citizen or resident of the State is entitled to engage in any occupation, profession, or vocation" and "the freedom of occupation must not be impaired except by another law conforming with the basic principles of the State of Israel that was enacted for a proper purpose, and as long as it does not exceed what is absolutely essential, or according to the above law, by virtue of the provision specified in it."

The potential of these laws was put to the test in 1993 when a company named Meatrael petitioned the High Court of Justice in 1993 to allow the import of nonkosher meat as part of the planned privatization of meat imports. Until 1992, the importing of frozen meat was controlled by the Ministry of Industry and Trade, which allowed only kosher meat. Critics argued that the government monopoly was unnecessary, detrimental to competition, and provided an overall low quality of imported meat (Arad, 1993). In 1992, following the recommendations of a professional committee that examined the advantages of opening the meat market to competition, the government decided to privatize meat imports and permit the free importation of meat by private entrepreneurs. Under pressure from the religious coalition partners, however, privatization was limited by a decision to provide import licenses only for kosher meat. Legal advisers at the Ministry of Industry and Trade and the Ministry of Finance were concerned that the limitations did not comply with the existing laws. Consequently, the government postponed the implementation of the reforms.

Meatrael's petition to the court demanded that the government's decision to delay the implementation be canceled so that it could import nonkosher meat (HCJ 3872/93, *Meatrael Inc. v. prime minister and the minister of religious affairs*). The company argued that because of narrow coalition interests, the government did not follow the recommendations of a professional committee and its decision contravened the Basic Law: Freedom of Occupation. The court ruled in favor of Meatrael and instructed the government to implement the professional committee's recommendations immediately and grant the company a license to import meat without further delay:

Every agency of the governmental authorities must respect the freedom of occupation of every citizen or resident. . . . Dismissing the petitioner's right to engage in the import of meat . . . is a *prima facie* case that contravenes the basic law's instruction. . . . [The administration] must be aware of its obligation to respect the freedom of occupation. It must also be mindful of the fact that the limitation on the freedom of occupation may only be considered for a proper purpose and on the grounds of the common good.

In discussing the "general good," the court adopted a distinctly liberal stance in accepting the petition and rejecting the religious claim that the sale of pork is offensive and should be banned. Justice Theodor Or, who presided over the panel of judges, explained the court's reasons:

A state where freedom of conscience exists alongside freedom of religion and culture cannot prevent any individual from eating nonkosher meat for the plain and simple reason that knowing about it might cause emotional offense to some other person, who is interested in seeing that every Jew should observe the kashrut laws, even if that person is convinced that eating only kosher meat is a desirable habit, or even essential, and when this behavior would be to the advantage of the person concerned. In considering the feelings of a certain individual in this case at the expense of another person means inequality: the individual who keeps the kashrut laws will continue with his daily life and which he believes to be the correct way, whereas the other person will be forced to live in contradiction to his belief, or go against his faith, in other words to suffer from religious coercion.

The victory in the court was short-lived. The religious SHAS party, a senior partner in the ruling coalition, took the initiative in changing the law with an amendment to the Basic Law: Freedom of Occupation. The amendment stipulated, "A legal provision infringing on the freedom of occupation will be valid under section 4, if the said provision was included in a law passed by a majority of the MKs and in which it was explicitly stated that it is valid even allowing for what is stated in the said basic law." The Meat and Its Products Law (1994) that followed the amendment specified an absolute prohibition on the import of frozen meat without a *hekhsher* (religious permit) from the chief rabbinate and thereby essentially blocked any possibility to import pork or other nonkosher meat into Israel. Meatrael petitioned the Court yet again (HCJ 4676/94), but this time the court decided not to intervene.

The amendment of the law and the ruling of the court prevented the importation of nonkosher meat but "internal" production, marketing, and consumption have increased. The growing demand, lax regulation, and the consequent "normalization" of pork, meant that secular entrepreneurs needed neither the state nor the court to expand their operations.

From Struggle to Growth

The growing demand for pork was met initially by small factories and family stores, some of which evolved to become major producers and set up retail chain stores with branches all over the country. Unlike in the past, these businesses have made little if any efforts to conceal their nonkosher merchandise. To cater to the immigrants, who in the early 1990s were generally poor, the new players – unlike Ma'adanei Mizra, which based its business over the years on meat products for the gourmet market – focused on more popular and less expensive products. Businesses that had been relatively small producers up to the 1990s began to expand their operations, the new immigrants being the "platform" that allowed them to grow and develop. Many of the secular entrepreneurs trading in nonkosher meat were veteran Israelis, mostly children of immigrants from eastern Europe who established family factories or small stores, who identified the new opportunities that opened up for them in the form of a new clientele of consumers and greater tolerance (or curiosity) demonstrated by the Israeli public with respect to nonkosher meat. In addition, scores of small delicatessen stores were opened by new immigrants in different cities that sold imported food products from Russia and local non-kosher meat.

Tiv-Ta'am's salami factory was established in 1988 in Rishon LeZion with a factory outlet store on the premises. Within a few years the company expanded, opening supermarkets and becoming the largest retail chain in Israel selling food to the FSU immigrants. In its early years, the company was hardly mentioned at all in the Israeli media, but in 2002 its CEO and owner, Kobi Tribitch, who inherited a small family business, was named by the Advertisers Association in Israel as the outstanding personality in marketing of the year. Tiv-Ta'am continued to expand, buying factory plants (including 50 percent of Ma'adanei Mizra) and opening new stores. By 2010, Tiv-Ta'am had twenty-eight stores and an annual sales turnover of 1.2 billion shekels.

Karl Berg, a family business producing sausages that was established in the 1940s by a new immigrant from Germany, ran into financial difficulties and was bought in 1994 by Hanan Abramovitch, who already owned a small store and was a partner in an old factory in Yafo. The business expanded to include a farm for raising pigs and about twelve stores all over the country. Ma'adanei Manya was founded by Yaakov and Meir Manya, whose father Herman owned a farm for rearing pigs that he established in northern Israel during the 1960s. The Ma'adanei Manya group includes a factory for producing smoked meat and sausages and a factory for the production of pastry products, as well as six supermarkets throughout the country. Ma'adanei Aviv was established in 1928 and began raising pigs in south Tel Aviv in 1942 and now runs a breeding farm in the north. Ma'adanei Aviv has about nine branches and markets its produce to additional delicatessen

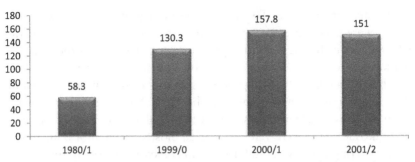

FIGURE 5.2. Pigs raised in Israel (in thousands). *Source:* Central Bureau of Statistics: Agriculture in Israel 2001–2003, p. 38.

stores. Waldman's factory in Holon is also an old family business catering mainly for the Russian sector; it owns two stores and has granted another three franchises, as well as marketing its products to delicatessen stores all over the country. Several additional small and medium-sized producers who entered the market during those years may be added to this list. Of all the companies concerned, it was the experienced Ma'adanei Mizra that found it difficult to cope with the new market conditions, suffered from managerial problems, and lost its leading position, until finally it was bought out by the Tiv-Ta'am company and other investors.

In 2007, the quantity of nonkosher meat sold in Israel was estimated at 1,200 to 1,400 tons per month, of which 400 to 500 were sold by Tiv-Ta'am, 300 by Ma'adanei Manya, 200 by Ma'adanei Waldman, about 120 tons by Mizra, and the remaining sales distributed among the small businesses (Walla business website, June 30, 2007; http://finance.walla.co.il/). The size of this market is estimated at about 39 billion shekels, divided between the recognized retail market, evaluated at 24 billion shekels, and the unofficial market, calculated at approximately an additional 15 billion shekels (Yefet, 2007). Agricultural production of pigs continued to increase even after the immigration decreased, probably because veteran Israelis also joined the consumers shopping at the stores selling nonkosher meat (Figure 5.2).

The large number of entrepreneurs relied on FSU immigrants and on their own products – pork, ham, and sausages – marketed to hundreds of smaller stores across the country. Whereas about two-thirds of Tiv-Ta'am's customers are veteran Israelis, at Ma'adanei Manya only 20 percent are veteran Israelis and the remainder are immigrants from the FSU (Yemini, 2003). Veteran Israelis, the owner of Ma'adanei Manya explained, may have become global consumers, but immigrants have a distinct taste:

I failed to bring them [the Israelis] to me with the quality salami products. . . . For if you take an Israeli and give him a culinary test he might get a score of 4 at best. Now what does the Israeli public know about meat, and if I talk to you about sausages and salami, what do you really know? You think that sausages are something very cheap and basic and you just know that salami is made from rubbish, and that's how it's labeled . . . ask ten Israelis and nine will tell you just that! At the same time our public, the Russian public. is a community that ate those products abroad. However, there are customers of mine who know what are good salamis and meat cuts . . . [but by contrast] the Israeli public is exposed only to the steak for entrecote, filet shrimps, calamari, and foods like those. (Yaakov Manya, interview).

Alongside the chain stores, a large number of small grocery stores emerged in the main concentrations of immigrants across the country. Although these stores attracted some curious veteran Israelis, they were characteristically "Russian." Interviews held with shop owners in Beersheba, Ashdod, and Hadera presented a similar picture regarding the reasons for opening up nonkosher businesses, the customers they cater to, and the ways they operate. The vast majority of the shopkeepers are immigrants who came to Israel during the 1990s, as are most of the customers (80–90% of the shoppers). Most store owners do not advertise their businesses, and the few who do so usually make do with several inches in the local Russian press. Store owners were aware of the sensitivities raised by that selling pork in previously traditional neighborhoods but also of the fact that demand for these products exists: "We were aware of the fact that a nonkosher store would bring in more customers, and for us this was the only consideration." At least one business opened up the store initially as a kosher establishment ("my wife and I come from traditional families") but eventually turned to selling nonkosher meat, yielding to pressure from the customers ("we noticed that the store was not attracting customers"; "we lost a lot of Russian customers"). In some cases, veteran Israelis, especially in traditional neighborhoods, viewed the stores with disdain and contempt, leading to some local conflicts, as discussed later. For other veteran Israelis, a visit to these shops was an "exotic" experience of unfamiliar smells and tastes. Located in the periphery, however, where the majority of the veteran population was traditional, the nonkosher stores remained largely a Russian domain.

The potential of Israeli consumers willing to try new foods was to be realized elsewhere and in different ways, befitting the new food culture of experience and lifestyle. Tiv-Ta'am defined its new target population as the new globalizing and consumerist middle-class or Bourgeoisie:

We decided to offer the new Israelis a multinational supermarket designed to meet their needs for a culinary festival. The new Israeli is exposed to all the various delicacies when abroad, knows what good food is, and demands to buy it in Israel. About twenty years ago flight attendants working for El Al were celebrities because they were the only ones who had French cheeses and Belgian chocolates, but nowadays all the people of Israel enjoy a lavish and abundant food supply. If twenty years ago the only fish you could get in the supermarket was carp, now you can also buy from us Coquilles St. Jacques. (*Yediot Aharonot*, Mamon business section, May 7, 2002)

For many young secular Israelis, the "taboo" surrounding the pig and the national significance associated with eating it were of no further importance. The entrepreneurs of the 1990s identified the considerable potential that existed in Israeli society but had not been realized owing to the very limited availability of the products (Kobi Tribitch, interview). According to Tiv-Ta'am's assessment, about half the Jewish population of Israel does not observe the rules of kashrut. Furthermore, as a high correlation was found between the nonobservance of kashrut and the upper income deciles, wherein the two highest deciles hold about 50 percent of the retail purchasing power, the growth potential of the nonkosher meat market was rated as substantial (Kobi Tribitch, interview, *Ha'aretz*, August 31, 2004). Based on these estimations, which might have been exaggerated, Tiv-Ta'am began to market itself as a place for gourmet shopping, attempting to entice both the veteran secular Israelis and immigrants from the FSU whose available income had already increased.

Tiv-Ta'am ... is based on the long-term processes taking place in modern Israel and reflects the increasing openness to international culture in the civil society in Israel. The company is determined to become a leader in this market, while emphasizing quality without any compromise and striving to achieve a national distribution system and constant improvement. (from the company website: http://www.tivtaam.co.il/)

The new strategy was interwoven with the socioeconomic and cultural transitions that accompanied the development of the consumer hedonistic society in Israel. Food was no longer a necessity, as in the old days, but became part of a lifestyle, often a status symbol, and a central element in the leisure culture and in the search for excitement and new tastes, emulating global developments, which the entrepreneurs sought to supply.

If the dream of Kobi Tribitch, one of the store's owners, who got his inspiration for this branch from Harrods, the exclusive London food store, is realized, then soon the retail food chains currently dominating the Israeli market will find themselves in competition with a secular alternative. This alternative will be a national food retail chain that is not kosher. Apart from the diverse products and the fact that the stores open for business on Shabbat, Tiv-Ta'am's advantage lies in the relative low prices it can offer the customers, which is made possible by savings in the costs incurred in ensuring that the products are kosher. (*Yediot Aharonot*, Mamon business section, May 7, 2002)

The marketing of nonkosher meat was not a political secular statement but rather a part of a wider "global shopping experience" that the store attempted to offer the new Bourgeoisie. Tiv-Ta'am prided itself on the variety on its shelves, like the selection of 400 different types of cheeses from around the world and the assortment of wines and meats consumers could choose from. The turning point was an opening of the retail chain's large branch in Netanya, an ambitious investment of more than $20 million, in which an especially large variety of products was to be offered to shoppers:

We decided to bring in wines from other European countries and not only from Russia, the Caucasus and Georgia but also wine from wineries in France in addition to those from California. When it came to cheese, at first we focused mainly on cheese from Russia because the customers were familiar with it, but slowly but surely we also introduced gorgonzola, types of cheddar, and other foods from England and France. (Kobi Tribitch, interview).

The large crowds the store attracted in the first weeks, including on the Sabbath, were indicative that the company was right. A journalist who visited the new store concluded, "This branch will have no option but to enlarge its parking lot considerably, and urgently, too. Apparently, even the owners of the retail chain did not anticipate such a large secular surge on Shabbat days, yet nevertheless an overtone of doing something out of spite was also in the air" (*Ha'aretz*, June 13, 2002). More than any imaginable secular protest, the crowds heading toward this branch expressed the desire to experience new tastes regardless of religious restrictions.

The tribal mentality has been breached as a different target population has now developed here.... Everyone has become more individualistic and self-centered... the customer that we seek to attract forms a secular target population living in the State of Israel, and with money in their pockets so that they can demand to enjoy life.... [In our campaign] We used the slogan "The others don't have it."... The other stores do not stock shrimps, the others don't have calamari, the other stores do not sell pork steak, they don't have eels, and the others do not have non-kosher cheese. The other stores do not keep nonkosher wines, the others do not sell nonkosher sushi, and the others do not stock nonkosher dim sum. All these items!" (Kobi Tribitch, interview)

In 2004, Tiv-Ta'am opened its largest store in Rishon LeZion, south of Tel Aviv, offering another "global shopping experience." The store offered products imported from Eastern Europe for immigrants but also from the rest of the world – including, shrimp, calamari, pork steak, and eel. The store included a sushi bar with a conveyor belt, dim sum, a huge grill at the entrance, a bar, and restaurants. The manager of the store explained the strategy of providing the consumer experience rather than just selling groceries: "I try to spread attractions out all over the store using the method that employs different stations, so that people will spend as much time as possible in the store and not simply take what they need off the shelves and go" (*Yediot Aharonot*, January 12, 2004). A newspaper recommended the store not for its prices, which were a bit higher than other retail stores, but "due to its distinct character when it comes to the shopping experience" (*Yediot Aharonot*, April 15, 2005). The decision of Tiv-Ta'am to decorate the stores at Christmas time with Christmas trees, colored lights, and images of Santa Claus was explained not as related to religiosity, but rather as another part of the global image of the stores:

We turn December into a festival of holy days – Chanukah, Christmas, *Eid al-Fitr* – and so we celebrate with the trees, because there is a clientele who want that, the Chanukah candles and the [other holiday] candles because we strive to hold a carnival. (Kobi Tribitch, interview).

By the late 1990s, the pork industry was well established and hard to miss, as the supermarkets were spread across the country, making nonkosher meat accessible and largely beyond the political debate (Figure 5.3).

The Economy of Pork: Secular Identities and Business Strategies

Until the 1990s, the nonkosher meat sector faced constant danger from political intervention and the threat to liquidate the industry. The struggle of the "veteran" entrepreneurs, such as Ma'adanei Mizra, relied on the liberal demand for freedom of occupation and individual liberty, as well as a republican discourse of contribution and attempted to mobilize public support against what was defined as "religious coercion." The new entrepreneurs who emerged in the 1990s operated in an entirely new reality, in which questions of identity and political struggles had become

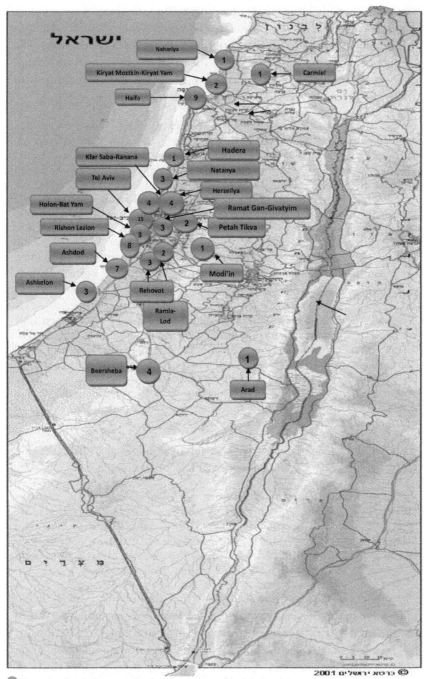

The number of non-kosher supermarkets that belong to the one of the chains in each town

FIGURE 5.3. Nonkosher supermarkets across the country.

marginal. Not all business owners interviewed, in spite of their trade, identified as "secular," but all of them described their business decision in pragmatic, calculated terms, brief and devoid of any ideology. The owners of major businesses – veteran Israelis, aware of previous struggles – placed themselves more firmly in the secular camp, at times with ambivalence to what that the concept entailed.

We have, in fact, kept up the tradition and continue to do so. We see tradition as part of a custom and not a religion; we usually attend the synagogue on holidays, pray and fast on Yom Kippur. . . . I ask myself, why do I fast on Yom Kippur? What transgressions have I committed that I am obliged to fast? In any case, I am dealing with a business that is not kosher and yet I fast on Yom Kippur. Not only do I fast, but I sit in the synagogue from morning till evening, and people are surprised. I tell them in reply that it does not matter, for faith is a separate entity, tradition is separate and religion is something else. (Yaakov Manya, interview)

Politically, the entrepreneurs remain unaffiliated and separate their business from politics, feeling that political identity would do more damage than good and that political struggle is a thing of the past.

Personally speaking, ever since my early childhood in Haifa I used to demonstrate with Meretz [the liberal party] on behalf of public transport on Shabbat. The reason was simply that I knew it was the right thing to do. [Is the issue of meat] a struggle? Somebody must want it, and now I have no need for crosswinds, the current situation is OK for me. . . . I am committed to a secular agenda but as far as the company is concerned we have no need for it as everyone already knows that Tiv-Ta'am is not kosher, so that for the moment it remains a question of personal choice. (Kobi Tribitch, interview).

Yaakov Manya, who supported the Shinui political party and the Am Hofshi (A Free People) movement reached similar conclusions:

[In the past] if they needed my assistance I would donate money, contribute the use of my car, and allow my stores to be used for distributing propaganda. My first expectation from the politicians was that [they] should abolish the municipal bylaw banning the sale of pork. . . . The second wish related to the issue of opening the stores on the Shabbat. . . . I used to champion the cause of freedom of occupation, I was a political activist, but nothing at all was achieved.

The owners of small businesses, mostly FSU immigrants, are even less political than their veteran colleagues. Not only have they not experienced the earlier struggles of veteran Israelis against government restrictions by having their store locations in areas with a large immigrant population, most of them encountered very little opposition from municipalities or local residents. Stiffer opposition was encountered by large chain stores that aimed to open their outlets in city centers and advertise their wares openly, attracting public attention. However, based on the logic described earlier, secular entrepreneurs tried to avoid a confrontation and developed a business strategy that would minimize conflict.

Actually, I have given in to the *haredim* and that is the reason why the stores are located in industrial zones, some of them in far-flung locations, and not in the city centers. A blind eye has been turned to the agreement with the *haredim* allowing the opening of nonkosher businesses in industrial zones, and that is a price to pay with which I can live. As a result of this agreement we lost some customers who now find it difficult to get to our branches. I am no rebel, and my philosophy calls for reconciliation. I am motivated mainly by commercial considerations and I have no wish to infuriate people to oppose me . . . therefore if the price I have to pay is moving my business to industrial zones, so be it! (*Yediot Aharonot*, Mamon business section, May 7, 2002).

Conflict is perceived as being unwarranted, and even damaging to business, so the preferred strategy of entrepreneurs is to select a typically "secular" location, which will not cause any confrontations, and to reach an agreement with the local authority and coordinate actions with them.

I have four stores in Haifa; three are open on Shabbat and the other one is not, because at first I failed to notice that it is near a high school for religious girls. The mayor asked me what do we intend to do about it. I replied, "We shall not open the store on Shabbat." I have no interest in getting involved in a disagreement, am I looking for places to create further friction? I shall not come to Jerusalem if the mayor objects . . . I am not some sort of scourge to be avoided like the plague. I bring employment for several hundred people, pay municipal rates, taxes . . . I stay away from wherever there may be potential strife . . . I tell the people working for me in advance: "there is plenty of space in Tel Aviv, look for a suitable site and see if within a certain radius there is no synagogue, no religious school." There is no need to run into trouble from the very outset, so we come across with only minimal trouble. (Kobi Tribitch, interview).

You have to check to see who supports you and which population is opposed to you. The difference between us and another business is that whereas you only check to see who your customer is, in our case you also check out to see who might kill you. I try to remain in the peripheral areas, in districts with a Russian population, and we still examine every single thing as the case may require. . . . We are planning to open a store soon at a certain location and the local businessman, a young person familiar with the neighborhood, said that he requested that at least on the opening day there should be several fire trucks standing by . . . people informed him that it is only a matter of time until the place is burnt down so I am waiting and biding my time. I had not come to confront them and I have no interest in doing so . . . previously [in a similar case] all the problems were solved thanks to a donation I made and then I had peace and quiet. (Anonymous, interview)

For some secular entrepreneurs, the large number of stores and the general acceptance of pork created a *fait accompli* that could not be challenged by religious opposition. Others were more skeptical, owing both to the feelings that an economic slowdown was just around the corner (some of the interviews were conducted in 2008–09) in addition to the possibility that the religious parties could still change the reality on the ground that had been created over the past two decades.

At first [the religious people] would still carry out provocations but no longer... because they know this will be of no use to them; they can no longer close down this business, the public won't allow it. In the first elections after the closure of nonkosher stores, the Shinui party will gain in strength again. [Additionally] a lot of money is involved in these shopping areas... not only Tiv-Ta'am... in the first elections after such a move a [secular] party with 30 seats will emerge. (Kobi Tribitch, interview)

I am always worried that SHAS is growing stronger because we can always be hindered in our efforts, and as evidence, although it is not necessarily linked with pig or not connected to pig, you can see what is happening with opening businesses on Shabbat. The people currently raising the issue now in legal domains are, in fact, owners of stores and grocers and not the general public that object to opening businesses on Shabbat but what are they doing about it? They are mobilizing the religious and *haredi* political bloc to their cause. (Yaakov Manya, interview).

In 2006, it appeared that Tiv-Ta'am's fortunes were waning, and a television investigation revealed that the retail chain had been selling spoiled chicken; large investments in new and prestigious branches, combined with other factors, all led to a drop in profits and the eventual sale of 50 percent of the shares to a new partner, at a price much lower than the estimates made by the company's owners several months earlier. The economic difficulties convinced the owners to look for new strategic partners or else to sell the company. Arkady Gaydamak, a businessman with political ambitions, declared in 2007 that he intended to buy Tiv-Ta'am (together with Ma'adanei Mizra, its associate company) and convert them into a kosher retail chain. Gaydamak explained that he predicted that

in the near future Tiv-Ta'am will be in a position to improve its commercial and financial performances dramatically. In keeping with my opinion as a Jew and a public figure in the Jewish society, the promotion, distribution, and sale of pork products in Israel are offensive to the Jewish tradition. Therefore, banning the distribution and sale of pork products throughout the Tiv-Ta'am supermarket chain will be the first task on my agenda. (*Ynet*, June 10, 2007)

The religious opposition could rejoice in the seeming collapse of the largest entrepreneur, but the other competitors declared that they were more than ready to step in and take over Tiv-Ta'am's clientele of veteran Israelis. "The moment that Gaydamak takes the pig out of Tiv-Ta'am we can enter their niche immediately," promised one entrepreneur; "this is a matter of fundamental importance. Just imagine what would happen if we did not exist, and Gaydamak were to decide to simply eliminate the industry?" (Yaakov Manya, *Ynet*, June 10, 2007). Others have followed suit. Ma'adanei Waldman, the third largest company, reported its intention to expand its business and declared that "if Tiv-Ta'am changes and becomes kosher, then there is no doubt that we shall become number one" (Walla News, June 30, 2007). In the end the Gaydamak deal did not materialize, Gaydamak himself disappeared from the political scene, and Tiv-Ta'am was purchased by a new owner that has not changed its concept.

Religious Authority and Consumer Choice: Beyond Pork

The majority of Israelis refrain from eating pork and declare that they keep at least some of the kashrut laws. However, this observance is an example of the gap between secularization as the decline of religious authority and the personal observance of religious rules. Certificates provided by the rabbinate signal to consumers that the restaurant or the supermarket is kosher. Business owners, however, may choose not to have the certificates. Some who abide by the rules of kashrut are reluctant to pay for the certificates and the inspection. Others also keep kashrut but operate on the Sabbath, which disqualifies them from receiving the certificate. For many Israelis, as Figure 5.4 demonstrates, a restaurant that describes itself as "kosher" even without a official certificate is acceptable. Similarly, they would shop in a nonkosher supermarket, but avoid the nonkosher meat. Kashrut, in other words, has become for those Israelis a personal set of preferences and decisions that is rooted in religiosity but, to a large extent, is independent of religious authority and regulation. This also explains the gap between the reluctance of the majority of Israelis to eat pork and, at the same time, their tepid support for regulation that would restrict the sale of pork.

■ Selects only restaurant with
   kosher certification

■ Declaration of the owner that
   he or she keeps a kosher kitchen
   is enough.

■ Can also choose a nonkosher
   restaurant, but does not eat
   meat

■ Chooses a restaurant without
   taking into account
   considerations of kashrut

■ No answer / refuse

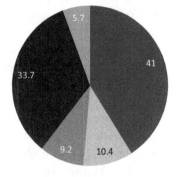

FIGURE 5.4. Regulation and authority. *Source:* Author's own survey, 2009.

Re-Politicized Pork? Minority Rights and Local Struggles

The rapid spread of pork sales and the limited support for restrictions frustrated religious groups and made them pessimistic about the prospects for comprehensive change. Religious struggles have not completely disappeared but have shifted to the local arena in what could be described as a rear-guard action. Shlomo Benizri, one of the SHAS party leaders, used a liberal discourse of minority rights to argue that a local ban on pork is required so that the religious minority be allowed to protect its way of life:

I am not opposed to selling pig, or rather, I would not like to see pig in Israel, but as we are speaking here about reciprocity, then why not? Eat pig, if you wish! We are not interfering with what you put on your plate, but as a Jew, when I go about my business where I live and there are shops there selling pig, it distresses me deeply, offends my way of life so I appeal to you: Listen, you can sell pig, but do so on the city outskirts, in an industrial zone. (cited in Barak-Erez, 2003)

The local struggle, and the legal fight associated with it, had stronger support than the general ban of pork sales. This struggle shifted the debate to the locations where pig could be sold and to the question of balance between the potential infringement on the right of the individual to consume pork and the offense to the religious way of life (Table 5.2). In addition, locally, in some areas, the religious could still exert political pressure to restrict or ban the sale of pork.

Municipalities, especially ones in which large religious groups were able to organize, have tried to kick-start the bylaws to prevent the sale of pig or relocate such trade far away to the outskirts of the cities. The

TABLE 5.2. *Enforcing Kashrut Laws*

	Ultra-Orthodox (%)	Religious (%)	Traditional (%)	Secular (%)	
Do you think the sale of nonkosher meat should be permitted in Israel?					
1 (Certainly yes)	1.5	5.8	9.6	44	Cramer's V = 0.374*
2	13.2	15.9	40	45.4	
3	8.8	20.3	17.4	5	Kendall's tau-c = −0.488*
4 (Certainly not)	76.5	58	33	5.6	
Do you think the sale of nonkosher meat should be permitted in neighborhoods where the majority of the residents are Jewish?					
1 (Certainly yes)	0	2.8	5.4	28.3	Cramer's V = 0.339*
2	4.4	11.3	21	40.1	
3	11.8	16.9	22.3	19	Kendall's tau-c= −0.456*
4 (Certainly not)	83.8	69	51.3	12.3	

$* P < 0.05; ** P < 0.01.$
Source: Author's own survey, 2009.

Local Authorities Law of 1956, known as the Special Enablement Law, states that a local authority is authorized to pass a bylaw restricting or prohibiting the sale of pork and its products. From the legal aspect, the question arose as to the legality of the restriction stipulated in the bylaws in view of the legal obligation to respect the freedom of occupation (Barak-Erez, 2003). In some cities, the limited enforcement capability enabled the stores selling nonkosher meat to disregard the municipal bylaws. In addition, the large population of immigrants encouraged the local elected authorities to turn a blind eye to the violations. However, in cities shared by large populations of immigrants and *haredim*, the latter demanded that the sale of pork be prohibited, or at least that the stores should be moved away from the city center. In Beit Shemesh, the pressure persuaded the city council to reach the decision to relocate the stores to the city's industrial zone. Moshe Abutbul, the deputy mayor, summed up the conflict and his own perspective in the following words: "We have expelled beyond our boundary the pig and the piggery" (*Ynet*, June 21, 2000).

In several cases, nonkosher butcheries have taken the municipalities to courts in order to challenge the bylaws, with differing results. An attempt by the municipality in Netanya in 1996 to impose a blanket ban on the sale of pork was annulled by the magistrate's court, which ruled that the ban does not meet the demand for proportionality. In Ashkelon, on the other hand, the magistrate's court turned down the petition of twelve butcher shops fined for selling pork. The judge ruled that by virtue of the fact that Israel is a Jewish and democratic state and as the pig "is a symbol of repugnance...a symbol of deceit and evil" there is good reason to take into consideration the position of prohibitions on the pig in the national heritage (Barak-Erez, 2003). The district court in Beersheba rejected the petition to cancel the fines and rescind the ban on the sale of pork for the reason that "the sale of pork is not in keeping with the values of the State of Israel as a Jewish and democratic state" (*Yediot Aharonot*, October 28, 1999).

In Netanya, a city in which one of the largest branches of Tiv-Ta'am is located in an industrial zone, a conflict took place that deteriorated into acts of violence perpetrated against the sale of pork after a large nonkosher store was opened in the city center. In August 2007, the opponents of the store in the city center demonstrated and smashed the windowpanes of other nonkosher delicatessen stores, and finally the Ma'adanei Aviv store was set on fire. Yielding to the pressure of this protest, the municipality decided that the stores selling nonkosher meat could trade only in the city's industrial zone. Similar decisions were taken in Carmiel, Tiberias, and Beit Shemesh, cities where the nonkosher delicatessen stores catered to a population of FSU immigrants, but met with the opposition of religious veteran residents.

The local struggles and attempts to use the municipal bylaws to restrict or prohibit the sale of pig sent the struggle back into the legal domain; the issue of the local authority's jurisdiction was brought in 2004 before the HCJ. The court, with an expanded panel of nine judges, discussed four petitions submitted against the municipalities of Beit Shemesh, Carmiel, and Tiberias (HCJ 953/01, *Solodkin v. Beit Shemesh Municipality*; HCJ 1355/01, *Shinui v. the minister of the interior and Beit Shemesh Municipality*; HCJ 7406/01, *Solodkin v. Carmiel Municipality*; HCJ 2283/02, *Maadanei Mania v. Tiberias Municipality*). Petitioners included a member of the Knesset, a political movement (Shinui), and a company producing and marketing nonkosher meat (Ma'adanei Manya). In Beit Shemesh and Carmiel, the petitions concerned the municipality's decision to permit the sale of pork only in the city's industrial zone, whereas in Tiberias it referred to the ban that the municipality imposed on selling pork throughout the entire city.

The petitioners claimed that the municipalities had overstepped their authority and that the municipal bylaws impeded the freedom of occupation as well as the individual freedom of the consumers. Furthermore, it was claimed that the municipality's decisions were disproportionate, disregarding the high percentage of FSU immigrants in those cities. The enforcement of the bylaws, they warned, would inflict severe losses on businesses and force the consumers to travel outside the area where they live, making consumption of nonkosher meat unreasonably expensive. As one of the petitioners, a store owner from Carmiel, explained the situation, "more than 50 percent of the town's residents shop at our stores, and 8 percent of the religious folk in the city do not want to allow us to make some money" (*Ha'aretz*, December 12, 2006). Petitioners asked the court to repeal the municipal bylaws and thereby permit the sale of pork throughout the city, with no limitation, except for the *haredi* neighborhoods.

During the court proceedings, Justice Mishael Heshin explained his objection to the said bylaws and, in so doing, expressed his own liberal perspective but also the normalization process that had come to affect pork:

Meat is bought in the local supermarket, where a person takes a cart, buys cheese, meat, bread, and goes home. That individual will not then travel especially to buy the meat for that is part of his or her daily sustenance. So where should pig be sold, outside in the fields? (*Ma'ariv*, December 8, 2003)

The court's ruling clarified even more the change that had occurred on the issue of the pig during the past two decades, as it shelved the bylaws and demanded that the municipalities revise them. The revisions, it explained, should consider, first, any potential offense to the feelings of those who object to the sale of pork, but, second, also the damage inflicted on those who wish to sell and buy pork and its products, and, third, the alternatives available to the potential sellers and buyers. The court's arguments in this case formed a part of the liberal discourse on the rights of individuals and community:

This decision must reflect the city's unique character, its division into the different neighborhoods, districts, and streets; the extent to which people and groups live together within the various neighborhoods, whether the issue concerns residents whose feelings might be upset if pork was to be sold openly in their vicinity, or those whose rights would be violated if pork and its products would not be sold near them; the practical solutions that may be implemented in these circumstances after considering the characteristics of each and every municipality, including the distances and travel time from one place to another, the possibility to designate places for the sale of pork and its products within the different neighborhoods or outside their boundaries.... Let us all remember that living together is not a matter of everything or nothing but rather an expression of mutual concessions, which in turn reflect coexistence in a multifarious society.... They are the outcome of the recognition that in order for us to be able to live together, we must recognize the uniqueness of every one of us, and therefore the fact that this uniqueness will be recognized only if we can live together.

The importance of the ruling and the discussion lies not only in transferring the focus of the debate from the national level to the local one, but also in setting the conflict between the two demands on a single plane, the right to eat pig and the demand to refrain from upsetting the feelings of the religious public (Barak-Erez, 2003). The court's decision has not ended the conflict. First, it was severely criticized by religious politicians who described the decision as a "final nail in the coffin of the state's Jewish identity" (MK Eli Yishai, *Yediot Aharonot*, June 16, 2004). Second, some municipalities, where religious residents continued to protest the sale of pork, attempted to use other means to restrict nonkosher shops, such as business licensing. In Kiryat Yam, for instance, where the municipality issued an order to close down a new store, claiming that it had no business license, the mayor did not hesitate to state his real motivation, a concern for "the delicate fabric of religious/secular relations in the city" and for "offending public feelings," and stressed that he would take whatever measures were available to him to prevent the opening of the store (*Ynet*, September 11, 2008).

What is unique about the local struggle is not just the simple transfer of the fight from the national domain to what is rapidly becoming a rearguard action against a trend that has already become firmly established but the strategies and arguments that the opponents employ. Unlike the past, when most of the contentions focused on the state's Jewish character and the pig as a distinct mark of the border between what is Jewish and Gentile, the local campaigns concentrate on the specific interests of religious groups fighting to protect their lifestyle (i.e., neighborhoods "free" of pig). This move became necessary because of the erosion of the special and despised status of the pig among the Jewish religious public in Israel (Barak-Erez, 2003). These groups now concentrate their energy on local struggles to exclude the pig from their environment while employing the existing means of enforcement; even more important their efforts were based on arguments such as "upsetting feelings" or protection of "a way of life," often associated with their minority rights, of all things, and not based on collective national values and a demand for a total ban. It is yet to be observed how the ruling of the HCJ requiring municipalities to devise policies that are "proportionate" and adjusted to local needs will be implemented.

Conclusion

The change in the pig's status in Israel over the past two decades can be described as dramatic. The pig, perceived previously by a majority of Jewish Israelis as an "abomination," for religious or national reasons, has turned into a commodity, detested by some, desired by others, and tolerated by many. Consequently, its status was determined by market laws of demand and supply rather than by political struggles and legislation. For many Israelis, FSU immigrants, and parts of the middle class, the avoidance of pork ceased to be a national symbol and remained a religious restriction and a matter of personal choice that required no political intervention or regulation. For immigrants, pork consumption was part of their diet, brought with them to Israel. For many of the middle class it became part of a wide range of culinary experiences and a matter of personal preference. These changes underpinned secular entrepreneurs' new strategies that no longer needed to appeal to republican arguments or to liberal freedoms. Rather, economic logic became the guide for entrepreneurs who employed business strategies in their decisions to sell pork, circumventing instead of confronting religious authorities. These initiatives required no coordination and political support, were connected only loosely to ideology and a secular agenda, but achieved a significant change in the public domain, virtually without conflict.

6

Live and Let Buy

Bargaining for the Sabbath

The declaration of the Sabbath as the official day of rest was one of the tenets of the status quo and, for many Israelis, also a principal expression of a Jewish state (Shaki, 2005). The proliferation of commerce on the Sabbath (Shabbat, in Hebrew) is a marked indication of the erosion of the status quo and the growing rift between religious and nonreligious Israelis, who hold different interpretations of the Sabbath and different expectations regarding its public status. For religious people, the Sabbath is a day dedicated to prayer and family life, when commercial activity is strictly prohibited. The religious position refuses to separate the perception of a day of rest from that of a holy day:

The Shabbat is supposed to be a holy day for those who observe it; the holiest day in the Hebrew calendar; a day whose religious-spiritual substance elevates the Shabbat time to a supreme level of sanctity and an uplifting of spirit and soul. It also raises the person keeping the Shabbat to the uppermost spheres of faith, spirit, philosophy and emotion, both religious and national. All these elements make the Shabbat a day of supreme spiritual pleasure, which is devoted, or which should be dedicated mostly to studying Torah [Jewish law]. Let it be clarified further that these are not symbolic matters and the Shabbat was not meant to stand for symbolism. (Shaki, 1995)

For the nonreligious public, strongly influenced by consumer culture, the Sabbath has come to mean something entirely different, a day of rest and leisure, as the large crowds that visit shopping centers and restaurants on the Sabbath indicate. The use of the term *nonreligious* rather than *secular* is purposeful, as many of those who shop on the Sabbath would not identify themselves as secular and their other practices and values may not demonstrate secularism. The expansion of commerce on Sabbath can be explained as a direct outcome of the emergence of a consumer society in which shopping is not just for satisfying basic needs, but is a cultural-leisure decision. This change can be described as a shift from "consumption," a mostly private and essential activity, to "consumerism," a social activity defining society's character, which becomes a central part of one's daily life (Bauman, 2007: 26). Accordingly, for nonreligious Israelis, the day of rest should have its unique character, but they nevertheless feel they should be allowed freedom of choice and all the recreational options should be available for them (Levi, 2004), including those that do not comply with religious restrictions.

Earlier secular struggles related to the Sabbath, such as the right to hold cultural activities like opening cinemas or theaters, required collective action, namely for the secular public to mobilize and launch a political struggle. By contrast, shopping on the Sabbath is a secular activity that violates religious rules but, as will be discussed later, these are often decisions connected loosely, at best, with the secular identity and struggle. The change in the nature of the Sabbath, similar to the examples in previous chapters, is not the outcome of a recognized political debate and is not registered in a change of the formal-political rules of the game. The economic entrepreneurs, rather than political authorities, responded to the increasing demand for shopping on Sabbath and, regardless of intent, undermined the formal rules of the game.

Regulating Rest Days

The organization of daily life in seven-day cycles serves not only to measure time but also to divide up time between working days and a rest day (or days). This division of time may be termed as being between the holy and the secular, between consumption and production, between freedom and obligations, between personal and public, and between the routine and spontaneous (Zerubavel, 1985: 91). In many states, the days of rest were institutionalized by laws that restricted work and commerce, intended to encourage religious participation or to guarantee workers and business owners a necessary break (Roucher, 1994). Opponents, such as the outraged Thomas Paine, perceived these laws as an unnecessary restriction and intervention in what should remain private decisions:

The word Sabbath means REST; that is, cessation from labor, but the stupid Blue Laws of Connecticut make a labor of rest, for they oblige a person to sit still from sunrise to sunset on a Sabbath-day, which is hard work. Fanaticism made those laws, for where such laws prevail hypocrisy will prevail also. (see Flanagan, 1979)

Laws restricting commerce on official days of rest continued to exist despite the criticism that they discriminated against people of other religions whose day of rest is on another day, hinder the freedom of occupation, or represent narrow economic interests (Flanagan, 1979). In secularizing societies and where consumerism became not only a way of life but the very essence of the good life, in the United States and elsewhere (Gabriel and Lang, 2006: 1), restrictions on commerce were more difficult to justify and sustain. Opponents of the laws, businesspeople and would-be customers, argued that restrictive laws were detrimental to the broader public, contravened the principle of separation of church and state, and ran contrary to the spirit of the time (Laband and Heinbuch, 1987: 48, 222; Roucher, 1994). Restrictions were supported by the church, small businesses, trade unions, and various groups and individuals concerned with the implications of extended commerce on the Sabbath for family life and society. The church regarded commerce on the day of rest not only as a religious transgression but also as competition in winning over the free time of the believers turned into shoppers (Laband and Heinbuch, 1987: 142–6). Consequently, the struggle has been described as a fight for the individual's time between "religious" participation (prayer or attending church services) and "secular" recreation such as shopping. Indeed, cancellation of the laws restricting trading on Sunday in the United States (blue laws) was found to have a negative effect on the number of church-goers and on donations to the church (Gruber and Hungerman, 2006).

Supporters of restrictive laws use not only religious arguments but also economic and social justifications to argue that the laws represent cultural values and protect workers, their families, and the community (Roucher, 1994; see also Kajalo, 2005). Large chain stores with large numbers of employees working in shifts were usually enthusiastic supporters of commerce on Sunday. Conversely, small businesses that found it difficult to open on the rest days had an interest in maintaining the restrictive laws. Similarly, employees and trade unions that feared that the abolition of the laws would compel them to work on the day of rest have often supported the restrictive laws. In the United Kingdom, religious groups highlighted the need for workers to enjoy the day off as a requisite for family life and demanded to "keep Sunday special" (Richter, 1994). Attempts to frame the debate in social – family values and workers' rights – rather than religious terms have often succeeded.

In the United States, Chief Justice Warren ruled in 1961 that the laws, even if they were religious in origin, served the secular goals of protecting the public's health and well-being and were therefore still proper and valid (Roucher, 1994).

The political-moral debate, however, was sidelined by economic developments. Shopping, as Benjamin Barber (1992), quoted earlier, noted, "has little tolerance for blue laws, whether dictated by pub-closing British paternalism, Sabbath-observing Jewish Orthodox, or no-Sunday liquor-sale Massachusetts Puritanism." In 1959, *Newsweek* magazine observed that on Sundays not only churches but also supermarkets, stores, car sales lots, and real estate offices attract crowds (see Roucher, 1994, April 21, 1958). This has been explained not only by the recreational perception of shopping but also by changes in the family structure – large number of families in which both parents work extended hours during the week, and single-parent families – that have made the weekend the only time for shopping. Shopping on days of rest, it was argued, would enable families in which both parents work to complete their shopping on weekends, make the shopping a relaxed family outing while allowing other individuals to take advantage of the opportunity to work on Sundays for a higher salary, and divide up the family chores between the spouses (Richter, 1994).

The debate over the restriction of commerce on the days of rest was, in many cases, dominated by social and economic arguments rather than religious and secular ones and, more important, by the growing power of business entrepreneurs. The unions, which previously supported the restrictive laws, either lost their political influence or changed their strategies (Price and Yandle, 1987), preferring to fight for extra pay for working on the rest day instead of campaigning to close businesses on Sundays (Roucher, 1994). Similarly, some new churches also adjusted their position to cope with the changes and no longer resist trade on Sundays while understanding that among their believers there are people who need or are interested in shopping on Sunday, including businesspeople and young careerists (Richter, 1994). By 1986, only eighteen of the states in the United States still retained laws closing businesses on Sunday, and the majority of them were dependent on local councils for enforcement and the councils' willingness to do so, as sometimes these laws simply became a dead letter (Roucher, 1994). In Canada also, beginning in 1985 most of the laws restricting trade on the official rest day were rescinded when the right to make the decision was transferred from the federal administration to the provinces (Skuterud, 2005). Similar processes are evident throughout Europe, where different countries have abolished the restrictive laws altogether or added various exemptions.

The regulation of the day of rest is a challenge for secularizing and multicultural societies in which differences between groups about the day and its public meaning are contested. The rules on commerce on the days of rest (Saturday or Sunday) were created in earlier periods when consumer society was in its infancy and religious and social concerns combined to restrict business. The emergence of a consumer society, however, put these rules under pressure from a public for whom shopping on the day of rest combined what they defined as a necessity with leisure, and businesspeople, who sought to exploit new opportunities and complained about the restrictions they perceived as anachronistic. Conversely, groups that previously defended the day of rest – churches, small business owners, and unions – weakened, as their attempt to describe restrictions as representing social and family values lost much of their public appeal, yet they continued to struggle to preserve the days of rest. States were now faced with the challenge to preserve restrictive laws, amend them, or ignore their breaching by entrepreneurs and the public. In some cases the pressure applied led to a formal change of the existing laws, whereas in other instances, independent initiatives bypassed the existing laws and, de facto, changed the rules of the game.

Israel: The Rules of the Game

The establishment of the Sabbath as the official day of rest was part of the status quo but, like some of its other components, its preservation also relied on a wider consensus and a convergence of perceptions. Secular leaders' agreement about its cultural and social importance minimized the gap between them and the religious groups and fostered a mutual understanding. The (secular) poet Haim Nahman Bialik perceived the Sabbath as "the keystone in building the revitalized Hebrew culture" (Zameret, 2004: 106). Worried that the new Hebrew culture might become detached from its Jewish roots, he proposed clear and explicit rules to prevail in the public sphere, especially regarding the Sabbath. Bialik objected to working, traveling, or even holding football games on the Sabbath. "It was the Shabbat and not the culture of oranges or potatoes that preserved the existence of our people throughout the years of its wanderings, and now that we have returned to the land of our forefathers, shall we turn our backs on it as though it was an unwanted item?" (see Zameret, 2004:

106). Berl Katznelson, one of the founding fathers of the Labor Party, expressed similar opinions and called the secular public "to turn our Shabbat days into beacons of culture" (ibid.).

The general agreement on the importance of the Sabbath as a day of rest, however, did not prevent conflicts. In the 1920s the pleas of the Chief Rabbi of Palestine that the leaders of the General Federation of Hebrew Labor (Histadrut) cease from organizing youth trips on the Sabbath were rejected out of hand. "We have no intention of entering into any negotiations over the cancellation of these trips whose cultural and national value is immense and important from many aspects," replied the Histadrut's cultural department (Friedman, 1994). Football matches played on the Sabbath not far from the *haredi* neighborhoods in Jerusalem attracted thousands of spectators and aroused protests, eventually leading to a demand by Agudat Israel in 1930 to stop the games in return for its agreement to cooperate with the Jewish Agency against the British White Paper. The agreement reached remained in force for only a short while (Friedman, 1994).

Disputes and confrontations were greater in Tel Aviv, where alongside a clear secular majority lived a sizable religious population. In the days of the British Mandate, a sound of a trumpet or shofar (ritual ram's horn) announced the commencement of Sabbath and the cessation of work. Many of the city's residents spent Sabbath on excursions, sometimes accompanied by shopping for various products (Helman, 2005). Businesspeople who worked on the Sabbath, such as photographers and cinema owners, justified their work by referring to the unfair competition from rival businesses, which opened undisturbed, and further claimed that their closing on Sabbath would benefit their non-Jewish competitors in nearby neighborhoods. A municipal bylaw was passed in Tel Aviv in 1926 prohibiting trade on the Sabbath, although the religious groups constantly complained that the law was not enforced (Helman, 2003).

On the national level, the assembly of the Knesset decided in 1932 to demand that Jewish local authorities respect the Sabbath, and in 1935 the Zionist congress decided to refrain from desecrating the Sabbath in all the national institutions, an agreement that served as the basis for stopping public transport in most of the districts controlled by the Jewish local authorities (Cohen, 1997). The decisions on the issue of the Sabbath had limited weight because the British government refused to approve religious laws that contradicted freedom of conscience (Shaki, 2005) but served as a reference point for the future. The status quo letter in which the Labor Party promised to establish the Sabbath as the official day of rest was another attempt to find a compromise between religious and secular.

The vague wording of the pre-state agreements had to be translated into formal rules and regulations after statehood. The new law (article 18a of the initial legislation of the State of Israel, Law and Administration Ordinance, 1948) again defined the Sabbath as the official "day of rest" but neither explicitly stated what is permitted or forbidden nor specified what sanctions would be imposed for violation of the rest day (Hacohen, 2002). The Working Hours and Rest Law in 1951 was more specific and stated that "unless stipulated otherwise in the regulations, the length of the weekly rest period for the worker is to be 36 consecutive hours. The rest day includes: For a Jew the Shabbat, while for non-Jewish citizens either Friday or Sunday according to his or her choice." Much to the disappointment of the religious parties, the legislation was backed by social and national arguments pertaining to the day of rest, without any reference to the sanctity of the Sabbath day and its Jewish spiritual and moral significance (Shaki, 2005).

The Working Hours and Rest Law stated that the Minister of Labor was entitled to permit work during the rest hours:

If he was convinced that halting the work for the weekly rest day, either in its entirety or only in part, might endanger the State's defense, or the safety of a person or property, or cause substantial damage to the economy, the work's performance or to the regular supply of services and commodities, which in the Minister of Labor's opinion, are essential for the public or some sectors of the population.

The authority to issue permits of a more general nature rested with a ministerial committee, whose decisions varied in line with the personality of the ministers serving in it and the balance of power therein (Cohen, 1997). This clause aroused arguments on occasions when the religious MKs claimed that the committee was prepared to grant the permits too easily and no serious attempt had been made to prevent the desecration of the Sabbath (Shaki, 2005).

Although the regulations concerning labor and work on the Sabbath were standardized by nationwide legislation, culture and entertainment remained open to debate. Events that involved the sale of tickets, use of electricity, and travel by car were perceived by the religious groups as constituting a violation of the Sabbath that should be forbidden or minimized. Decisions regarding theatres and other events were often made at the local level and, at times, involved disputes between religious and secular residents. The Municipalities' Ordinance Law of 1991 affirmed the authority of municipalities to regulate the opening and closing times of shops, restaurants, cinemas, and theaters. It became apparent time and time again that defining what is prohibited and what is permitted is not a simple technical question, but is rather a part of a more fundamental debate about the nature of the Sabbath.

The rules of the game after statehood remained a general and a fairly loose framework that depended on broader agreements, which themselves were ingrained in the cultural context, more than on specific laws and regulations. Until the 1990s, the secular population had a limited motivation to change the rules, owing to a basic common denominator with the religious public, the desire or need for a political compromise, and the ability to find solutions in many cases where local disputes occurred. Consequently, the conflicts to be discussed in the following sections were also limited in scope and intensity.

Struggle I: The Right to Culture

In the early years of statehood, conflicts surrounding the Sabbath focused mostly on questions of cultural events that pitted the secular against the religious, especially the *haredim* in Jerusalem. The refusal of the owner of the Edison movie theater to yield to religious demands to close on the Sabbath led to a stormy demonstration on May 25, 1949, which was broken up forcefully by the police, thereby arousing an additional storm of protest by the *haredi* public; eventually, a committee of inquiry was set up to investigate those events (Friedman, 1994). Another confrontation was centered on the Sabbath Square in Jerusalem, where the *haredim* tried to prevent both military and civilian vehicles from passing through the area on the Sabbath. Members of the socialist Hashomer Hatza'ir and secular kibbutzim showed up in the square to confront the *haredim* who obstructed traffic and the transport of their dairy products to the markets. These secular groups, which regarded themselves as having borne the brunt of Jerusalem's defense during the war two years previously, now sought to prevent the *haredim* from taking control of the city. In a manifesto they issued, the republican equation emphasized their contribution while the *haredim* were castigated as a group

that played no active role in the war in defense of Jerusalem, unfurled a white flag in the hour of need, and were prepared to surrender. These same people who rejected everything that is precious to the nation and the homeland have risen up and are now using violence in efforts to impose a regime, which the majority of the people completely rejected in the recent elections to the Knesset.

The manifesto praised the work of the police, who dealt firmly with the protesters and called on the rest of society to take a firm stance to protect liberal freedoms:

Down with this atrocious propaganda by the dark forces in the *Yishuv*!

Down with the attempts by thugs to impose a religious regime on the *Yishuv*!

Let the workers and the progressive forces who form the majority of Jerusalem's residents mobilize against these conspiracies!

For the sake of a regime of freedom!

For a regime of democratic rule!

For a regime that maintains human rights!

For a regime protecting law-abiding citizens doing their jobs! (Friedman, 1994)

The struggle in Jerusalem was unique, as the *haredim* were insistent in defending the Sabbath, and secular groups, including some from outside the city, were organized to thwart the *haredim*'s intentions. In one of the fiercest demonstrations in 1956, a haredi protester was killed; his image became a symbol of the struggle to keep the Sabbath among the *haredi* circles, and especially in the *haredi* community (Cohen, 1997). Secularists, organized in the Israeli Association for the Prevention of Religious Coercion founded in 1951, described the anxiety felt by those who perceived the religious drive to enforce their way of life on the secular population. In a declaration, intended also for the religious public, the liberal argument was directed against the religious:

We do not disturb you during your prayers, interfere with your eating kosher food or studying in yeshivot as you wish... so do not bother us. Observe the Shabbat day in your own homes and allow every person to act in accordance with his or her conscience. (see Segev, 1984: 230–1)

In Jerusalem, the concept of "live and let live" was difficult to implement but in other cities, struggles of that magnitude were rare, as secular people were not so quick to mobilize and were largely satisfied with loopholes that enabled them to enjoy the Sabbath on the beaches or at soccer games. Struggles did occur, however, over questions regarding cultural activities inside some of the cities where religious and secular ways of life clashed. In 1984, the mayor of Petah Tikvah decided to allow the open-ing of movie theaters on Friday evenings and declared, "The residents of Petah Tikvah who would like to watch movies on the Sabbath eve will no longer have to travel to Tel Aviv" (Gutkind-Golan, 1990: 71). For the secular public, the mayor explained, "recreation has become a major part of... family life.... In nearby Tel Aviv with its scores of places of enter-tainment a new norm of consumer habits has been created.... I cannot ignore all this." The opening was accompanied by a mass demonstration of about 10,000 religious demonstrators, and intensive political pressure was brought to bear on the mayor to close the theater. It was only in 1987 that the demonstrations, which were declared illegal about a year previously, began to die down.

The struggle in Petah Tikvah over the right for ("secular") culture on the Sabbath was replicated elsewhere, but not with the same intensity. The attempt, adopted later by other groups and institutions, to separate culture from commerce and to emphasize that the struggle was about the right for culture on the day of rest was only partially successful as consumer culture expanded to blur the difference between the two. An indication for the future was the struggle in 1986 against a flea market in Kibbutz Nir Eliyahu that operated on the Sabbath. The kibbutz, which accrued heavy debts due to the crisis in agriculture, described the initiative as "a desperate attempt to extricate themselves from economic distress" (*Yediot Aharonot*, August 25, 1986). Ironically, it was the kibbutzim again, self-described as socialist, that established themselves as economic entrepreneurs at the forefront of a commercializing process. Other kib-butzim also began to operate stores, kiosks, and additional activities, which prompted the religious parties to protest and threaten a coalition crisis over "mass desecration of the Sabbath" (*Yediot Aharonot*, August 27, 1986 and September 3, 1986). These struggles indicated two impor-tant developments. First, the secular public began to view shopping as part of recreation, challenging the limitations of the status quo. Second, economic entrepreneurs were ready to take advantage of the changes and expand their activities on the Sabbath.

Struggle II: Sabbath and the Consumer Society

In 2003 the daily *Yediot Aharonot* reported that during the previous year, Israelis spent 5.2 billion shekels shopping on the Sabbath: "Some people prefer to attend synagogue, others go to the swimming pool, and a large number of people prefer to spend their time shopping," as one store owner explained the obvious fact (*Yediot Aharonot*, June 15, 2003). According to some estimates, 600,000 Israelis visit shopping malls every Sabbath, attesting to the changes of the past two decades. Israeli society was no longer insulated from foreign cultural influences or occupied with the nation- and state-building project associated with an ethos of simplicity and frugality. Rather, since the 1970s, more and more Israelis began to adopt new "Western" modes of consumption, recreation, and status. This development reached its climax during the 1990s, when the globalization or Americanization of Israeli society was felt almost everywhere.

The large malls so typical of the consumer society first appeared in Israel during the 1970s. The Ayalon mall in Ramat Gan, which opened in 1986, was the first to imitate the American model of a covered mall with "anchor" stores at the forefront. In the 1990s, scores of additional malls opened in large and medium-sized cities throughout the country and more shopping centers were built in rural regional council areas, close to major intersections. In almost every important city in Israel, leading international chain stores also integrated into the new commercial centers. American fast-food chains, toy stores, and clothes outlets, along with local brands, offered the Israeli consumer public a new kind of "shopping experience." By 2005 about seventy new malls had been constructed in Israel, which accounted for more than 40 percent of the commercial turnover in Israel and placed Israel in fourth place globally in terms of the size of commercial areas per resident (Gilboa, 2007). As elsewhere, the air-conditioned malls became a focal point for shopping and recreation. The competition among the malls became especially aggressive, a factor that led these malls to intensify their marketing efforts to attract shoppers, including opening the stores on the Sabbath.

In addition to the malls in the city centers, the new era saw the development of shopping centers outside the cities, which offered businesspeople stores at discounted rents and provided the customers with easier access, abundant parking, and, in many cases, bargains. The shopping centers outside the cities gave yet another advantage to the chain stores that rented space there – the opportunity to open on the Sabbath. The distance from the cities, with their religious communities, often coupled with the support of the relevant regional council in whose area the mall was located, kept public opposition and the limitations imposed by municipal bylaws to an absolute minimum. The decision of stores to operate on the Sabbath was, first and foremost, economic, and the positive response indicated by the number of shoppers led many businesses to follow suit and open as well. The radical change of leisure patterns (and Sabbath observance) in the 1990s led to broad public debate in the political, legal, and civil arenas. Proposals for new religious–secular compromises (detailed later) sought to redraw the distinction between religious and commercial activity but it was "market forces" – secular entrepreneurs and shoppers – setting the new rules of the game.

Secular Entrepreneurs: Value for Money

Shopping on the Sabbath did not begin in the 1990s. In Jewish towns almost all businesses were closed but Israelis, at least those who owned cars, could always visit the non-Jewish towns and villages, where there were busy markets; after 1967, they could also visit towns in the West Bank and Gaza. Jewish businesses that opened on the Sabbath were few and small in scale until the 1990s. In 1967, Kibbutz Gan Shmuel opened a "kiosk," a small store selling agricultural produce grown on the kibbutz that operated on the Sabbath and was frequented by local residents or travelers driving along the main road. In the 1990s the small store expanded to a large supermarket (open on the Sabbath); shortly afterward, the kibbutz partnered with a prominent businessman to build a shopping mall where the small kiosk once stood. For the secular kibbutz, opening for business on the Sabbath was not a principled issue. As elsewhere, the expansion of the operation on Sabbath was an economic decision and the natural response of entrepreneurs to the changes in Israeli society:

Nowadays you can come to Ashdod on Shabbat and much to my regret – or perhaps satisfaction, for my opinion is irrelevant – you can see on the beach scores, if not hundreds, of families with their barbecues. If fifteen to twenty years ago somebody had lit a barbecue on Shabbat. he would have been stoned.... But during the 1990s all this changed with the arrival of the *Aliyah* [immigration] from Russia. Despite their particular needs, the number of commercial sites that opened on Shabbat were few and far between. However, the Russians believed that it was perfectly legitimate to do their shopping on the weekend and they were soon joined by the secular population, as well as by traditional people, including me. Although I do not light a fire on the Shabbat, I am willing, however, to drive to do my shopping on Shabbat. (Jacky Ben-Zaken, interview)

The change in outlook was evident. Furthermore, it did not happen only in the kibbutzim or in Tel Aviv but also spread to cities such as Ashdod, where, even allowing for the presence of a large religious population, the Star Center opened its doors on Sabbath in 2005 for the benefit of the city's residents, who previously used to travel to shop on the Sabbath, and visitors from outside the city.

A change has occurred in shopping patterns. Nowadays shopping has become a kind of recreation for the family and the wife.... As there are coffee bars, restaurants, and fashion stores, the visit to the mall has become an experience lasting several hours. During this time the customers can go into cosmetics stores, sit around in coffee bars so that all these activities have become an accepted form of recreation, and you can see that as time progresses, so the activities on Shabbat are on the increase and the income from business on Shabbat increases steadily. (Jacky Ben-Zaken, interview)

Similar decisions have been made by entrepreneurs across the country that have met with little or no resistance from the religious public, a tremendous response from the shopping public, and the blind eye of the municipalities. Not all the chain stores choose to open on the Sabbath for a variety of reasons, such as being owned by religious people or for social or economic reasons. Moreover, companies that do operate on the Sabbath use strategic considerations to decide which stores to open and where it would be better to remain closed on the Sabbath.

First of all, it is an initiative of the shopping center and the company renting out the available space, and then it is up to the store owners. When it comes to opening on Shabbat, one owner looks at another and observes what is happening. These business people do not call a meeting, do not talk with one another, and in fact do nothing except look at what each one is actually doing; when we see that the majority are opening so we also open the store.... It is a system of trial and error, and within a week or two things sort themselves out one way or the other. (A.A., interview).

The question here is the volume of trading on Shabbat.... If the income fails to justify bringing in the workers and paying them overtime at Shabbat rates to keep the store open on Shabbat then the store will close, and consequently the mall will gradually see more stores closing until eventually it will be categorized as a closed mall. This development has a snowball effect – the fewer shops there are that open on Shabbat, fewer customers come along because they find it less interesting to come on Shabbat because there is a spiral effect here which converges inwards and eventually leads to a total closure. (Eitan Bar-Zeev, interview).

Accounts in the financial press, as well as many of the interviewees in this research, reported large profits from Sabbath sales, which sometimes came to more than twice the profits on a regular weekday (*Ha'aretz*, real estate section, December 15, 2005). However, as in other examples discussed in previous chapters, economic incentives could not always be separated from ideological considerations that served to legitimate the decision to operate on the Sabbath. For some businesspeople, operation on the Sabbath was not only an economic decision justified by freedom of choice arguments but also a service they provided for clients or the public good.

> Based on a profit-and-loss calculation for opening on Shabbat, I make no profit. In fact it is a zero-sum game, and I have absolutely no way to prove that economically the Shabbat contributes anything to my business. However, this is a service, and our chain stores are a specialist business, so that service is the essence of our trade and as far as I am concerned, providing a service for people who work all week long and wish to go out at weekends to a place where they disturb nobody and buy what they want at their leisure is important. (Eyal Fishman, interview).

Secular entrepreneurs not only responded to the changes they identified in Israeli society – the expanding consumer culture and its new leisure patterns – but also promoted them through their business decisions. Thus, the decisions to open business on the Sabbath and the large number of consumers shopping on that day have rapidly changed the character of the day of rest.

The Israeli Public: Let Us Shop

Compared with the previous cases discussed in the book, shopping on the Sabbath has the strongest support and, consequently, limited resistance. Opinion polls show the public's broad support for commerce on the Sabbath; support expressed directly in the profits of those companies doing business on the Sabbath. The vast majority of Israeli Jews agree that the Sabbath is a day of rest, different from other days, but the significance attributed to the day does not necessarily rule out shopping. A comprehensive survey carried out in 1999 found that between 48 and 55 percent of the Jews in Israel keep the Sabbath commandments and traditions, such as lighting candles and having a Sabbath dinner or *Kiddush* (sanctification with wine and bread), and the decisive majority described Sabbath as a "family" day (Levi, Levinson, and Katz, 2002). But, perception of the Sabbath as a family day means different things for religious and secular individuals. For the latter, it is also a day for leisure that includes different activities, some that contravene religious restrictions, including shopping. Thus, more and more Israelis do not perceive shopping on the Sabbath as problematic and a majority supports the opening of shops, even if they rarely shop on the Sabbath.

Shopping on the Sabbath contravenes explicit religious rules – using money or driving to the mall – but many of those who shop continue to define themselves as "traditional" rather than "secular,"and report they observe other Jewish commandments and even some of the traditional rituals of the Sabbath. As elsewhere, shopping on the day of rest is explained by Israelis as part of family leisure or a result of an overloaded work schedule that does not allow shopping during the week. The act of shopping on the Sabbath, therefore, is not considered by many shoppers as an expression of a "secular" identity or related to a religious–secular struggle. Individuals interviewed offer a flexible view of the Sabbath that combines rest, traditional rituals, family leisure, and shopping, a combination that rests on a general liberal attitude of "live and let live." This attitude was also adopted by some who observe the Sabbath and refrain from shopping.

I don't go to these places on the Sabbath . . . other people do go there because they enjoy it and that is ok. . . . I don't think we need a law to prevent this. You cannot force people to behave or believe, people should be free to choose the way to live. If you don't want to observe Sabbath or to rest, I don't see anything wrong with it. (Boaz, interview)

Those who shop on the Sabbath tended to describe the shopping as a minor part of Sabbath activity, done when necessity rises or combined with other activities. Thus, even traditional Jews who observe the Sabbath may shop occasionally.

We don't cook on the Sabbath, we don't clean the house or work in the garden on Sabbath . . . we live nearby a shopping center that is open on Sabbath and sometime we hang out there. If we see something we want, we buy it, but this is not the purpose of the visit . . . we don't plan to shop on the Sabbath but sometimes it just happens. (Shaul, interview)

Some of the people interviewed, traditional and secular alike, including those who shop on the Sabbath, expressed concerns and regret over the rapid commercialization of the Sabbath. People referred to the Sabbath as the day of rest and were nostalgic for times when they could feel the change on Friday afternoon when the Sabbath began. "The bustle of Friday afternoon and the calm of the Sabbath," described one woman, "I love this shift, without the religious connotations." But, interviewees were reluctant to support legislation that would prevent commerce, based on their preference to educate people to value the Sabbath for social and cultural reasons and their skepticism that legislation could reverse the trend. "I would be happy to see more businesses closed on the Sabbath," explained one interviewee, "but I am realistic and know you can't fight it."

TABLE 6.1. *Support for Commerce on the Sabbath*

	Ultra-Orthodox (%)	Religious (%)	Traditional (%)	Secular (%)	
Opening stores on the Sabbath (location: outside city center)					
1 (Strongly against)	58.8	32.9	6.4	2.0	Cramer's $V = 0.421^*$
2	41.2	43.8	20.9	7.5	Kendall's tau-c $= 0.490^*$
3	0	13.7	17.9	9.3	
4	0	9.6	41.7	49.3	
5 (Strongly support)	0	0	13.2	31.9	
Opening stores on the Sabbath (location: inside city center)					
1 (Strongly against)	71.6	47.2	15.3	5.2	Cramer's $V = 0.389^*$
2	28.4	38.9	37.9	14.5	Kendall's tau-c $= 0.492^*$
3	0	5.6	14.5	13	
4	0	8.3	27.2	41.7	
5 (Strongly support)	0	0	5.1	25.5	

* $P < 0.05$; ** $P < 0.01$.
Source: Author's own survey, 2009.

The increase in commercial activity on the Sabbath received strong popular support but was restricted by existing laws. It also sparked objections on both religious and social grounds, as its opponents wished to preserve the Sabbath's character and place limitations on commerce (Table 6.1). The struggle over the Sabbath between the secular entrepreneurs and their opponents proceeded in the legal and political domains and led to proposals for compromise together with new strategies for resistance. Regulation of the Sabbath, as elsewhere, was a challenge for the political system that had to decide between enforcement of the old rules – perceived by the nonreligious as outdated – or acceptance of the new reality and face religious opposition.

The support for shopping on Sabbath and the act of shopping itself, more than the examples in previous chapters, blur the lines between traditional and secular individuals. About 70 percent of those who describe themselves "traditional" travel on the Sabbath by car and about 45 percent do not refrain from shopping on Sabbath (Table 6.2).

TABLE 6.2. *Shopping on the Sabbath*

	Ultra-Orthodox (%)	Religious (%)	Traditional (%)	Secular (%)	
In general, how often do you shop on the Sabbath?					
Very often	0	1.4	3.8	8.7	Cramer's $V = 0.311^*$
Often	0	4.1	10.1	17.1	
Rarely	0	1.4	16.9	29.8	Kendall's tau-c $= -0.377^*$
Very rarely	0	0	15.2	19.1	
Never	100	93.2	54.0	25.2	

* $P < 0.05$; ** $P < 0.01$.
Source: Author's own survey, 2009.

Shopping on the Sabbath also blurs the differences between ethnic groups. The vast majority of those who preferred civil marriage and civil burial were Ashkenazim and FSU immigrants, whereas Mizrahim attributed a high importance to the traditional ceremonies. Mizrahim, more than other ethnic groups, observe kashrut rules and refrain from eating pork. Shopping on the Sabbath, conversely, provides a different picture, in which the differences between the groups are small (Table 6.3).

TABLE 6.3. *Ethnicity and Commerce on the Sabbath*

	1 (Strongly Oppose) (%)	2 (%)	3 (%)	4 (%)	5 (Strongly Support) (%)
Do you support allowing commerce on the Sabbath outside city centers?					
Mizrachim	11.7	20.2	14.5	39.5	14.2
Ashkenazim	12.3	18.6	9.3	34.8	25
FSU immigrants	1.0	8.1	10.1	54	26.3
Israelis	18.3	22.3	10.3	31.4	17.7

	Often (%)	Rarely (%)	Never (%)
Do you shop on the Sabbath?			
Mizrachim	17.3	29.7	53
Ashkenazim	16.7	36.0	47
FSU Immigrants	19.2	44.4	36.4
Israelis	17.7	31.4	50.9

Source: Author's own survey, 2009.

Politics: An Empty Debate?

Historically, the operations of businesspeople on the Sabbath continued almost unfettered as the government and local authorities chose to
minimize their interference. Actions and statements drew some media
attention and public debate but, in practice, had limited influence on the
growing commercial activity on the Sabbath. By the mid-1990s, Israelis
across the country could choose to shop on the Sabbath not far from
home.

In 1996, Eli Yishai of the SHAS party, the new Minister for Labor and
Social Welfare, announced that he intended to take firm action against
violations of the Sabbath laws (*Yediot Aharonot*, economic supplement,
August 23, 1996). This decision prompted a well-publicized fight against
McDonald's and between Omri Padan, the CEO of McDonald's in Israel,
and Eli Yishai. This struggle was largely symbolic of the changes that were
taking place in Israel and the new character of similar confrontations in
Israel and worldwide. Padan, a former soldier in an elite military unit,
an economist, and one of the founders of Peace Now, was perceived as
embodying the Israeli image of the global and secular "McWorld." Yishai,
the leader of a religious party, was depicted as being at the opposite pole
of the local, communal, and religious-traditional world. The Israeli media
also did not miss this image:

These two individuals – Yishai and Padan – constitute the two extremities of
Israeli society: the religious individual against the secular one, the Sephardic Jew
as opposed to the Ashkenazi Jew, the symbol of the deprived classes in contrast
to the representative of the elite, a symbol of one rooted in Jewish culture as
opposed to a symbol of Americanization. To put it differently, it could be said
that Yishai represents everyone who is not a customer of Padan. (Kadosh, 2000)

Minister Yishai used a clause in the Youth Employment Law that prohibits employing Jewish youth on the Sabbath. The ministry's inspectors,
accompanied by police officers, fined restaurants, and in the courts the
company had to pay out thousands of shekels in fines. Padan reacted
by placing advertisements in the newspaper warning that Israel could
"become another Iran" and asked the secular public to support him. The
arguments he used combined liberal economics, secular ideology, and the
religious threat to both:

Where economics are concerned, Shabbat is very important to me. Our branch
at Bilu Junction sells eight times more on Shabbat than it does on the rest of the
weekdays because then crowds of people come there to shop and spend time, and
whoever plans to close us down on Shabbat cuts our income. The other side of

the coin in this struggle is the quality of my life as a citizen of this country. It is unthinkable that inspectors from the Ministry for Labor should come along and dictate to the secular public, which is still the majority in the State of Israel, how to live their lives and what to do on Shabbat.... I think that an all-out war may break out here and I have no idea where it might end, and even though the religious groups gained in strength in the last elections and will not yield here, the secular people will fight back. (Meidan, 1997)

Padan also made it perfectly clear that he would continue to sell cheeseburgers and dairy ice cream, regardless of kashrut laws, invoking his republican contribution to bolster his position:

Now that we are in the twenty-first century, the state must stop telling its citizens what to do and definitely what to eat. This is my economic and cultural personal philosophy and therefore it is perfectly clear to me that we shall do everything possible to defeat them.... I did not serve in the army and neither did I fight in the wars to defend this country so that we would turn into another Iran. (Meidan, 1997)

The struggle between McDonald's and the Ministry of Labor was symbolic also for the gap between political statements, actions, and impacts. Sending out the inspectors to enforce the Working Hours Law was the decision of the minister responsible for the law, in keeping with his considerations and especially his religious-political position. The decision to send (or to refrain from sending) the inspectors became a political ritual but had, in practice, only a negligible influence on businesses opening on Shabbat. Religious ministers' decisions to reinforce the law were met by secular protests against religious coercion. Conversely, the decisions of nonreligious ministers to freeze the inspectors' work led to a religious furor and, in 2003, to the suspension of the participation by the NRP in the government and the coalition "that uproots the Shabbat" (*Ma'ariv*, March 30, 2003).

Legislative initiatives for a new Sabbath law that would redefine the rules of the game have failed. The different initiatives adopted a largely similar formula, replicated in other arenas, that, first, established the universal importance of the Sabbath and, second, separated cultural from commercial activities to allow the former and restrict the latter. Proposals, usually the result of cooperation between religious and secular MKs, emphasized the uniqueness of the Sabbath in Israel and the importance of the state's Jewish character, but also integrated social-economic justifications for a new Sabbath law. In December 2001, the daily *Yediot Aharonot* reported on "a revolutionary law bill to change the status quo with respect to the Sabbath" that was initiated by secular and religious

members of the parliament. "As soon as an explicit law prohibits commerce and manufacturing work in factories on Sabbath then everything
which is not mentioned can in actual practice be permitted," explained
MK Nahum Langenthal, the proposal's initiator, who continued, "As
long as the tide in the malls and the factories is stopped, the religious
population is willing to turn a blind eye and ignore what is going on in
cultural or other activities on Shabbat" (*Yediot Aharonot*, December 31,
2001).

Religious politicians could find partners among secularists who supported the restrictions on commerce for cultural, ecological, and social
reasons. A day without commerce, it was argued, would allow people
to engage in other activities, reduce waste, protect small businesses that
cannot operate on the Sabbath, and guarantee workers a day of rest.
Business interests and the opposition of more radical secular and religious politicians, however, rendered the proposed bills irrelevant. Secular
entrepreneurs rejected any attempt to separate cultural from commercial
activities, which they described as unjustified intervention:

This is a religious law that has been painted in social colors. This situation is due
to the fact that no one at all in the coalition is prepared to go ahead and deal
with the Shabbat issue, and this is what I have to say to you, if you people are so
brave, then go ahead and pass a law dealing with Shabbat; let us see how you can
get the support to pass this law through the coalition. Moreover, how are you
going to decide what is permitted and what is prohibited – yes to gas stations, yes
to the airport, and no to something else? Why? For what reason?" (Eyal Fishman,
interview).

I believe that when it comes to democracy there is no room at all for legislation
based on religion, for that is my own private affair. I do not believe in legislation
that is religious by definition and orders people to close or open their businesses
on Shabbat, as the case may be. (Eitan Bar-Zeev, interview).

The entrepreneurs' arguments received support from secular politicians
that claimed the proposal constituted a submission to religious coercion.
"In the proposed law bill, what the secular people are forbidden to do
is written down, but what they are allowed to do is not stated overtly.
What advantage do the secular people gain here?" asked MK Yosef Lapid.
Orthodox politicians had their own reservations on the compromise: they
claimed it granted a permit to violate Shabbat and therefore they could
not agree to it (*Yediot Aharonot*, January 1, 2002). Similar proposals
were raised several more times by parties and individuals, based on the
same compromises and rejected for the same reasons. Minister Eli Yishai
of the SHAS party vowed to prevent any compromises and scolded the

"initiative by these so-called religious parties who have suddenly become Reform Jews in matters concerning Shabbat." Other religious leaders explained that the most they would be willing to concede would be to turn a blind eye to activities on the Sabbath that they could not prohibit by law (Goldstein, 2007).

Another creative attempt to solve the Sabbath controversy was the suggestion to make Sunday an additional day of rest in which commerce would take place. In June 2000, Natan Sharansky, the interior minister at the time, came up with a proposal to declare Sunday an official day of rest and Ehud Barak, the prime minister, promised to look into that possibility (*Yediot Aharonot*, June 26, 2000). Two years later, another bill that proposed making Sunday a rest day and prohibiting work on the Sabbath was submitted (*Ma'ariv*, March 30, 2002). Business owners expressed support for the idea but industrialists and economists warned that in practice this proposal meant a transition to a working week of only four and a half days (because Friday is, in any case, a short working day), which would result in serious damage to the economy (*Yediot Aharonot*, February 18, 2003). The debate over the proposed bill, as with many others that were submitted and debated, ended without any practical results.

More concrete debates and struggles occurred in municipalities where mayors, caught between the demands of residents for and against commerce on the Sabbath and between the businesses in the malls that operated on the Sabbath and those inside the city that were prevented from doing so, have had to make decisions. However, like their counterparts in the national government, mayors have also tried to evade making a clear decision. In Tel Aviv, where a bylaw requiring Sabbath observance had existed since 1926, the city council deliberated in 1998 whether to add the words "except for cultural and educational activities" but, under pressure from the mayor, decided to defer making a decision on the proposal (*Ha'aretz*, January 15, 1998). In any event, the municipality has refrained ever since from implementing these bylaws against cultural institutions and businesses open on the Sabbath. In Herzliya, the mayor, identified with the Meretz liberal party, permitted the opening of a mall on the Sabbath and even supported the idea. In Netanya, the decision was taken to suspend the enforcement of the bylaw, which allowed the municipality to impose fines of 490 shekels. "This is not a local issue, but a matter for which the state must find the solution and there must be a law that applies to everyone equally. It is not the mayor's responsibility to take a stand

and decide policy on this issue," explained the mayor (*Ynet*, December 9, 2003).

The mayors had to contend not just with the demand of a large public for commerce on the Sabbath, but also with economic considerations, which were quite clear to the secular entrepreneurs as well.

As far as the municipality is concerned . . . they have internalized the fact that on the whole, if a project outside residential areas is open on Shabbat . . . it makes a substantial economic contribution. In conclusion, if you assess the complex [the mall in Ashdod] as a whole, then the facts are that we have created employment for about 3,000 people here that did not exit previously . . . and apart from that advantage you produce an impressive source of income for the municipality. . . . We calculated that during the past four years we have paid 50 million shekels in taxes and other charges to the Ashdod municipality. (Jacky Ben-Zaken, interview).

Religious business people, on the other hand, were frustrated with the governments that avoided their duty to enforce existing laws. As one of them explained:

Speaking as a businessman I can tell you for sure that if this option [fines] was implemented then businesses would close on Shabbat. It would not be viable to pay fines for trading on Shabbat, when wages are double and most of the business is done in the afternoons. Add also the risk involved that the opening a criminal record entails, then this would ensure the closing of businesses on Shabbat, but so far no Minister of Industry and Commerce has applied the law, even though he has the authority to do so. (Avi Katz, quoted in Goldstein, 2007)

The regulation of the Sabbath is a striking example of the weakness of the political system, expressed in the inconsistent and ineffective enforcement of the existing regulations as well as the inability to formulate innovative compromises. Although the media gave extensive coverage to the regulations' enforcement as well as the work of the inspectors who fined businesses that were open on the Sabbath, in actual practice these measures had little, if any, effect on the expansion of commerce. The department responsible for enforcing the labor laws at the Ministry of Industry and Commerce employed only four inspectors responsible for enforcing the employment of Jewish workers on the Sabbath (Levi, 2004), allowing entrepreneurs to evade enforcement (discussed later). Attempts to reach a compromise – bills introduced in the formal political domain and social pacts agreed outside it – also failed to change the reality in which the state had little, if any, regulative capacity on the Sabbath.

The Legal Domain

Secular entrepreneurs were largely comfortable with the political vacuum and did not need the protection of the courts. Rather, in recent years, they found themselves in the courts mainly as defendants, when they were prosecuted for opening their businesses on the Sabbath or when they attempted to appeal fines imposed on them for the same reason. The courts repeatedly ruled that the legal restrictions on activities on the Sabbath were lawful and proper, but allowed essential services to be maintained and protected the right to hold cultural activities on the Sabbath. These decisions, made in the heyday of the status quo, preceded the compromise formula described earlier. In these decisions, the court followed (and cited) the American example: laws restricting trade on Sundays were upheld for their social value. Public needs, however, had also to be protected even when they do not comply with religious restrictions. The attempt to balance between protecting the day of rest and liberal freedoms appeared in several rulings.

When, in 1968, a gas station owner in Ramat Gan appealed against his conviction for an offense against a municipal bylaw committed when he opened the gas station on Sabbath, the court was able both to uphold the Sabbath law and side with the owner. The Sabbath laws, the court explained, are not illiberal, and cited U.S. Chief Justice Earl Warren's support for Sunday closing laws:

"Sunday closing laws, like those before us, have become part and parcel of this great governmental concern wholly apart from their original purposes or connotations. The present purpose and effect of most of them is to provide a uniform day of rest for all citizens; the fact that this day is Sunday, a day of particular significance for the dominant Christian sects, does not bar the State from achieving its secular goals." (cited in Yizramax HCJ 217/68).

However, the court overruled the municipality's decision, arguing that a gas station does not fall within the definition of the municipal bylaw that enables municipalities to order the closing of "business and places of entertainment" that operate on the Sabbath. The court ruled that vital public services should be exempted from the restrictions and that a gas station constitutes a vital public service on Sabbath too, and especially so in view of the changing circumstances.

Private vehicles are becoming an increasingly popular form of transport and constitute a vital element in maintaining the economy and the various industries as well as in satisfying the social and cultural needs of the general public and the individual, and furthermore, public transport services do not usually operate on

Shabbat. The fuel used in running modern vehicles is the very "life blood" of the living body without which it could not exist. (Judge Berenson in HCJ 217/68, *Yizramax v. the State of Israel*)

The court continued to uphold the Sabbath laws but established another important distinction between cultural and commercial activities. Citing examples from liberal democracies such as the United States and Canada and acknowledging the particular cultural significance of the Sabbath, the court affirmed the restrictions on commerce:

In fixing the principle of a weekly day of rest and designating that day as Shabbat the legislator aimed at implementing several integrated goals: First, a social objective, by which it was only proper to designate a weekly rest day for every individual so that he or she may rest from all their labor, spend time with the family or friends, and also to find the time for relaxation and entertainment according to their choices and personal preferences. Moreover, the rest day was meant to protect the worker's health and ensure fair working conditions. Second, setting aside the Shabbat for the rest day was decided in keeping with the commandments in the *halakhah* and traditions of Israel. (HCJ 5073/91; Israel Theaters v. Municipality of Netanya)

By emphasizing the social and cultural significance of the Sabbath, the court was able to distinguish between commerce and culture. Thus, in 1991, when owners of movie theaters and secular groups petitioned the court against the city of Netanya that ordered them to close down on Friday nights, the court sided with the petitioners. The ruling against the municipality explained that the municipal bylaw allows cultural and educational activities, and theaters should clearly be recognized as such. According to the court, the concepts of culture and education are

clear and lucid. There may be an argument about the fringes of this policy, but nowadays there is no room to argue the point that culture does not include literature, art, music, dance, theater and the cinema. The order relating to the closure of a place and prohibiting cultural and educational activities constitutes a limitation on the individual's freedom to choose for himself a cultural form of recreation in line with his personal taste, and sometimes this just might occur on the official day of rest when he has time off from work. (HCJ 5073/91, *Israel Theaters v. Municipality of Netanya*; HCJ,5609/91, *Koren v. Municipality of Netanya*; HCJ 5799/91, *Feit and others v. Municipality of Netanya*)

The distinction between "culture" and "commerce" was reaffirmed also when companies fined for employing workers on the Sabbath, in violation of the Working Hours and Rest Law, claimed that this law contradicted the Basic Law: Freedom of Occupation. The court rejected the submission for two main reasons. First, the limitation clause appended to the basic law allows for an infringement of the freedom of occupation if the law is in accordance with the values of the state and is intended for a proper purpose. Second, the court ruled that the Working Hours and Rest Law is not a "religious" law, but a social and national one. Highlighting the law's social aspects, the court drew attention to Canada, where even allowing for the separation of church and state there, some of the provinces make the closing of businesses on Sunday mandatory.

> The social purpose serves an important public goal, namely, it was designed to protect the individual (worker and employer) and was intended to ensure the well-being of the entire family, while also including an assurance of equality between the religious person and whoever is not religious... and it also serves a proper religious-national purpose. It takes into consideration the feelings of the religious public in Israel and also expresses that national link that connects us together as members of one people. (HCJ 5026/04, *Design 22 and others v. Rosenzweig and others*)

By shifting the focus to the national significance of the Sabbath, the court could turn the law into an example of the compatibility of the Jewish and democratic values of the state. The law, explained Chief Justice Aharon Barak:

> [b]efits the values of the State of Israel as a Jewish and democratic state. It was enacted for a proper purpose – a public-social goal implemented in a manner that applies a religious-national element. (ibid.; see also Handyman affair, 10687/02; *the State of Israel v. P.K.P. Design Ltd.*, 1168/00).

The National Labor Court adopted a similar approach when it ruled that the Working Hours and Rest Law also applies to kibbutzim. The judges did not forget to include quotations from secular intellectuals such as Berl Katznelson – "For me, the Shabbat is one of the pillars of Hebrew culture" and the poet Bialik, who wrote to the members of Kibbutz Geva that "the Land of Israel without Sabbath will not be built but will end up in ruins and all your labor will be in vain" (*Ha'aretz*, December 12, 2006).

In contrast to the issues discussed in the previous chapters, these rulings clearly proved to the secular entrepreneurs that the courts are not the domain in which a change can be effected or in which they can even defend themselves against the enforcement of the law, which they tried to depict as "religious" or as "religious coercion" and as impairing the freedom of occupation. What was even more important was the fact that the court made it abundantly clear that its liberal position is not at variance with the Working Hours and Rest Law, which it interpreted as a law that comes with inherent social and national values. Following the clear-cut rulings by the courts, the majority of the entrepreneurs abandoned legal efforts to argue against the law's legality or defend themselves against the fines.

Covenants and Pacts

The failure of the political system to regulate the Sabbath and the expanding commercial activity concerned not only religious Israelis but also some secular Israelis. For the latter, the Sabbath as a day of rest was valued for its social and cultural significance and the preoccupation with shopping was viewed with disdain. Their desire for a cultural Sabbath with Jewish substance was different from the religious interpretations but similar in objection to the commercialization of the day of rest. This agreement replicated the formula adopted in political and legal circles but sought to overcome the political system's failure to manage religious–secular relations and the radicalization among religious and secular perceived as a threat to the core consensus of society (Cohen and Rynhold, 2005). The covenants contained different aspects of religious–secular debates (marriage and conversion, for example), but the Sabbath occupied an important part in many.

The first covenant attempt was in 1986, led by a secular law professor, Ruth Gavison, and a rabbi within the settler movement, Yoel Bin-Nun. In 1988, the moderate religious kibbutz movement and, in 1990, the moderate religious party Meimad produced more covenant proposals (Cohen and Rynhold, 2005). The covenants were initiated and supported by nongovernmental organizations and involved religious and secular elites, not necessarily politicians. The covenants' aim was to forge an agreement that would galvanize public support (ibid.) and, eventually, translate to a formal compromise. These attempts were continued in the 1990s, when government failure and radicalization seemed to increase.

In the Forum for National Consensus, an apolitical body founded in 1998, a "Sabbath team" consolidated understandings on the issue of work and rest on the Sabbath, public transport and cultural activities, and a general proposal for a Sabbath law (Yaffe and Rosenthaler, 2005). Another covenant, drafted by Professor Ruth Gavison and Rabbi Yaakov Medan and supported and adopted by various institutions, represented to a large extent all the agreements reached between religious and secular groups. It proposed to establish, in a basic law, that the Sabbath is an official rest day; guarantee the right of the workers to a day of rest on the Sabbath; allow the activities of cultural institutions, restaurants, and a limited number of businesses to be defined as essential; and permit some public transport on the Sabbath, and all the above while making every effort to maintain the Sabbath's special character. Similar guidelines appeared in the framework for a constitution proposed by the Israel Democracy Institute, another effort to mend relations between different parts of society and stabilize the political system. The proposed bill stated that the Sabbath is the official day of rest, that every Jewish worker has an undeniable right to not work on the Sabbath, and that no industrial or commercial activities will be allowed nor any activities of the national institutions, except for cases in which a special license is granted. On the other hand, the proposed law bill stipulated that "the right to hold activities for recreation, culture and entertainment on Sabbath should not be hindered, as long as due care is exercised where the restrictions on location and noise are concerned."

Covenants replicated understandings reached in the political realm and decisions made in the courts that set the Sabbath as a day of rest and separated commerce from culture. Many secular ideologists had no trouble in identifying with issues relating to the rights of workers who are forced to work on the Sabbath, the damage done to small businesses, and the longing for a day's rest free from consumerism and dedicated to the family or quality leisure and culture. However, the secularization of the Sabbath continued its momentum almost entirely within the economic realm and was based on the entrepreneurs' economic considerations. As far as the vast majority of the consumers and businessmen were concerned, trading on Sabbath had already become a *fait accompli*.

The Market Economy and the Sabbath: Secular Strategies

Public demand was the major factor in entrepreneurs' decisions to open their business on the Sabbath. However, entrepreneurs also had to contend with religious opposition and regulation by local and national authorities. The legitimacy of opening a business was based on three principal arguments: (1) the location of the business far from major population centers, (2) its offering a service that meets the needs or demands of a large public, and (3) the competition that drives business owners to work on the Sabbath, as long as others do. The location of the malls that operate on the Sabbath – mostly outside the main population centers and from religious neighborhoods, according to the entrepreneurs – enables a free choice and underscores a liberal position of "live and let live."

We work at those locations where it is permitted.... Even if we are allowed to work at a specific location where I might cause trouble, such as near a religious neighborhood or beside a city residential area, or at a place where our activities causes noise and a disturbance, then as a matter of principle, we shall not open the business. Our approach states the following: "We are not going to disturb you, so please do not bother us." What religious person is bothered by the fact that I am working in Shefayim? It is only when that person thinks about what we are doing there, it is only when he starts getting involved with us, that I really do disturb him. We respect that [religious] individual and all we want from him is that he should respect us. (Eyal Fishman, interview)

All the malls within the cities are closed on Shabbat, so the stores opening are those located in power centers beyond the cities' boundaries and locations where the local authority is not religious. That is the whole philosophy in a nutshell behind all those malls located outside the cities, a philosophy that states that we will build malls outside the cities' boundaries so that we shall indeed avoid causing a disturbance and avoid desecrating the Sabbath overtly, and thereby refrain from upsetting the religious or traditional population. (Kobi Moise, interview)

In addition to the malls' locations, the secular entrepreneurs also emphasized the need and the desire of a large public for shopping on the Sabbath. This demand, they argued, justified the opening of their businesses on the Sabbath. Moreover, the distinction drawn between culture and commerce was rejected by the entrepreneurs as being "outmoded" or "elitist." The choice, they argued, adopting again the liberal discourse, must remain with the public – which, to all intents and purposes, had already decided.

All over the Western world shopping as a pastime has already become part of the prevailing culture.... On one day you can take a trip to the Galilee while on another day you can travel to the commercial center at Gan Shmuel, spend three to four hours taking the boy to the games center they have here; you can also go bowling, and in the meantime the wife takes the daughter shopping.... I do not know if you can define the culture as something specific... For you, buying food is a form of recreation while for somebody else going to the theater is recreation. (Oded Levi, interview)

Office Depot is committed to serving the secular clientele as well.... The purchases made on Shabbat are concentrated on a regular and sympathetic crowd who need products for the home and the family, and we are committed to giving them that service. (Zachi Fishbein, CEO at Office Depot; see Chen, 2000)

Economic competition and necessity were other reasons entrepreneurs provided for operating on the Sabbath. For some kibbutzim, for example, the economic projects operating on the Sabbath constituted an integral part of their plans for economic recovery. In Kibbutz Mizra, when defending the right of the restaurant to operate on the Sabbath, as in the case of pork (Chapter 5), ideological and economic arguments converged, as one kibbutz member explained:

> Just imagine what will happen if the religious groups succeed in closing us down and closing the other places of recreation. Where will the hundreds of thousands of Israelis go on Shabbat? Who will speak up for their basic freedom to eat wherever they wish? If the religious groups close us down it will not end here with restaurants but will spread to affect beaches and other places of recreation.... This is a campaign against the secular way of life. (Ben-Simon, 1998)

Similarly, the general secretary of the kibbutzim warned that the problem is not confined to the right of the consumers to shop on the Sabbath, but also concerns the right of business men and women to make a living, in Mizra and elsewhere:

> If somebody tries to close them down he will hurt hundreds of thousands of people who travel every Shabbat from the center of the country to spend time elsewhere. Additionally, as the income from the business on Shabbat accounts for some 40% of the annual turnover for those kibbutzim, the closure of these enterprises on Shabbat would certainly mean their liquidation. (Ben-Simon, 1998)

The kibbutzim, as mentioned before, had no problem with adopting the capitalist principles of the consumer society and using them to explain that shopping on the Sabbath constitutes a genuine need on the part of the citizens, just as it is for the business community, kibbutzim, and others, especially when competition dictates operating on the Sabbath. "If we were to close on Shabbat, then we could distribute the load over six days in the week at a lower cost," the CEO of Dafna Shoes justified the decision, "but I am not willing to be the only righteous person at this site where all the businesses are open on Shabbat, for this would not be fair competition" (Chen, 2000).

The economic considerations and justifications of entrepreneurs underscored a laissez-faire approach demanding to keep government intervention minimal and leave the decision to individual choice, unless operation on the Sabbath would directly upset religious communities. The distinctions drawn between businesses located outside the cities and those situated within the cities' boundaries could have emerged as an amended status quo according to which the Sabbath was observed within the city limits. It was soon revealed, however, that this distinction was problematic to maintain. Businesses in the city center could not remain indifferent to the expanding Sabbath trade at the expense of weekday shopping. These small businesses, regardless of their location, wanted to preserve the status of the official rest day, as explained by the organization's chairperson:

Ninety-five percent of the retailers have no interest in opening on Shabbat for the average trader works 68 hours per week compared to a 43-hour working week for a salaried employee. Is the retailer not entitled to relax together with his family on the day when his wife who is employed does not work and his children are not at school? As part of the war against the religious sector, the law and the Shabbat in Israel are being crushed. (Chen, 2000)

Whereas the store owners and the merchants' organizations could only demand the strict enforcement of the existing laws, the mall owners within the city insisted on being allowed to open on Sabbath and sometimes took the initiative. In Beersheba, for example, the mall located in the city center decided to open its doors on Sabbath, to compete with the rival shopping center located out of town. Religious groups demanded that the mayor enforce the law and made an explicit differentiation between the two malls. The city's rabbi explained that "the mall is located at the very heart of the city and there are seven synagogues in its immediate vicinity, merely a stone's throw away, so this step is a callous affront to a very large public" (*Negev Times*, April 2, 2004). The mall's owners explained that they opened the mall in reaction to unfair competition, but in this case the company chose to close the mall on the Sabbath after only three months for economic reasons (Pe'er Nadir, interview). In other cities, such as Herzliya and Kfar Saba, the malls opened on the Sabbath with support from the secular public and protests from the religious. The mall owners also used an economic justification to explain their decision:

We are facing unfair competition from the shopping centers in the *moshavim* and kibbutzim . . . so that if a client has no other shopping options on Shabbat, he will go there instead of shopping with me in midweek.

I would prefer not to work on Shabbat. . . . I believe that both the workers in the stores and the public should be given a rest, but you cannot allow others to make progress while you are left behind. (*Ma'ariv*, December 10, 2002).

You have your competitors to consider, because if they are working on Shabbat then you have no choice but to adjust to the prevailing market conditions. My principal competitor opens on Shabbat and therefore if the law is enforced today and everything closes on Shabbat, then I have no problem with that and I will be pleased to close too. If the reality of the situation was that everyone closes on Shabbat then I would not swim against the tide and I could close, because then I could be sure that whoever does not shop on Shabbat would show up during the week and I have no problem. (A.S., interview)

The debate over the Sabbath since the 1990s was hardly ideological, as entrepreneurs could rely on economic demand and minimal, localized, opposition to their operation. Officially, operation on the Sabbath was restricted by laws and regulations that were also upheld by the courts. In practice, however, this enforcement had negligible influence.

Enforcement and Evasion

In the absence of a comprehensive "Sabbath law," the Working Hours and Rest Law constitutes the most significant legal restriction for operating businesses on the Sabbath. Inspectors from the Ministry of Industry and Trade are authorized to hand out fines when they find Jewish people working on the Sabbath. These fines, as the ministry itself acknowledges, are not very effective:

Although you fine them, the business concerns continue to open on Shabbat.... The law is a labor law and not a Shabbat law and so I have no authority to come along and close down a business on Shabbat even if it employs Jews. The only action I can take here is to fine the offender or prosecute him because I cannot come and put a seal on the door. (Yehezkel Ophir, interview)

During the 1990s, the fines were rather small and had a marginal impact on the businesses operating on Sabbath. The increase in the fines afterward did not change their limited impact. The small number of inspectors and the considerable profits to be made by working on the Sabbath did not change the reality of the situation but only led to increased antagonism between the ministry and the entrepreneurs, as well as diverse strategies used by the latter to evade the fines.

All this enforcement is just a gesture to placate the religious groups and nothing more, for if they really wanted to enforce the law then the inspectors would come every Shabbat and all day long, and this is not the case at present. What happens now is only for appearances' sake in order to say that something is being done ... because if they really wanted to take action they would come every Shabbat with four or five inspectors because once a single inspector shows up at the site then within seconds everyone at the site knows and the workers vanish into thin air. (A.S., interview)

I have no ID card, what can you do? Shoot me? What can you do to me? Once you instruct your workers to give the inspector the right answers then inspectors can do nothing. Remember that the companies' CEOs are opportunists and employ every conceivable maneuver and use their creativity to their fullest advantage; and believe me when I say that the business sector's creativity far outweighs anything that the government sector has to offer. (Eitan Bar-Zeev, interview)

In some cases, the confrontation between entrepreneurs had a principled angle when businesspeople chose to confront the ministry, the politicians in charge, and their policies. Making this a principled issue, they vowed to resist the attempts of religious parties to close down their businesses on the Sabbath.

As soon as they dominate the government ministries and control them according to their own specific demands then, in my opinion, they have crossed the bounds of democracy. That, then, is the current situation, as they occupy the Ministry of Labor, they control that ministry and there is no separation of the enforcement authorities and the legal system, and both of them work in tandem – nd this is what bothers me.... Once they succeed in finishing me off, then the very next day they will proceed to their next target and this is what people in this country don't understand... they will go on to gas stations, and next they will target the beaches and it could even reach other places of culture. (Eyal Fishman, interview)

Confrontations, however, were the exception as most entrepreneurs, like in the case of nonkosher meat, felt no need to take upon themselves a political commitment. In contrast to Eyal Fishman and Omri Padan before him, who chose a well-publicized head-on confrontation, most of the entrepreneurs preferred to avoid clashing with that policy and with relative ease found ways to evade the law that prohibits the employment of Jews on the Sabbath. Jewish workers present in the store would have no signs of identification (shirts or tags) and would "disappear" or pretend to be customers when the inspectors showed up (what some interviewees described as a "game of cat and mouse"). An easier way to evade the law, available especially for larger businesses, was to hire temporary non-Jewish employees for the Sabbath. These included either Arab workers or non-Jewish FSU immigrants. These non-Jewish workers filled the positions at the cash desks and sales counters, allowing the Jewish workers to be less visible. In cases in which the companies have no alternative but to employ Jewish workers and they are eventually caught by the inspectors, the entrepreneurs prefer to pay the fines and avoid confrontations (Figure 6.1):

We do not go to court but try to end the matter outside the courts even if for one reason only, namely the legal costs incurred in defending the case are higher than

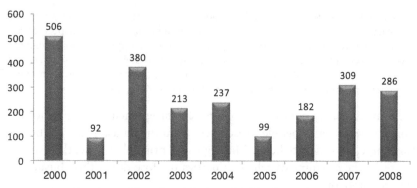

FIGURE 6.1. Number of fines for violation of Sabbath regulations. *Source:* Ministry of Industry, Trade, and Labor website, accessed November 2010.

any penalty. We are not a company dedicated to promoting a principle but for making a profit.... We do not view the issue as a banner to wage war against, but rather we see it as a business matter. We look upon the issue as a business affair, pure and simple, not political and not ideological. The economic forces driving us to open on Shabbat are very powerful, as far as the business's viability is concerned, and for that reason it works. Should some external political pressure emerge then it may prevent this development, but as long as it depends on market forces it will continue. (E.A., interview)

The rapid expansion of commerce on the Sabbath indicated that the policies of governments and the ministry in charge had no influence on the developments, regardless of the political personas involved. The political vacuum was evident in the inabilities of governments not only to make decisions, but also to enforce existing rules and regulations. Consequently, the entrepreneurs had no inclination to engage in political principled struggles to change the rules of the game, nor to accept the compromises suggested.

Local Struggles and Consumer Boycotts

The weakness of the political system and the framing of the commercialization of the Sabbath in economic cost-benefit calculations also influenced the religious counter-strategies. In the 1990s, the religious, and particularly the *haredi*, public realized the gap between their formal political power and their actual ability to influence the developments in the public sphere in general, and the Sabbath in particular (Shamir and Ben-Porat, 2007). Not only did the prospects for a comprehensive "Sabbath law" or a binding agreement not appear on the horizon, but the existing laws were also hardly implemented and commerce on Sabbath expanded rapidly. The religious struggle over the Sabbath, as with the fight against the sale of pork outlined in the previous chapter, was transferred to the local level and, more recently, the consumer power of the religious has been used to counter the commercial activity on the Sabbath.

Demonstrations over the closure of roads in *haredi* neighborhoods on Sabbath, as on Bar-Ilan Street in Jerusalem, ended in compromises to the *haredi* public's satisfaction. Similarly, struggles against the opening of malls on the Sabbath within cities such as Beersheba and Kfar Saba resulted in a successful outcome for the religious. Their success in protecting their own neighborhoods, however, contrasted sharply with the developments elsewhere. The disappointment from the meager achievements made in the political realm encouraged new religious leaders, including businesspeople, to take the lead. For religious businesspeople, the expansion of commerce on Sabbath was also an economic problem they described as unfair competition. In tenders issued for running the stores at the new airport, for example, participants were required to open their stores on Sabbath; consequently, religious businesspeople had to withdraw their proposals. Religious businesspeople also reported that the management of malls open on the Sabbath pressured them to open their stores too (Chen, 2004). Not only business owners, but also religious employees reported they were discriminated against after they refused to work on the Sabbath (*HaZofeh*, December 8, 2004).

Religious citizens, frustrated with formal political channels, attempted to use their consumer power through a boycott, whereby an organized public avoids purchasing certain products, or a "buycott," according to which consumers prefer to buy specific products that are not offensive to their point of view or do not harm their interests. One way or another, a consumers' boycott is a "collective action" whose success demands cooperation and the willingness to make a sacrifice to attain a common goal (Shamir and Ben-Porat, 2007). At first glance, the potential of the religious population in general, and the *haredi* public in particular, to conduct an effective consumers' boycott is large, thanks to a general, clear, and agreed agenda; an effective leadership; and social capital for the cooperation a boycott requires. Previously, a campaign against the mobile phone companies to demand that they supply telephones without certain advanced services such as the Internet, owing to the possible inflow of "improper" content, succeeded, and several companies agreed to supply "kosher mobile phones" (Shamir and Ben-Porat, 2007). The Sabbath, however, was a greater challenge as religious-*haredi* purchasing power (and collective commitment) was pitted against the growing popularity of shopping on the Sabbath.

The struggle included threats to boycott companies working on the Sabbath as well as an effort to encourage shopping at stores that remain closed on the Sabbath. Stickers indicating that the business in question closed on the Sabbath, a list of stores observing the Sabbath that was publicized on various websites, or even dedicated credit cards not for use on the Sabbath all formed a part of the campaign to encourage religious people to prefer businesses that observe the Sabbath (Shamir and Ben-Porat, 2007). In February 2006, it was reported that 3,000 customers carried the credit card issued by one of these companies, whereas about 10,000 customers had joined the loyalty program of another company (*Ha'aretz*, February 28, 2006). Other campaigns were directed at specific businesses and shopping malls that operated on the Sabbath. In 1999, the *haredi* Council of Torah Sages called for a boycott of a center near Petah Tikvah. The council explained its call for a boycott:

> We order that everything in our power should be done to prevent and terminate this wicked decree, and hereby instruct and call upon every household in the city and its environs to stop shopping at these stores every day of the week until they turn aside from their evil way.

A local rabbi explained the strategy:

> Let us assume that the profits made from opening on Shabbat are 20 percent and the profits to be made from religious customers are 30 percent. The stores open on Shabbat not for ideological reasons, but for commercial goals, and if the profits to be made on Shabbat are offset [by a boycott] then the owners will do their own calculations.

It soon emerged, however, that businesspeople's calculations were different. As explained by one store owner:

> Rabbi Solomon told me that if we would close on Shabbat he would look after my interests in several different ways. As Shabbat brings in more than 50% of our business, I decided to continue opening on Shabbat. (Ilan, 1999)

In March 2008, a publicized boycott was declared against Dudi Weissman, the owner of the AM-PM chain store. Weissman, who had bought the supermarket chain that year, removed from the shelves the nonkosher food products previously sold there but continued to operate the stores on the Sabbath, one of them near a religious center in Tel Aviv. The rabbis' Committee for the Sanctity of Shabbat issued a public appeal calling for a boycott of all Weissman's businesses, including a chain of stores catering to the *haredi* sector (*Ynet*, March 14, 2008). Despite public declarations by secular individuals that they would buy at Weissman's establishments to compensate for the *haredi* boycott, during the months when the boycott was in force the food chain lost about 30 percent to 50 percent of its income. All efforts to find a compromise between Weissman and the religious leaders failed, yet the AM-PM stores continued to operate on the Sabbath.

Commerce on the Sabbath did not slow down as religious economic-based efforts failed to change the cost-benefit calculations of entrepreneurs. The large profits to be made from opening for business on the Sabbath, the limited size and poverty of the *haredi* communities, and the reluctant response of the religious public all diminished the boycott's impact. Religious businesspeople expressed their skepticism about the chances for the campaign's success and voiced severe criticism of members of the religious public who refrain from eating at a nonkosher restaurant but willingly purchase goods at a store that violates the Sabbath (Shamir and Ben-Porat, 2007). As the interviewees in this research study confirmed, the chain stores selling clothes and electrical appliances did not feel intimidated by the religious public and the threat of a consumer boycott.

Conclusion

Commerce on the Sabbath, like the trade in pork, is powered by economic considerations, but its expansion has required even less political action or legal protection. Rather, as the change in perceptions toward the Sabbath included a majority of Israelis, and as the decision to shop was almost completely separated from ideology or identity, entrepreneurs could operate almost without interference. Earlier secular struggles to allow theaters to operate on the Sabbath used liberal arguments of freedom and individual rights. These liberal arguments played a rather minor role in later developments as liberal ideologists remained reluctant to use them and the courts, usually an address for such claims, refused to accept them. Shopping has become an integral part of the day of rest as a result of consumer demands, entrepreneurial actions, and a weak political system that failed to regulate the day of rest, leaving the decisions to private, market-based calculations.

The economic and social changes and the development of a consumer society in Israel marked the wide gap that evolved between the status quo arrangements and the nonreligious lifestyle. This gap also defied new compromises forged by politicians, the courts, and nongovernmental organizations based on the differentiation of commerce from culture and the supposedly common desire for the Sabbath as a special day. As long as regulations were hardly enforced and demand for shopping was on the rise, secular entrepreneurs felt no need to engage in an ideological or practical confrontation. Rather, entrepreneurs adopted "evasion" strategies, from locating their businesses outside the city centers to employing non-Jewish workers, who were permitted to work on the Sabbath. Thus, it was the practices of entrepreneurs, motivated by considerations of profit, and consumers' demands that redefined the public Sabbath, indicating again the political vacuum described in other chapters and the limited impact of politics on everyday life.

7

Conclusions

The unpacking of secularization attempted here allows us to come to terms with its inconsistencies and contradictions. This unpacking includes distinguishing secularization as a process from secularism as an ideology; measuring secularization in the decline of religious authority; accounting also for non-ideological forces behind the process; observing the unfolding of secularization in a bricolage of inconsistent changing beliefs, practices, and affiliations; recognizing that the outcomes of secularization depend on particular, local conditions; looking for secularization also outside formal political process; and being skeptical regarding the relation between secularization as a process and a tolerant liberal society as its outcome.

As this account of the secularization of Israel has demonstrated, ideology and political struggles explain only part of the changes that have occurred in the past two decades. Civil marriage, civil burial, shops selling pork, and the rapidly expanding commerce on the Sabbath are all evidence for a secularization process unfolding in Israel since the early 1990s. During the same period, however, not only have religious parties and institutions continued to hold formal power, but many Israelis have also declared that they feel closer to religion than ever before and take part in different religious activities. Moreover, when this book was written, women in Israel were still prevented from eulogizing in some state cemeteries and religious leaders order their disciples serving in the military to refuse to serve alongside women and to leave the room when women singers appear. These are just a few examples that demonstrate that Israel, in spite of secularization, is nowhere close to being a secular state or society.

The establishment and resilience of religious or religiously inspired institutions are often attributed to the power of religious parties able to successfully negotiate pacts against the weakness of secular parties and the secular public at large. But, as argued here and elsewhere, religiosity is ingrained deeply in the Israeli state and society. The complex relationship between national identity and religion born in the formative stage of the Zionist movement remains a powerful limitation on secularism and secularization. The secular culture that the Zionist founders attempted to create was riddled with messianic elements and religious terminology. This tension was observed by the philosopher Gerschom Scholem, who wrote in 1926:

People here [in Palestine] are unaware of the implications of their deeds. They believe that they have turned Hebrew into a secular language after they rescued the apocalyptic sting out of it, but that is not the truth... [E]very word that was not created anew but taken from the "good and old" treasure, is full to its brim with explosives.... God will not remain silent in a language in which he was sworn thousands of times to come back to our lives. (in Kimmerling, 2004: 85)

Secularism, much like Scholem's prediction, was sidelined by other developments and, in spite of the founders' disdain toward religious orthodoxy and a declaration of a "break" from the past, failed to become politically dominant. This is not to say that secularism did not exist. Philosophically, long before Zionism, Jewish "free thinkers" challenged the religious establishment. Ideologically, secular Israelis advocated the separation of religion and state in order to grant religious freedom and freedom from religion. Politically, struggles were waged in the name of secularism with different demands associated with religious freedoms. However, this liberal position was shared only by a minority.

Collective national identity in Israel, shared by religious and secular Jews, is deeply anchored in Jewish religion. This pertains not only to symbols and shared memories but also to the instrumental role religion performs in drawing boundaries and providing the legitimacy they require. Religion, in other words, continues to play a critical role in the definition of national boundaries translated into immigration laws, citizenship, and rights. Because it is difficult, if not impossible, to distinguish the (Jewish) nation from (Jewish) religion, the majority of nonreligious Israelis were (and still are) ambivalent toward religion and its role in public life as, on the one hand, it places limitations but, on the other hand, secures privileges. Consequently, many are suspicious of a secularism that seemingly threatens the secure boundaries of the Jewish state. It is hardly surprising that, in this context, secularism (an ideology related to liberalism) would be marginal and secularization (a process) could challenge only informally and only particular elements of the status quo.

The secularization that took off in the late 1980s was different. This process, underpinned by economic and demographic changes, included new players, goals, and strategies that responded to new needs and demands, as well as to the new opportunities that emerged. The decline of religious authority was not registered in formal changes in the status quo. Rather, it was new informal institutions and secularized spaces that provided alternatives by circumventing, rather than clashing with, religious authority. In previous chapters, the interactions among the state and formal rules, secular entrepreneurs, and the public were analyzed to explain how and where secularization unfolded. In this concluding chapter, the overall impact and limitations of this secularization are assessed.

Secularization as Institutional Change

The institutional explanation of the status quo used here locates its establishment at a particular historical moment, as a political compromise that responded to particular needs, demands, and compromises. Relations between religion and the state, between religious and secular ways of life, and between religion and the economy have found different compromises and settlements manifested in institutional arrangements best understood as established rules of the game. The status quo included not only a formal division of authority between the religious and the political but also informal rules, norms, and procedures that structured the choices and behavior of groups and individuals. The power and stability of the status quo can be attributed to the will and ability of leaders, a wide societal consensus, and a path-dependent "normal politics" that operated within the confines of the status quo. In the 1980s, however, the material and ideational foundations of the status quo were shaken and its internal contradictions were exposed so that it no longer seemed a "coherent, self-reinforcing, let alone functional, whole" (Thelen, 1999).

The alterations in domestic and international environments – social, political, and economic – provided new opportunities and incentives for new agents (secular entrepreneurs) to challenge the status quo, even if their goals were far more modest. Secularization, therefore, is measured first and foremost by the general decline of religious authority and challenges to existing religious institutions. It is driven not only by ideological but also by practical preferences and everyday life choices that respond to economic and social changes. Consequently, as the chapters here demonstrated, secularization unfolds in a bricolage of changing beliefs, practices, and affiliations that do not always move in lockstep with one another.

A similar trajectory can be discerned in all four cases studied here that underline the developments in Israel. First, new challenges to the status quo combined ideological and non-ideological-secular elements with more practical and materialist ones, with the latter becoming more and more dominant. And, second, the focus was shifted from the formal political sphere to the courts and, more importantly, to private initiatives and informal processes. Previous challenges to the status quo were usually undertaken by groups and individuals, self-defined as secular and holding a political agenda that sought to restrict religious power. Even when struggles were waged over particular and concrete issues, a comprehensive ideology was at the background. More recent challenges to the status quo, conversely, were presented by FSU immigrants and the consumerist middle class, with different goals and strategies, often not described in secular terms or in political language. FSU immigrants, especially those not recognized as Jews by religious orthodoxy, suffered directly from the Orthodox monopoly, not being allowed burial in Jewish cemeteries and prevented from marriage in Israel. Their demands (Chapters 3 and 4) were usually concrete, pragmatic, and particular. Economic liberalization provided another momentum for secularization. The rising consumer culture had the obvious impact on shopping on the Sabbath but also on a growing gourmet culture often oblivious to religious restrictions, as well as a commercialization of marriage and burial services that included secularized elements. Legitimacy still drew on liberal-universal arguments of freedom but more and more on economic rationality.

Secularization entered a new phase in the 1990s when it changed from a minority position against a consensual status quo to a wider, often incoherent, movement against an eroding status quo. These new demands were met, and at times created, by new entrepreneurs with different motivations, from ideological-secular ones hoping to bring about a secular society to ones addressing particular needs in return for profits. In practice, goals and strategies are often a mixed bag that defies rigid categorizations. Economic entrepreneurs who sell pork or operate on the Sabbath will use liberal arguments of freedom to fight restrictions, and ideological entrepreneurs who promote civil marriage and burial may become professional providers of secular services or use economic means to advance their cause. Individual choices display the same dynamics. Choosing a civil burial can be a private, aesthetic preference, eating pork a habit brought from the FSU, civil marriage an alternative for being rejected by the Orthodox rabbinate, and shopping on Sabbath a leisure choice. Nonetheless, these actions and choices, individually, whether intended or not, defy religious authority. This defiance is even more important when actions of different entrepreneurs with different goals and ideologies can, without planning or coordination, render existing arrangements optional and challenge institutions' cohesion. Secularization, as an institutional change, therefore, is shaped not only by conscious and ideological action but also by everyday choices and actions of entrepreneurs or individuals. These choices and actions, behind the backs of individuals; and possibly separated from their political desires, aggregate to form new secularized spaces.

New preferences, demands, and choices of Jewish Israelis, regardless of their goals and intentions, amounted to what can be described as an institutional change. By the late 1990s, civil marriage and burial services were accessible, restrictions on the Sabbath were minimized, and nonkosher establishments were widely available. However, in spite of these changes, the formal status of the Orthodox rabbinate remained intact, Israelis continued to profess religious attachments as before, and nonliberal policies toward minorities and women seemed to increase. These contradictions and limitations can be explained by three distinctions developed earlier in this book. First, expanding the definition of politics from the formal arena of parties and elections incorporates new channels of activity that formal analysis may overlook. Second, understanding secularization as a decline of religious authority, rather than a comprehensive value change, allows us to come to terms with inconsistencies and contradictions within the process. Third, separating secularization, a process driven by different forces, from secularism, an ideology associated with a liberal worldview and a commitment to individual freedoms, enables us to grasp the gap between secularization and a liberal order.

The Politics of Secularization

The new secularization differed in the way demands were framed and justified and in the political channels used by secular entrepreneurs to advance their goals. Claims against the status quo of veteran, ideological secularists combined liberal arguments of freedom with republican claims of rights based on their contribution to the collective. When religious legislation attempted to curtail the operation of a kibbutz meat factory that produced pork, not only were liberal arguments of freedom to choose what to eat raised, but also the contribution of the kibbutz members to the country – namely, their army service – was highlighted and contrasted with ultra-Orthodox exemption. The republican discourse was used again in the 1990s. FSU immigrants serving in the army but not recognized as Jews and prevented from marriage provided an effective symbol to challenge the Orthodox monopoly. Similarly, the outrage over fallen soldiers who could not be buried in a Jewish cemetery had a far stronger impact than ordinary citizens treated the same way and strengthened demands for reform. Republican arguments of contribution (or its lack) are still effective to mobilize the nonreligious public against the ultra-Orthodox, as the popular campaigns for an "equal draft" that demand the conscription of yeshiva students demonstrate.

Liberal arguments remain a common secular strategy, especially for non-Orthodox groups that demand freedom of choice in marriage and burial, equality for women, and formal recognition of their institutions. Gradually, however, the liberal freedoms and republican claims gave way to economic arguments and new political strategies in new arenas. Republican and liberal freedoms belong in the political or legislative sphere in which struggles to change existing legislation and regulations take place. Thus, secular entrepreneurs who sought to change rules that applied to marriage, burial, nonkosher meat, and commerce on Sabbath initially concentrated their efforts in formal political channels and liberal arguments. These efforts met not only the resistance of religious or religiously inspired institutions, but also wider public ambivalence or apathy that hindered significant mobilization. Most important, as the different cases indicate, secular entrepreneurs encountered a stagnant political system unable or unwilling to introduce significant reforms or to adapt the institutional arrangements to the changes – demographic and economic – and the new needs and demands they entailed.

The Supreme Court, which since the 1980s had adopted an activist doctrine, became an alternative channel for secular entrepreneurs and for individuals who believed they unjustly suffered the consequences of the Orthodox monopoly. The liberal discourse dominated the debate in the courts as civil marriage and burial were presented in terms of individual rights, equality, and freedom of choice. This language, used by secular entrepreneurs or individuals seeking the help of the court, applied both to questions of marriage and burial and to issues that pertain to commerce, where the logic of the law and the logic of the market (Mautner, 2011: 6) intertwined. The court rulings, as in the case of marriage, provided important outlets for secular individuals who could register their marriage abroad or enjoy rights as cohabitants. The court also restricted municipal

TABLE 7.1. *Regulation of Religious Life*

	Ultra-Orthodox (%)	Religious (%)	Traditional (%)	Secular (%)	
Do you think that the Knesset should legislate on questions of Jewish law – for example, the Sabbath or kashrut?					
1 (Definitely yes)	47	29.6	19.1	7.9	Cramer's $V = 0.210^*$
2	24.2	39.4	39.5	26.2	Kendall's tau-c $= 0.242^*$
3	12.1	14.1	24.8	35.7	
4 (Definitely not)	16.7	16.9	19.6	30.2	

* $P < 0.05$; ** $P < 0.01$.
Source: Author's own survey, 2009.

decisions on closing businesses operating on the Sabbath or selling pork and demanded that the government implement its decisions to build civil cemeteries. The court, however, in spite of its liberal inclination, was confined by the political system as well as by religious groups' growing public resentment of its activism. Secular entrepreneurs, by the late 1990s, seemed to have exhausted much of the potential of the court as an agent for change.

For many Israelis, religious and secular alike, the political system is perceived as being incapable of regulating religious affairs, but secular Israelis strictly object to political involvement in legislation on religious issues (see Table 7.1). The weak political system, the rulings of the court, and the demands of a growing number of individual citizens have opened new opportunities for secular entrepreneurs. Even though a comprehensive political change seemed a remote possibility, the loopholes in the system allowed entrepreneurs to operate comfortably and, because or the weakness of the political system, could be widened. Loopholes have rapidly turned through entrepreneurial actions into alternative channels, underpinned by market logic, and into secularized spaces where religious authority has had a limited influence. Subpolitics, a term borrowed from Ulrich Beck and used here to explain this phenomenon of new political channels, captures well the dynamic in which citizens who lost faith in formal politics channel their political activity to new arenas. In Beck's account, subpolitics includes different political strategies that take place outside formal politics. In this study of secularization, subpolitics is stretched to incorporate also actions that are political in their consequences but not necessarily in their intentions or motivations. These actions include those taken by both entrepreneurs and their "clientele," who have contributed to secularization in their choices and practices even if their intentions were entirely different.

The secularization process described here unfolded outside the sphere of formal politics, but remained political in its outcomes and implications, unfolding in an "economic story" and a "geographic story." Economically, pork turned from a symbol to a commodity, marriage and burial services were offered (also) by business entrepreneurs, and commerce on the Sabbath became a business decision of store owners. Geographically, secularization can be mapped in real spaces where nonkosher meat is sold, private cemeteries offer their services, and commerce on the Sabbath takes place. These spaces, placed on a real map, stretch across the country from north to south. This secularization was not necessarily the outcome of a planned campaign or a conscious secular individual orientation. As demonstrated before, the decisions of entrepreneurs to open their businesses on the Sabbath can be a simple cost-benefit calculation and the decisions of people to shop on the Sabbath a choice of leisure. Civil burial can be the result of entrepreneurial business decisions and aesthetic preferences for a coffin. Similarly, the decision of people to get married outside the rabbinate may be a result of necessity, as for FSU immigrants not recognized as Jews, rather than a secular preference. Citizens responding to secular entrepreneurship (and some of the entrepreneurs) will associate their choices to practical everyday preferences rather than to a coherent secular commitment. Accordingly, secular entrepreneurs are likely to be more successful outside the formal political sphere and would generally prefer strategies that avoid conflict and confrontation.

The choices of entrepreneurs and individuals, regardless of their intentions, aggregate to a series of institutional changes often not formally registered in rules and regulations. The choices are "political," therefore, in their outcome but the limitations of this politics, both in regard to the potential for a wider comprehensive change and for the needs of individuals and groups outside the consensus, should not be missed. In practice, civil marriage and burial became an option for Israelis willing and able to use private services, shopping on the Sabbath became popular among Israelis of different orientations, and pork ceased to be a taboo in Israel. Alongside these changes, however, religion continued to hold significant power over other aspects of public and private life and individual religiosity thrived alongside secularization. This incongruence requires, first, attention to the contradictions within secularization and, second, an assessment of the overall importance of these institutional changes.

The Contradictions of Secularization

Secularization, it has been argued here and elsewhere, is a process that does not necessarily end with a secular state and society. Israeli secularization, reflected in the choices and identities of Jewish Israelis, is fraught with ambivalence, inconsistencies, and contradictions. These contradictions are the result, first, of the inherent insecurity of Israeli secularism and its difficulty in disengaging from religion and, second, of the different forces that underpin secularization. Three sources and paths of secularization were identified in this book that are independent of one another but interact in different choices and struggles: ideological or principled secularism, secularization of everyday life, and demographic secularism.

Ideological or "principled" secularism is a mixture of ideologies and worldviews that share the desire to restrict religious authority over private and public lives. For some, this restriction should involve a complete religion–state separation; for others, it is about providing space for non-Orthodox versions of Judaism. Although this secularism emphasizes individual rights and freedoms, secularists, in some cases, can be more antireligious than liberal, especially when tolerance, respect, and minority rights are concerned. Nevertheless, Israelis who are committed to equality and freedom, and who vote for left-wing parties, are likely to hold a secular worldview. In the secularization process described here, principled secularism can be observed in entrepreneurs who offer alternative marriage and burial rituals and individuals who choose to take part in those rituals. Participants in this process are usually Ashkenazi, educated, and upper-middle class, with a "secular" identity. Secularization and secularism, in this case, match as identities, beliefs, and behaviors display a (relative) coherence, albeit for a small number of Jewish Israelis.

"Demographic" secularism, propelled by FSU immigrants, was of a somewhat different character. As do the veteran Israelis described earlier, FSU immigrants generally identify themselves as secular and are agnostic in their beliefs. However, their political attitude, described as "pragmatic-secular-rightist and ethnic" (Al Haj, 2002), keeps them apart from other secular activists. This right-wing secularism challenges Jewish Orthodoxy but adheres to the basic consensus among the Jewish majority in Israel regarding the Jewish ethnocentric political culture of the state (Shumsky, 2001). This secularization, therefore, is not based on an all-encompassing liberal perception, but is particularistic in regard to its aims and is restricted mainly to the internal Jewish discourse.

Finally, the secularization of everyday life, underscored by economic changes, involves Israelis of different ethnic and class backgrounds. This participation – most evident in shopping on the Sabbath – is often devoid of any ideological component and is regarded as a practical decision or a leisure preference. Consequently, it includes not only secular Ashkenazim and FSU immigrants, but also those identified as "traditional," combining a religious identity with secular practices. Mizrahim and Ashkenazim who developed a strategy of cultural accommodation could take part in this part of secularization yet maintain a conservative position regarding the role of religion in their communities and remain strict in observance of some rituals and practices, respect for religious authority (against liberal reforms), and rejection of political liberalism.

The descriptions of ideological, demographic, and everyday life secularizations are ideal-types set against a dynamic reality. Mixed displays of religiosity and secularity defy attempts to place individual Jewish Israelis on a continuum from "religious" and "secular," to delineate a linear course of secularization, or to place them in one category of secularization. Although religious Orthodox Jews and committed secularists demonstrate a more or less coherent pattern, the majority of Israelis show different levels of beliefs and attitudes, a selective choice of practices and rituals, and different responses toward various opportunities associated with secularization. Thus, the majority of Israelis express support for allowing commerce on the Sabbath, but at the same time would like the Sabbath to remain a "special day." Furthermore, many Israelis support the idea of civil marriage and burial, but would prefer to be married by an Orthodox rabbi and have an Orthodox funeral themselves.

The incoherence has a direct bearing on the strategies of secular entrepreneurs. Ideological secularism and secularization driven by FSU immigrants have had common goals, especially the desire to allow secular services of burial and marriage. However, whereas secular activists aimed for a secular or pluralist setting that would maximize freedom, FSU immigrants and their leaders were looking for practical solutions. Thus, solutions that included specific provisions for immigrants not recognized as Jews were acceptable for parties representing the immigrants, to the dismay of secular activists who hoped to achieve a comprehensive change. FSU immigrants, for their part, were reluctant to take part in liberal struggles, because of either a general political apathy or a more particular suspicion of liberal secularists.

Conversely, adopting immigrants as their main clientele proved a double-edged sword for secular entrepreneurs who wanted, beyond legitimacy, to become an appealing alternative for mainstream Israelis.

Immigrants, on one hand, provided a strong case for reforms in marriage and burial in order to answer to real and immediate needs. The "republican equation" of images of immigrant soldiers in military fatigues who served in the army but were prevented from marriage in Israel because they are not Jewish, or, fallen soldiers who could not be buried next to their Jewish comrades, evoked strong sympathy for their hardship and resentment toward the rabbinate. However, on the other hand, entrepreneurs were concerned that turning secular alternatives into solutions for the needy would turn away veteran Israelis. Burial provided a striking example of this dilemma, as the state-run civil cemetery developed an image of a "Russian" cemetery and, conversely, in some of the prestigious private secular cemeteries non-Jews were buried separately or were refused burial altogether. Secular Israelis, it turned out, may wish for a civil funeral but would like to be buried in a Jewish cemetery.

Between Secular, Secularized, and Liberal

The secularized spaces described previously developed amid the religious monopoly, the varying religious identities and attachments of many Israelis and alongside a political culture that has been described as a nonliberal democracy. The seeming mismatch between secular behavior and religious affiliations has been explained, first, by defining secularization as a decline of religious authority rather than of religiosity and, second, by a bricolage form of secularization in which beliefs, practices, and identities unfold in a set of personal or group choices that are not necessarily coherent. Thus, shopping on the Sabbath or even eating pork does not necessarily contradict adherence to other religious commandments and practices, either because of the overlap between religion and national identity or because people continue to identify with religion or some of its aspects. Similarly, choices of nonreligious Israelis often did not stray too far from traditional habits. New marriage patterns include new family structures but largely affirm traditional family patterns, and the ceremonies tend to replicate parts of the traditional ceremony. Similarly, secular funerals often include religious elements, such as the Kaddish prayer, alongside burial in a coffin. Non-Orthodox marriage and burial, therefore, have defied (Orthodox) religious authority but often maintained Jewish cultural attachments.

Secularization develops independently not only from a coherent secular belief system, but also from liberal values. This split between secularization as a process and secularism as a liberal worldview with a commitment to tolerance and equality has significant implications for the status of minorities and marginalized groups in Israel. Israel's description is as a "nonliberal democracy" that, in contrast to the liberal democracy, whose first priority is the individual and his or her rights, relates to the strong emphasis on the collective or community and the hierarchies and exclusions it entails (Ben-Porat and Feniger, 2009). Israel is not only a nonliberal democracy but also an "ethnic democracy" (Smooha, 1997) with a stratified citizenship structure that excludes and marginalizes groups according to ethnicity or gender. Participation is more a privilege than a right and is reserved to those who act in the collective interest. The term "nonliberal democracy," however, pertains not only to the regime structure but also to the particular society and political culture (Ben-Porat and Feniger, 2009). Antiliberalism and ethnocentrism, therefore, are entrenched characteristics of Israeli society and include three principal aspects: the priority of security over democratic values, the aspiration for consensus, and the exclusion of minorities (Ben-Dor, Pedahtzur, and Hasisi, 2003).

The illiberal character of Israeli democracy has significant consequences for the status of women, homosexuals, and Arab citizens of the state. The secularization of Israeli society described here seems to have a limited, if any, effect on the illiberal character of Israeli state and society. Differently stated, liberalization, measured in commitment to values such as tolerance and equality, either lags behind secularization or is completely independent from it. Previous research found that people who shop on the Sabbath were not more tolerant toward marginalized groups in Israeli society – homosexuals and especially the Arab minority (Ben-Porat and Feniger, 2009). The data used in this work show similar trends (see Table 7.2). As discussed throughout this book, secular behavior (measured in defying religious rules and authority) is often devoid of any political or ideological commitment and can be removed from a liberal worldview. Even a secular identity can be only partly liberal, supporting civil marriage and burial but reluctant to support equality for Arabs. Whereas people who identify themselves as secular tend to be more liberal than others regarding questions of equality to Arabs, a significant number among them express explicitly nonliberal attitudes as they support preferences for Jews, reject measures to reduce economic gaps between Jews and Arabs, and oppose mixed neighborhoods (see Table 7.2).

These findings explain why Israeli society remains illiberal in many measures and are indicative that secularization, a result of everyday life practices, and liberal democracy can follow separate trajectories and that even secularism, a liberal worldview, can be restricted in its application to certain "others" excluded from the collective.

TABLE 7.2. *Religiosity/Secularity and Liberalism*

	Ultra-Orthodox (%)	Religious (%)	Traditional (%)	Secular (%)	
Israel should give preference to Jews in government jobs					
1 (Strongly oppose)	1.5	0	3.0	6.7	Cramer's $V = 0.213^*$
2	3.0	8.5	9.8	23.3	
3	1.5	9.9	13.2	16.6	Kendall's tau-c $= -0.265$
4	28.4	33.8	43.6	32.1	
5 (Strongly support)	65.7	47.9	30.3	21.3	
The state should invest more resources in the Arab sector schools to reduce the gap between Jews and Arabs in Israel					
1 (Strongly oppose)	30.8	11.0	9.8	8.2	Cramer's $V = 0.169^*$
2	27.7	30.7	32.5	19.9	
3	18.5	15.1	19.2	17.3	Kendall's tau-c $= 0.186^*$
4	21.5	34.2	27.8	40.8	
5 (Strongly agree)	1.5	2.7	33.3	13.8	
Arabs should be allowed to buy or rent apartments in Jewish neighborhoods					
1 (Strongly oppose)	50.7	41.7	27.4	13.2	Cramer's $V = 0.239^*$
2	41.8	31.9	37.6	26	
3	6.0	8.3	15.4	14.6	Kendall's tau-c $= 0.317^*$
4	1.5	18.1	17.1	36.5	
5 (Strongly agree)	0	0	2.6	9.6	

$^* P < 0.05$; $^{**} P < 0.01$.
Source: Author's own survey, 2009.

Secularized but Not Secular

Secularization is a process whereby religious authority declines but religion may still hold enough public and private resonance to ensure that secularism remains a nondominant ideology rather than a political order. In the past decades, Israeli society has gone through a secularization process but Israel is unlikely to become secular. Secularization, as argued throughout this book, is constrained not only by politically entrenched religious institutions and personal religious identities but also by the ambivalence of secularism itself. National identity, symbols, exclusive claims for land, and the national boundaries all relied upon and were all closely tied to religion. These limitations did not exclude the possibility of a secular version of nationalism and the continuous attempts of Israelis to carve an identity that is either secular or independent from religious Orthodoxy and its institutions. This search included not only political struggles but also cultural alternatives that challenged the Orthodox hegemony institutionalized in the status quo. In many cases, however, these new identities challenged the contents but have simultaneously re-affirmed the boundaries of the Jewish state. Israeli secularism was bound up with more generic characteristics of its nemesis more than some of its proponents are willing to acknowledge, exposing the shaky ground on which secularism often stands and the constant need for critical self-reflection.

Ideological struggles associated with secularism that sought a formal institutional change have largely failed. It was a secularization process advanced through nonideological forces and nonformal channels that created new opportunities for ritual and leisure choice. These new secularized spaces were the result not of struggles but rather of the ability to take advantage of loopholes and circumvent rather than confront existing institutional arrangements. Thus, even though formally, for reasons discussed earlier, rules and regulations have hardly changed, it was the informal processes that mattered. In these new comfort zones – secularized spaces – Israelis had new choices regarding significant rituals and everyday practices of shopping and leisure. Secularization, consequently, was both political and de-politicizing: political, in bringing institutional change but de-politicizing in allowing individuals to settle for comfort zones achieved with limited if any struggle.

This de-politicized secularization falls short of a secular order and is likely to remain so for the near future for several reasons. First, religion, especially in the current political atmosphere, will continue to serve an indispensible role in consolidating and demarcating national boundaries, guaranteeing secular ambivalence. Second, the political vacuum that enabled secular spaces allows also the creation of religious ones. In recent years, Orthodox demands have led to new private and public services in which strict separation of men and women is maintained and to demands to extend strict religious rules into more spaces. In the military, for example, some religious recruits, with the support of their leaders, demand not to serve alongside women and to receive food with a kosher certificate from ultra-Orthodox rabbis. This development can be explained, third, by the religious reaction to demographic and economic changes. As elsewhere, global and local changes in Israel bring forth religious fundamentalism. Finally, fourth, although the division of Israelis into self-identification categories (religious, traditional, and secular) remains stable, there is an indication that younger Israelis tend to be more traditional and religious, possibly as a result of higher birth rates among these groups. What this religiosity would mean is yet to be seen, but a secular identity and worldview seem unlikely.

Secular and nonreligious Israelis, especially of the middle class and in the Tel Aviv area, have been freed to a large extent from religious authority and can live much of their life (and even beyond), if they choose to, free of religious interference. The alternatives they take advantage of – nonkosher supermarkets or civil marriage – were created or sustained by the market, largely independent from the political realm, or by loopholes of the weakening political system. Ironically, these processes seem to provide the political protection to sustain the status quo and the Orthodox monopoly as struggles against religious authority are jettisoned for the purchase of an alternative – a private cemetery, or a wedding abroad. Thus, on one hand, the secular camp is made up of a large majority with little commitment to struggle and an ideological minority with limited power. On the other hand, alternative solutions dissipate the political energy that exists on particular issues of secularist concerns in everyday life. It is not accidental that secular struggles for the equality of women, recognition of non-Orthodox Jewish communities, or the right of every citizen to marry have all but disappeared from the political landscape. Principled struggles for freedom and equality, the core of secularism, remain beyond the pale of secularization. More than sixty years ago, Israel's Declaration of Independence stated:

The state of Israel will be open for Jewish immigration and for the Ingathering of the Exiles; it will foster the development of the country for the benefit of all its inhabitants; it will be based on freedom, justice, and peace as envisaged by the prophets of Israel; it will ensure complete equality of social and political rights to all its inhabitants irrespective of religion, race or sex; it will guarantee freedom of religion, conscience, language, education, and culture; it will safeguard the Holy Places of all religions; and it will be faithful to the principles of the Charter of the United Nations.

Is secularization likely to close the gap between the promise of the declaration and contemporary reality? Secularization, as the Israeli case demonstrates, is propelled by individual interests and choices of entrepreneurs and ordinary citizens. These choices, commercial or cultural, can be loosely related to a secular worldview and may not require political organization, effort, or commitment. Although these choices can aggregate to an institutional change measured in the decline of religious authority, this change is likely to be limited in scope and to leave questions of freedom and inequality unanswered. Secularism, conversely, if it remains true to its liberal ethos, will require generosity, openness, solidarity, and a real political commitment.

Bibliography

Abramov, Zalman S. 1979. *Perpetual Dilemma: Jewish Religion in the Jewish State*. Cranbury, NJ: Fairleigh Dickinson University Press.

Abramovitz, Henry. 2000. "A Funeral in Jerusalem: An Anthropological Viewpoint," in Abohev et al. (eds.), *Israel: A Local Anthropology*. Tel-Aviv: Cherikover (Hebrew).

Al Haj, Majid. 2002. "Ethnic Mobilization in an Ethno-National State: the Case of Immigrants from the Former Soviet Union in Israel," *Ethnic and Racial Studies* 25(2): 238–257.

Ammerman, Nancy. 2007. "Introduction," in N. Ammerman (ed.), *Everyday Religion; Observing Modern Religious Lives*. Oxford: Oxford University Press.

Appadurai, Arjun. 1990. "Disjuncture and Difference in the Global Cultural Economy," *Public Culture* 2(2): 1–15.

Arad, Nurit. 1993. "A Story with Beef," *Yediot Aharonot*, October 25 (Hebrew).

Archer, Margaret. 1990. "Foreword," in M. Elbrow and E. King, *Globalization, Knowledge and Society*. London: Sage.

Arian, Asher, David Nachmias, Doron Navot, and Daniel Shani (2003). *The Israeli Democracy Index*. Jerusalem: The Israel Democracy Institute (Hebrew).

Arian, Asher, Tamar Hermann, Nir Atmor, Yael Hadar, Yuval Lebel, and Hila Zaban. 2008. *Auditing Israeli Democracy 2008: Between the State and Civil Society*. Jerusalem: Israeli Democracy Institute (Hebrew).

Arrighi, Giovanni. 1994. *The Long Twentieth Century*. London: Verso.

Audi, Robert. 1989. "The Separation of Church and State and the Obligations of Citizenship," *Philosophy and Public Affairs* 18(3): 259–296.

Barak-Erez, Daphne. 2003. "Metamorphosis of the Pig," *Gilgulo Shel Hazir, Mishpatim* 33: 403–457 (Hebrew).

———. 2007. *Outlawed Pigs: Law, Religion, and Culture in Israel*. Madison: University of Wisconsin Press.

Barber, Benjamin. 1992. "Jihad vs. McWorld," *The Atlantic Monthly*, March 1992.

Bauer, Yehuda. 2005. "The Intellectual Development of the Jewish Humanist Movement," in Y. Malkin (ed.), *Jewish Secular Culture*. Tel-Aviv: Keter (Hebrew).

Bauman, Zygmunt. 1992. *Intimations of Postmodernity*. London: Routledge.

———. 2007. *Consuming Life*. Cambridge, UK: Polity Press.

Beck, Ulrich. 1996. "World Risk Society as Cosmopolitan Society? Ecological Questions in a Framework of Manufactured Uncertainties," *Theory, Culture & Society* 13(4): 1–32.

———. 1997. "Subpolitics," *Organization & Environment* 10(1): 52–65.

———. 1999. *World Risk Society*. Cambridge, UK: Polity Press.

Beckford, James. 2002. *Social Theory and Religion*. Cambridge: Cambridge University Press.

Beit Daniel. 2007. *There is an Equal Jewish Marriage*. http://www.beit-daniel. org.il/pics/page_files/file56.PDF (Hebrew).

Beit-Halahmi, Benjamin. 1992. *Despair and Deliverance: Private Salvation in Contemporary Israel*. New York: SUNY Press.

Belasco, Warren. 2002. "Food Matters: Perspectives on an Emerging Field," in W. Belasco and P. Scranton (eds.), *Food Nations: Selling Taste in Consumer Societies*. New York: Routledge, pp. 2–23.

Bell, Daniel. 1980. "The Return of the Sacred? The Arguments on the Future of Religion," in *The Winding Passage, Essays and Sociological Journeys 1960–1980*. Cambridge, MA: Alt Books.

Bell, David and Gill Valentine. 1997. *Consuming Geographies: We Are Where We Eat*. London: Routledge.

Bellah, Robert N. 1967. "Civil Religion in America," *Daedalus* 96: 1–21.

Ben-Amos, Avner and Eyal Ben-Ari. 1995. "Resonance and Reverberation: Ritual and Bureaucracy in the State Funerals of the French Third Republic," *Theory and Society* 24(2): 163–191.

Ben-Dor, Gabriel, Ami Pedhazur, and Badi Hasisi. 2003. "Anti-Liberalism and the Use of Force in Israeli Democracy," *Journal of Military Sociology* 31, 1: 119–142;

Ben-Porat, Guy. 2000. "In a State of Holiness; Rethinking Israeli Secularism," *Alternatives* 25(2): 223–246.

———. 2005. "Same Old Middle East? The New Middle East and the Double Movement," *International Relations* 19(1): 39–62.

Ben-Porat, Guy and Yariv Feniger. 2009. "Live and Let Buy, Consumerism, Secularization and Liberalism," *Comparative Politics* 41(3): 293–313.

Ben-Rafael, Eliezer. 2007. "Mizrahi and Russian Challenges to Israel's Dominant Culture: Divergences and Convergences," *Israel Studies* 12(3): 68–91.

Ben-Rafael, Eliezer and Nissim Leon. 2006. "Ethnicity, Religiosity and Politics: The Question of the Sources of Ultra-Orthodoxy among Mizrahim," in U. Cohen, E. Ben-Rafael, A. Bareli, and E. Yaar (eds.), *Israel and Modernity*. Sde Boker: Merkaz le-moreshet Ben-Gurion (Hebrew), pp. 285–312 (Hebrew).

Ben-Simon, Daniel. 1998. "Who Will Stop the Haredi Sledge?" *Haaretz*, December 11 (Hebrew).

Berger, Peter L. 1996. "Secularism in Retreat," *The National Interest*, Winter: 3–12.

———. 1969. *The Sacred Canopy*. New York: Anchor Books.

———. 1999. "Desecularization of the World," in P. Berger (ed.), *The Desecularization of the World*. Washington, DC: Ethics and Public Policy Center.

Berger, Peter, Grace Davie, and Effie Fokas. 2008. *Religious America. Secular Europe?* Surrey, UK: Ashgate.

Boggs, Carl. 2000. *The End of Politics: Corporate Power and the Decline in Public Sphere*. New York and London: Guilford Press.

Broide, Haim. 1977. *Life Paths*. Private publication (Hebrew).

Bruce, Steve. 2003. *Politics and Religion*. Cambridge, UK: Blackwell.

———. 2006. "Secularization and the Impotence of Individualized Religion," *The Hedgehog Review*, Spring and Summer: 35–45.

Cady, Linell. 2005. "Secularism, Secularizing and Secularization: Reflections on Stout's Democracy and Tradition," *Journal of the American Academy of Religion* 73(3): 871–885.

Calderon, Ruth. 1999. "The Marriage as Midrash," in O. Piltz (ed.), *Towards Weddings*. Tel-Aviv: Alma (Hebrew).

Caplan, Kimmy. 2007. *Internal Popular Discourse in Israeli Haredi Society*. Jerusalem: Shazar Center (Hebrew).

Caplan, Pat. 1997. "Approaches to the Study of Food, Health and Identity, in P. Caplan (ed.), *Food, Health and Identity*. London: Routledge, pp. 1–31.

Carmeli, Yoram and Kalman Appelbaum, 2004. "Introduction," in Y. Carmeli and K. Appelbaum (eds.), *Consumption and Market Society in Israel*. New York: Oxford University Press.

Casanova, Jose. 1994. *Public Religions in the Modern World*. Chicago: University of Chicago Press.

———. 2006. "Rethinking Secularization: A Global Comparative Perspective," *The Hedgehog Review*, Spring/Summer: 7–22.

———. 2009. "The Secular and Secularism," *Social Research* 76(4): 1049–1066.

Chaves, Mark, 1994. "Secularization as Declining Religious Authority," *Social Forces* 72(3), pp. 749–774.

Chen, Shoshana. 2000. "Sabbath Morning, a Beautiful Day," *Yediot Aharonot*, Yom Kippur Supplement, October 8 (Hebrew).

———. 2004. "Who Loves the Sabbath?" *Yediot Aharonot*, Economic Supplement, February 17 (Hebrew).

Cherlin, Andrew J. 2004. "The Deinstitutionalization of American Marriage," *Journal of Marriage and Family* 66: 848–861.

Cohen, Asher. 1997. "Religion and State: Secularists, Religious and Haredim," in Z. Zameret and H. Yablonka (eds.), *The First Decade*. Jerusalem: Yad Ben-Zvi (Hebrew).

Cohen, Asher and Jonathan Rynhold. 2005. "Social Covenants: the Solution to the Crisis of Religion and State in Israel?", *Journal of Church and State* 47, 4:725–746.

Connolly, William E. 1999 *Why I Am Not a Secularist* Minnesota: Minnesota University Press.

Coontz, Stephanie. 2004. "The World Historical Transformation of Marriage," *Journal of Marriage and Family* 66: 974–979.

Cott, Nancy. 1998. "Marriage and Women's Citizenship in the United States, 1830–1934," *American Historical Review* 103: 1440–1474.

Coussin, Orna. 2001. "How Much Does it Cost," *Ha'aretz*, December 27 (Hebrew).

Cox, Harvey. 1965. *The Secular City*. New York: Macmillan.

Cristi, Marcela and Lorne L. Dawson. 2007. "Civil Religion in America and in Global Context," in J.A. Beckford and N.J. Demerath III (eds.), *The Sage Handbook of the Sociology of Religion*. Los Angeles: Sage, pp. 267–292.

Dalton, Russell. 2004. *Democratic Challenges, Democratic Choices*. Oxford: Oxford University Press.

Davie, Grace. 1994. *Religion in Britain since 1945: Believing Without Belonging*. Oxford: Blackwell.

———. 2007. "Vicarious Religion: A Methodological Challenge" in N.T. Ammerman (ed.), *Everyday Religion: Observing Modern Religious Lives*. Oxford: Oxford University Press.

Degani, Avni and Rina Degani. 2004. "Patterns of Russian Food Consumption Habits," research for the Manufacturers Association, Geokartography (Hebrew).

Demerath, N.J. 2000. "The Varieties of Sacred Experience: Finding the Sacred in the Secular Glove," *Journal for the Scientific Study of Religion* 39(1): 1–11.

Devetak, Richard and Richard Higgot. 1999. "Justice unbound? Globalization, states and the transformation of the social bond," *International Affairs*, 75(3): 483–498.

Diamond, Larry and Richard Gunther. 2001. "Introduction," in L. Diamond and R. Gunther (eds.), *Political Parties and Democracy*. Baltimore, MD: Johns Hopkins University Press.

Dobbelaere, Karel. 1981. "Secularization: A Multi-Dimensional Concept," *Current Sociology* 29(2): 3–153.

———. 1999. "Toward an Integrated Perspective on the Process Related to the Descriptive Concept of Secularization," *Sociology of Religion* 60(3): 229–247.

Don-Yehia, Eliezer. 2000. "Conflict Management of Religious Issues: The Israeli Case in a Comparative Perspective," in R. Hazan and M. Maor (eds.), *Parties, Elections and Cleavages*. London: Frank Cass, pp. 85–108

Don-Yehia, Eliezer and Charles Liebman. 1984. *Civil Religion in Israel: Traditional Judaism and Political Culture in the Jewish State*. Berkeley, CA: University of California Press.

Dovrin, Nurit. 2006. "Marriages of Israelis Abroad and the Role of FSU Immigrants," *Megamot* 44(3): 477–506 (Hebrew).

Eichner, Maxine. 2006. "Marriage and the Elephant: State Regulation of Intimate Relationships between Adults," *Bepress Legal Series*, Paper 1646.

Ein, Jason. 2004. "The Future of the "Death-Care" Industry," http://www.forbes.com/2004/10/08/cz_1008findsvpdeathcare.html.

Eisenstadt, S. N. 2000. "Multiple Modernities," *Daedalus* 129(1): 1–29.

Elam, Yigal. 2000. *Judaism as a Status Quo*. Tel-Aviv: Am Over (Hebrew).

El-Or, Tamar and Eran Neriah. 2003. "The Haredi Wanderer," in E. Sivan and K. Caplan (eds.), *Israeli Haredim: Integration without Assimilation?* Jerusalem: Van Leer (Hebrew).

Ettinger, Yair. 2011a. "A Canopy that Bypasses the Rabbinate," *Ha'aretz*, October 21 (Hebrew).

———. 2011b. "The Kibbutz Is Secular, the Funeral Religious," *Ha'aretz*, October 11 (Hebrew).

Fantasia, Rick. 1995. "Fast Food in France," *Theory and Society* 24: 201–243.

Fieldhouse, George. 1995. *Food and Nutrition*. London: Chapman and Hall.

Ferziger, Adam S. 2008. "Religion for the Secular," *Journal of Modern Jewish Studies* 7(1): 67–90.

Fineman, Martha. 2006. "The Meaning of Marriage," in A. Bernstein (ed.), *Marriage Proposals: Questioning a Legal Status*. New York: New York University Press.

Flanagan, Daniel Otto. 1979. "Sunday Blue Laws: A New Hypocrisy," *Notre Dame Lawyer* April: 716–729.

Fogiel-Bijaoui, Sylvie. 1999. "Families in Israel: Postfeminism, Feminism and the State," in D. Izraeli, et al. (eds.), *Sex, Gender, Politics: Women in Israel*. Tel Aviv: Hakibbutz Hameuhad, 1999, pp. 107–167 (Hebrew).

———. 2005. "Families in Israel: Post Modernity, Feminism and the State," in J.L. Roopnarine and U.P. Gielen (eds.), *Families in Global Perspective*. Boston: Allyn & Bacon, pp. 184–204.

Foster, Bernard. 1984. *Living and Dying, A Picture of Hull in the Nineteenth Century*. Hull, UK: Abbotsgate Publishers.

Fox, John. 2008. *A World Survey of Religion and the State*. Cambridge: Cambridge University Press.

Friedman, Menachem. 1994. "Neturei Karta and the Sabbath Demonstrations in Jerusalem: 1948–50," in A. Bareli (ed.), *The Divided Jerusalem 1948–1967*. Jerusalem: Yad Ben-Zvi (Hebrew).

Friedman, Thomas. 1985. "Israel Debates the Politics of Pork," *New York Times*, August 25, p. 2.

Fulton, Robert L. 1961. "The clergyman and the funeral director: A study in role conflict," *Social Forces*, 39:317–323.

Gabriel, Yiannis and Tim Lang. 2006. *The Unmanageable Consumer*. London: Sage.

Gal, Avraham. 2001. "Principles and Goals of Menuha Nekhona," Internal document.

———. 2007. "Just Don't Say a Kaddish for Me," *Ynet*, December 19 (Hebrew).

Gal, Limor. 2007. "Carved in Stone," *Ha'aretz*, August 24 (Hebrew).

Gans, Herbert, J. 1994. "Symbolic Ethnicity and Symbolic Religiosity: Towards a Comparison of Ethnic and Religious Generation," *Ethnic and Racial Studies* 17, 4:577–592.

Giddens, Anthony. 1971. *Capitalism and Modern Social Theory*. Cambridge: Cambridge University Press.

———. 1992. *The Transformation of Intimacy: Sexuality, Love, and Eroticism in Modern Societies*. Stanford, CA: Stanford University Press.

Gilboa, Shaked. 2007. *Shopping Mall Consumption Patterns in Israel.* Jerusalem: Ministry of Industry, Trade and Labor (Hebrew).

Gill, Anthony and Arang Keshavarzian. 1999 "State Building and Religious Resources: An Institutional Theory of Church-State Relations in Iran and Mexico," *Politics and Society* 27(3): 431–465.

Glickman, Anya, Anat Oren and Noah Levin-Epstine. 2003. *The Institution of Marriage in Israel at the 21st Century. Israeli Public Opinion* (published by B.I. and Lucille Cohen Institute for Public Opinion Research at Tel-Aviv University), Issue No. 7 (November 2003) (Hebrew).

Goldstein, Yaffa. 2007. "An Agreed upon Sabbath?" *Besheva*, May 31. http://www.inn.co.il/Besheva/Article.aspx/6652 (Hebrew).

Goodman, Yehuda. 2003. *The Return to Religion and Jewish Identities in the Early 2000s.* Discussion Paper 15–2002. Tel Aviv University: Sapir Center (Hebrew).

Gorski, Philip S. and Ates Altmordu. 2008. "After Secularization," *Annual Review of Sociology* 34: 55–85.

Gottlieb, Beatrice. 1993. *The Family in the Western World from the Black Death to the Industrial Age.* New York and Oxford: Oxford University Press.

Gross, Netty C. 2000. "Pigging Out," *The Jerusalem Report*, January 31, pp. 16–19.

Gruber, Jonathan and Daniel M. Hungerman. 2006. "The Church vs. the Mall: What Happens When Religion Faces Increased Secular Competition," NBER Working Paper 12410.

Gutkind-Golan, Naomi. 1990. "Heikhal Cinema Case as a Symptom to Religious-Secular Relationship in Israel in the Eighties," in C. Liebman (ed.), *Religious and Secular: Conflict and Accommodation between Jews in Israel.* Jerusalem: Keter Publishing (Hebrew).

Gvion, Liora. 2005. "Hummus-Couscous-Sushi: Food and Ethnicity in Israeli Society," in A. Kleinberg, (ed.), *A Full Stomach: A Different Look on Food and Society.* Jerusalem: Keter (Hebrew).

Hacohen, Aviad. 2002. "The Sabbath in a Jewish and Democratic State," *Da'at*, http://www.daat.ac.il/mishpat-ivri/skirot/66–2.htm (Hebrew).

Hadden, Jeffrey K. 1987. "Towards Desacralizing Secularization Theory," *Social Forces* 65(3): 587–611.

Haider-Markel, Donald P. and Mark R. Joslyn. 2005. "Attributions and the Regulation of Marriage: Considering the Parallels Between Race and Homosexuality," *PS: Political Science and Politics* 38: 233–239.

Hall, Peter. 1986. *Governing the Economy: The Politics of State Intervention in Britain and France.* Cambridge, UK: Polity Press.

Hammond, Philip and Kee Warner. 1993. "Religion and Ethnicity in Late-Twentieth Century America," *Annals of the American Academy of Political and Social Science* 527: 55–66.

Harvey, David. 1989. *The Urban Experience*, Baltimore, MD: Johns Hopkins University Press).

Hay, Collin. 2007. *Why We Hate Politics.* Cambridge, UK: Polity Press.

Haynes, Jeff. 1998. *Religion in Global Politics.* London and New York: Longman.

_____. 2006. "Religion and International Relations in the 21st Century: Conflict or Cooperation?," *Third World Quarterly*, 27(3): 535–541.

Heclo, Hugh. 2001. "Religion and Public Policy: An Introduction," *Journal of Policy History*, 13: 11–18.

Held, David, Anthony McGrew, David Goldblatt, and Jonathan Perraton. 1999. *Global Transformations*. London: Polity Press.

Helman, Anat. 2005. "Torah, Work and Coffee Shops: Religion and Public Life in Tel-Aviv during the British Mandate," *Kathedra*, 105: 85–110 (Hebrew).

Heruti-Sover, Tal. 2007. "Burial in the Kibbutzim: A Growing Business," *Ha'aretz De-Marker*, March 11 (Hebrew).

Hirst, Paul. 2000. "The global economy: myths or reality?" in D. Kalb (ed.), *The Ends of Globalization; Bringing Society Back In*. Oxford: Oxford University Press, pp.107–123.

Holzer, Boris and Mads Sorensen. 2001. *Subpolitics and Subpoliticians*. Arbeitspapier 4 des SFB 536 Reflexive Modernisierung. Munchen: University of Munchen.

Howes, David. 1996. "Introduction: Commodities and Cultural Border," in D. Howes (ed.), *Cross-Cultural Consumption*. London: Routledge, pp. 1–18.

Hunt, Stephen. 2005. *Religion and Everyday Life*. London: Routledge.

Hunter, James D. 1991. *Culture Wars: The Struggle to Define America*. New York: Basic Books.

Huntington, Samuel. 1968. *Political Order in Changing Societies*. New Haven, CT: Yale University Press.

_____. 1993. "The Clash of Civilizations?," *Foreign Affairs* 73(3): 22–49.

Iannaccone, Laurence R. 1995. "Voodoo Economics? Defending the Rational Choice Approach to Religion," *Journal for the Scientific Study of Religion* 34 (March): 76–88.

IDI (Israel Democracy Institute). 2007. *The 2007 Israeli Democracy Index*. Jerusalem: IDI.

Ikenberry, John. 1988 *Reasons of State: Oil Politics and the Capacity of the American Government*, Ithaca, NY: Cornell University Press.

Ilan, Shahar. 1998. "Burial Pays," *Ha'aretz*, July 4 (Hebrew).

_____. 1999. "Petach Tikvah Shows: Sabbath War II," *Ha'aretz*, June 15 (Hebrew).

Inglehart, Ronald and Wayne E. Baker. 2000. "Modernization, Cultural Change and the Persistence of Traditional Values," *American Sociological Review* 65: 19–51.

Itim Institute. 2011. *Report on Burial in Israel*. (Hebrew), http://www.itim.org. il/_Uploads/dbsAttachedFiles/burial_2011.pdf (Hebrew).

Itzhaki, Yedidya. 2000. *The Uncovered Head*. Haifa: Haifa University Press (Hebrew).

James, Allison. 1996. "Cooking the Books: Global or Local Identities in Contemporary British Food Cultures?" in D. Howes (ed.), *Cross-Cultural Consumption*. London: Routledge, pp.77–92.

Jelen, Ted and C. Wilcox. 2002. "Religion: the One, the Few and the Many," in T. Jelen and Clyde Wilcox (eds.), *Religion and Politics in Comparative Perspective*. Cambridge: Cambridge University Press.

Josephson, Jyl. 2005. "Citizenship, Same-Sex Marriage, and Feminist Critiques of Marriage," *Perspectives on Politics* 3(2): 269–284.

Jurgensmeyer, Mark. 1995. "The New Religious State," *Comparative Politics* 27: 379–391.

Kadosh, Orna. 2000. "The Social Gospel of Omri McDonalds," *Ma'ariv* weekend supplement, June 23 (Hebrew).

Kajalo, Sami. 1997. "Sunday Trading, Consumer Culture, and Shopping – Will Europe Sacrifice Sunday to Recreational Shopping?," paper presented at the Sosiologipaivat 1997 Conference.

———. 2005. "History and Politics of Deregulation of Retail Hours in Finland: Theoretical Considerations and Empirical Evidence," paper presented at the ANZMAC 2005 Conference.

Kama, Amit. 2000. "From *Terra Incognita* to *Terra Firma*: The Logbook of the Voyage of Gay Men's Community into the Israeli Public Sphere," *Journal of Homosexuality* 38(4): 133–162.

Kempner-Kritz, Mali. 2002. "The Mother of the New Family," *Yediot Aharonot*, February 6 (Hebrew).

Kaplan, Dana. 2001. *Marriage of the Middle Class in Israel*. MA thesis, Tel-Aviv University (Hebrew).

Karpel, Motti. 2003. *The Revolution of Faith: The Decline of Zionism and the Religious Alternative*. Alon Shvut: Lechatchila (Hebrew).

Keddie, Nikki R. 2003. "Secularism and Its Discontents," *Daedalus* 132(3):14–30.

Kedem, Peri. 1991. "Dimension of Jewish Religiosity in Israel," in Z. Sobel and B. Bet-Hallahmi (eds.), *Jewishness and Judaism in Contemporary Israel*. Albany, NY: State University of New York Press.

Kelley, Jonathan, M.D.R. Evans, and Bruce Headey. 1993. "Moral Reasoning and Political Conflict: The Abortion Controversy," *British Journal of Sociology* 44(1): 589–611.

Kiernan, Katherine. 2002. "Cohabitation in Western Europe: Trends, Issues and Implications," in A. Booth and A.C. Crouter (eds.), *Just Living Together: Implications of Cohabitation on Families, Children, and Social Policy*. Mahwah, NJ: Erlbaum, pp. 3–31.

Kimmerling, Baruch. 2004. *Immigrants, Settlers, Natives: The Israeli State and Society Between Cultural Pluralism and Cultural Wars*. Tel-Aviv: Am Oved (Hebrew).

Kobrin, Stephen. 1998. "Back to the Future: Neomedievalism and the Postmodern Digital Economy," *Journal of International Affairs* 51(2): 361–386.

Kopelowitz, Ezra. 2001. "Religious Politics and Israel's Ethnic Democracy," *Israel Studies*, 6(3): 166–190.

Kopp, Steven W. and Elyria Kemp. 2007. "The Death-Care Industry, a Review of Regulatory and Consumer Issues," *Journal of Consumer Affairs*. 41, 1:150–173.

Kosmin, Barry and Ariela Keysar. 2009. "American Nones: The Profile of the No Religion Population," http://www.americanreligionsurvey-aris.org/reports/NONES_08.pdf.

Krasner, Steven. 1984. "Approaches to the State: Alternative Conceptions and Historical Dynamics," *Comparative Politics* 16(2): 223–246.

Laband, David and Deborah Hendry Heinbuch. 1987. *Blue Laws: The History, Economics and Politics of Sunday-Closing Laws*. Lexington, MA: Lexington Books.

Lambert, Yves. 1999. "Religion in Modernity as a New Axial Age: Secularization or New Religious Forms?," *Sociology of Religion* 60(3): 303–333.

Lechner, Frank J. 1991. "The Case Against Secularization: A Rebuttal," *Social Forces* 69: 1103–1119.

Lehman-Wilzig, Samuel N. 1991. "Loyalty, Voice and Quasi-Exit," *Comparative Politics* 24: 97–108.

Leon, Nissim. 2009. "A Post-Orthodox View on Mizrachi Traditionalism," *Pe'amim* 122/123: 89–115 (Hebrew).

Leshem, Elazar. 2001. "The Immigration from the Former USSR and the Religious-Secular Schism in Israel," in M. Lissak and E. Leshem (eds.), *From Russia to Israel: Identity and Culture in Transition*. Tel-Aviv: Hakibutz Hameuchad Press (Hebrew).

Levi, Gal and Zeev Amreich. 2001. "Shas and the Mirage of Ethnicity." in Y. Peled (ed.), *Shas: The Challenge of Israeliness*. Tel-Aviv: Miskal, pp. 126–158 (Hebrew).

Levi, Shlomit. 2004. "The Private and Public Sabbath in Israel," in J. Blidstein (ed.), *Sabbath: Idea, History and Reality*. Beersheba: Ben-Gurion University Press (Hebrew).

Levi, Shlomit, Hanna Levinson, and Eliahu Katz. 2002. *Jews, Israelis: A Portrait*. Jerusalem: Israeli Democracy Institute (Hebrew).

Levi, Yagil. 2008. "Israel's Violated Republican Equation." *Citizenship Studies* 12, 3:249–264.

Lévi-Strauss, Claude. 1956. "The Family," in Harry L. Shapiro (ed.), *Man, Culture, and Society*. New York: Oxford University Press, p.147.

Liebman, Charles. 1997. "Prospects for Jewish Secularism," *Alpayim* 14: 97–115 (Hebrew).

Liebman, Charles and Eliezer Don-Yehia. 1984. "Traditional Culture in a Modern State: Changes and Developments in the Civil Religion of Israel," *Megamot* 24(4): 461–485 (Hebrew).

Liebman, Charles and Bernard Susser. 1998. "Judaism and Jewishness in the Jewish State," *Annals AAPSS* 555: 15–25.

Lifshitz, Shahar. 2005. *Cohabitation Law in Israel from the Perspective of a Civil Law Theory of the Family*. Haifa: Haifa University Press (Hebrew).

Livneh, Neri. 2004. "The Dead and the Living," *Ha'aretz* weekend supplement, October 15 (Hebrew).

———. 2005. "A Radical Departure," *Ha'aretz* weekend supplement, October 14 (Hebrew).

Lori, Aviva. 1998. "To Cyprus with Love and Protest," *Haaretz*, April 3 (Hebrew).

Lyon, David. 1985. "Rethinking Secularization: Retrospect and Prospect," *Review of Religious Research* 26(3): 228–243.

Marin, Yuval. 2004. "The Right to Family Life and Civil Marriage under International Law and Its Implementation in the State of Israel," *Bepress Legal Series*, Paper 275.

Marx, Karl and Friedrich Engels. 1848. Manifesto of the Communist Party. http://www.anu.edu.au/polsci/marx/classics/manifesto.html.

Maoz, Asher. 2007. "Ben-Gurion's Mistake," *Haaretz*, July 24 (Hebrew).

Mautner, Menachem. 2011. *Law and the Culture of Israel*. Oxford: Oxford University Press.

Mazori, Dalia 2005. "Into the Coffin?," NRG, April 19 (Hebrew).

McClay, Wilfred M. 2001. "Two Concepts of Secularization," *Journal of Policy History* 13(1): 47–72.

McCleary, Rachel and Robert Barro. 2006. "Religion and Economy," *Journal of Economic Perspectives* 20(2): 49–72.

McCracken, Grant. 1990. *Culture and Consumption*. Bloomington, IN: Indiana University Press.

McKendrick, Neil, John Brewer, and J.H. Plumb. 1982. *The Birth of a Consumer Society: The Commercialization of Eighteenth-Century England*. Bloomington: Indiana University Press.

McLeod, Hugh. 2000. *Secularisation in Western Europe 1848–1914*. New York, NY: St. Martin's Press.

McMullen, Mike. 1994. "Religious Polities as Institutions," *Social Forces* 73(2): 709–728.

Meidan, Anat. 1997. "Until the Last Cheeseburger," *Yediot Aharonot* weekend supplement, January 24 (Hebrew).

Mennel, Stephen. 1985. *All Manners of Food: Eating and Taste in England and France from the Middle Ages to the Present*. Oxford: Basil Blackwell.

Metz, Tamara. 2010. *Untying the Knot: Marriage, the State and the Case for Their Divorce*. Princeton, NJ: Princeton University Press.

Mey-Ami, Naomi. 2007. "The Implementation of the Civil Burial Law," Knesset Research and Information Center (Hebrew).

Meydani, Assaf. 2010. "Political Entrepreneurs and Public Administration Reform: The Case of Local Authorities' Unification Reform in Israel," *International Journal of Public Administration* 33: 200–206.

Meyer, John W., John Boli, and George M. Thomas. 1987. "Ontology and Rationalization in the Western Cultural Account," in G.M. Thomas, J.W. Meyer, F.O. Ramirez, and J. Boli, *Institutional Structure: Constituting State, Society, and the Individual*. Newbury Park, CA: Sage, pp. 12–38.

Migdal, Joel. 2001. *State in Society*. Cambridge: Cambridge University Press.

Miles, Steven 1998. *Consumerism as a Way of Life*. London: Sage.

Mills, C. Wright. 1959. *The Sociological Imagination*. Oxford: Oxford University Press.

Mintz, Sidney. 2002. "Food and Eating: Some Persisting Questions," in W. Belasco and P. Scranton (eds.), *Food Nations: Selling Taste in Consumer Societies*. New York: Routledge.

Mintz, Sidney and Christine M. Du Bois. 2002. "The Anthropology of Food and Eating," *Annual Review of Anthropology* 31: 99–119.

Mitchell, Claire. 2006. "The Religious Content of Ethnic Identities," *Sociology* 40(6): 1135–1152.

Mittelman, James. 2000. *The Globalization Syndrome*. Princeton, NJ: Princeton University Press.

Mizrahi, Shlomo and Assaf Meydani. 2003. "Political Participation via the Judicial System: Exit, Voice and Quasi-Exit in Israeli Society," *Israel Studies* 8: 118–138.

Modelski, George. 1999. "From Leadership to Organization: the Evolution of Global Politics," in A. Bornshier and C. Chase-Dunn (eds.), *The Future of Global Conflict*. London: Sage, pp.123–156.

Mosse, George. 1979. "National Cemeteries and National Revival: The Cult of the Fallen Soldiers in Germany," *Journal of Contemporary History* 14(1): 1–20.

Moyser, George. 1991. "Politics and Religion in the Modern World: an Overview," in George Moyser (ed.), *Politics and Religion in the Modern World*. London: Routledge, pp. 1–27.

National Insurance Institute. 2007. *Single-Parent Families in Israel*. Jerusalem: NIS Working Papers.

Naor, Ravit. 2005. "My Cypriote Wedding" http://cyprus-wedding.co.il/newspaper.html (Hebrew).

Nock, Steven L. 2005. "Marriage as a Public Issue," *The Future of Children* 15(2): 13–27.

Norris, Pippa. 1999. "Introduction: The Growth of Critical Citizens?" in P. Norris (ed.), *Critical Citizens*, Oxford: Oxford University Press.

Norris, Pippa and Ronald Inglehart. 2004. *Sacred and Secular: Religion and Politics Worldwide*. Cambridge: Cambridge University Press.

Nye, Joseph S. 1997. "Introduction: The Decline of Confidence in Government," in J. Nye, P. Zelikow, and D. King (eds.), *Why People Don't Trust Government*. Cambridge, MA: Harvard University Press.

Ohmae, Kenichi. 1995. *The End of the Nation State*. New York: The Free Press.

Oren, Guy. 2008. "A Secular Wedding: Only What Is Relevant for Your Relationship," *Ynet*, January 15 (Hebrew).

Peled, Yoav. 1998. "Towards a Redefinition of Jewish Nationalism in Israel? The Enigma of Shas," *Ethnic and Racial Studies* 21(4): 703–727.

Peres, Yohanan and Eliezer Ben-Rafael. 2007. *Cleavages in Israeli Society*. Tel-Aviv: Am Oved (Hebrew).

Peters, B. Guy, Jon Pierre, and Desmond S. King. 2005. "The Politics of Path Dependency: Political Conflict in Historical Institutionalism," *The Journal of Politics* 67(4): 1275–1300.

Pharr, Susan J. and Robert D. Putnam. 2000. *Disaffected Democracies – What's Troubling the Trilateral Countries?* Princeton, NJ: Princeton University Press.

Philipov, Michael and Evgenia Bystrov. 2011. "All by Myself? The Paradox of Citizenship among the FSU Immigrants in Israel," in G. Ben-Porat and B. Turner (eds.), *The Contradictions of Israeli Citizenship: Land, Religion and State*. London: Routledge.

Pierre, Jon. 2000. *Debating Governance: Authority, Steering and Democracy.* Oxford: Oxford University Press.

Pinchasi, Hava. 2009. "My Feminine Funeral," *Ynet*, December 29 (Hebrew).

Pine, Vanderlyn R. and Derek L. Philips. 1970. "The Cost of Dying: A Sociological Analysis of Funeral Expenditures," *Social Problems* 17(3): 405–417.

Prashitzky, Ana. 2011. "The Construction of Collective Memory in the Realm of Orthodox and Alternative Jewish Marriage Ceremonies," *Megamot* 48(1): 86–108 (Hebrew).

Price, Jamie and Bruce Yandle. 1987. "Labor Markets and Sunday Closing Laws," *Journal of Labor Research* 8(4): 407–414.

Poggi, Gianfranco. 1990. *The State: Its Nature, Development and Prospects.* Stanford, CA: Stanford University Press.

Ram, Uri. 2008a. *The Globalization of Israel: McWorld in Tel-Aviv, Jihad in Jerusalem.* New York: Routledge.

———. 2008b. "Why Secularism Fails? Secular Nationalism and Religious Revivalism in Israel," *International Journal of Politics, Culture and Society* 21: 57–73.

Raz-Krakotzkin, Amnon. 2000. "Rabin's Legacy: On Secularism, Nationalism and Orientalism," in L. Grinberg (ed.), *Contested Memory: Myth, Nationalism and Democracy.* Beersheba: Humphrey Institute, Ben-Gurion University.

Richter, Philip. 1994. "Seven Days' Trading Make One Weak? The Sunday Trading Issue as an Index of Secularization," *The British Journal of Sociology* 45(3): 333–348.

Ritzer, George. 1996. *The McDonaldization of Society.* Thousand Oaks, CA: Pine Forge Press.

Rivlin, Paul. 2010. *The Israeli Economy from the Foundation of the State through the 21st Century.* Cambridge: Cambridge University Press.

Rodrik, Dani. 1997. *Has Globalization Gone Too Far?* Washington, DC: Institute for International Economics.

Rosecrance, Richard. 1996. "The Rise of the Virtual State," *Foreign Affairs*, 75(4): 45–61.

Rosenblum, Irit. 2004. "A Revolution in Noah's Ark," *Eretz Acheret*, July–August (Hebrew). http://acheret.co.il/?cmd=articles.152&act=read&id=681.

Roucher, Alan. 1994. "Sunday Business and the Decline of Sunday Closing Laws: A Historical Review," *Journal of Church and State* 36: 13–36.

Rugg, Julie. 2006. "Lawn Cemeteries: The Emergence of a New Landscape of Death," *Urban History* 33:213–233.

Safran, William. 2003. "Introduction," in W. Safran (ed.). *The Secular and the Sacred, Nation, Religion and Politics*, London: Frank Cass.

Sagiv, Talia and Edna Lomsky-Feder. 2007. "An Actualization of a Symbolic Conflict: The Arena of Secular 'Batei Midrash'," *Israeli Sociology* 8(2): 269–300 (Hebrew).

Sagiv-Shifter, Tami and Michal Shamir. 2002. "Israel as a laboratory for the study of political tolerance," Tel-Aviv: Cohen Institute for Public Opinion Research (Hebrew).

Sapir, Gidi and Daniel Statman. 2009. "Religious Marriage in a Liberal State," *Cardozo Law Review de novo* 30(6): 2855–2880.

Sartori, Giovanni. 1995. "How Far Can Free Government Travel?," *Journal of Democracy* 6(3): 101–111.

Sassen, Saskia. 1998. *Globalization and its Discontents*. New York, NY: New Press.

Scholte, J.A. 2000. *Globalization, a Critical Introduction*. London: Macmillan.

Schneider, Mark and Paul Teske. 1992. "Toward a Theory of the Political Entrepreneur: Evidence from Local Government," *American Political Science Review* 86(3): 737–747.

Schwartz, Dov. 1999. *Religious Zionism: Between Rationality and Messianism*. Tel-Aviv: Am-Oved (Hebrew).

Segal, Israel. 1999. "Fallen Asleep While on Guard," in D. Tzuker (ed.), *We, Secular Jews*. Tel-Aviv: Yediot Aharonot (Hebrew).

Segev, Tom. 1984. *The First Israelis*. Jerusalem: Domino (Hebrew).

Seltzer, Judith. 2000. "Families Formed Outside of Marriage," *Journal of Marriage and Family* 62: 1247–1268.

Shafat, Gershon. 1995. *Gush Emunim: The Story Behind*. Beit-El Library (Hebrew).

Shafir, Gershon and Yoav Peled. 2002. *Being Israeli: The Dynamics of Multiple Citizenship*. New York: Cambridge University Press.

Shaki, Hai Avner. 1995. "The Legal Status of the Sabbath in Israel," *Moznei Mishpat D*: 147–217 (Hebrew).

Shalev, Meir. 2001. *The Blue Mountain*. Edinburgh, UK: Canongate.

Shalom, Efrat 2003. "A Religious Marriage, with Shrimps." *Haaretz*, July 30 (Hebrew).

Shamir, Omri and Guy Ben-Porat, 2007. "Boycotting for Sabbath: Religious Consumerism as a Political Strategy" *Contemporary Politics* 13(1): 75–92.

Shapira, Anita. 1992. *Land and Power*. New York: Oxford University Press.

Sharot, Stephan, Hannah Ayalon, and Eliezer Ben-Rafael. 1986. "Secularization and the Diminishing Decline of Religion," *Review of Religious Research* 27: 193–207.

Sheingate, Adam D. 2003, "Political Entrepreneurship, Institutional Change, and American Political Development," *Studies in American Political Development* 17: 185–203.

Shifman, Pinhas. 1995a. *Who is Afraid of Civil Marriage?* Jerusalem: The Jerusalem Institute for Israel Studies (Hebrew).

———. 1995b. *Family Law in Israel*. Jerusalem: Jerusalem: Hebrew University (Hebrew).

———. 2001. *Civil or Sacred: Marriage and Divorce Alternatives in Israel*. Tel-Aviv: Association for Civil Rights in Israel (Hebrew).

Shokeid, Moshe. 1984. "Cultural Ethnicity in Israel: The Case of Middle Eastern Jews' Religiosity," *AJS Review* 9(2): 247–271.

Shumsky, Dimitry. 2001. "Ethnicity and Citizenship in the Conception of the Israeli-Russians," *Theory and Criticism* 19: 17–40 (Hebrew).

———. 2004. "Post Zionist Orientalism? Orientalist Discourse and Islamophobia among the Russian-Speaking Intelligentsia in Israel," *Social Identities* 10(1): 83–99.

Shupe, Anson and Jeffrey K. Hadden. 1989. "Is There Such a Thing as Global Fundamentalism?," in A. Shupe and J.K. Hadden (eds.), *Secularization and Fundamentalism Reconsidered, Vol. III*. New York: Paragon.

Simoons, Fredrick J. 1967. *Eat Not This Flesh*. Madison: University of Wisconsin Press.

Sinai, Ruthi. 1997. "No Rest Yet," *Ha'aretz*, September 29 (Hebrew).

Singerman, Diane. 1995. *Avenues of Participation*. Princeton, NJ: Princeton University Press.

Skuterud, Mikal. 2005. "The Impact of Sunday Shopping on Employment and Hours of Work in the Retail Industry: Evidence from Canada," *European Economic Review* 49: 1953–1978.

Sommerville, C. John. 1998. "Secular Society/Religious Population: Our Tacit Rules for Using the Term 'Secularization'," *Journal for the Scientific Study of Religion* 37(2): 249–253.

———. 2006. *The Decline of the Secular University*. New York: Oxford University Press.

Smooha, Sami. 1997. "Ethnic Democracy: Israel as an Archetype" *Israel Studies* 2(2): 198–241.

Stadler, Nurit, Edna Lomsky Feder, and Eyal Ben-Ari. 2008. "Fundamentalism's Challenges to Citizenship: The Haredim," *Citizenship Studies* 12(3): 215–231.

State Comptroller. 2009. Report on Civil Burial on Agricultural Lands. http://www.mevaker.gov.il/serve/showHtml.asp?bookid=568&id=2&frompage=395&contentid=11065&parentcid=11058&filename=131.htm&bctype=2&startpage=12&sw=1382&hw=794 (Hebrew).

Stark, Rodney. 1996. "Bringing Theory Back In," in L. Young (ed.), *Rational Choice Theories of Religion*. London: Routledge.

Stark, Rodney and Roger Finke. 2000. *Acts of Faith: Explaining the Human Side of Religion*. Berkeley and Los Angeles: University of California Press.

Stark, Rodney and Laurence Iannaccone. 1994. "A Supply-Side Reinterpretation of the 'Secularization' of Europe," *Journal for the Scientific Study of Religion* 33: 230–252.

Stav, David. 2007. "Tzohar Rabbis Fight Back," http://www.nrg.co.il/online/11/ART1/610/685.html (Hebrew).

Stearns, Peter N. 2006. *Consumerism in World History*. New York: Routledge.

Stephenson, Peter H. 1989. "Going to McDonald's in Leiden: Reflections of Concept of Self and Society in the Netherlands," *Ethos* 17(2): 226–247.

Sternhell, Zeev. 1998. *The Founding Myths of Zionism: Nationalism, Socialism and the Making of the Jewish State*. Princeton, NJ: Princeton University Press.

Stolle, Dietland, Marc Hooghe, and Michele Micheletti. 2005. "Politics in the Supermarket: Political Consumerism as a Form of Political Participation," *International Political Science Review* 26: 245–269.

Susser, Bernard and Asher Cohen. 2000. *Israel and the Politics of Jewish Identity: The Secular-Religious Impasse*. Baltimore, MD: Johns Hopkins University Press.

Swatos, William H. Jr. and Kevin J. Christiano. 1999. "Introduction – Secularization Theory: The Course of a Concept," *Sociology of Religion* 60(3): 209–228.

Tessler, Ricki. 2003. *In the Name of the Lord: Shas and the Religious Revolution*. Tel-Aviv: Keter (Hebrew).

Thelen, Kathleen. 1999. "Historical Institutionalism in Comparative Politics." *Annual Review of Political Science* 2:394–404.

Thomas, Scott M. 2005. *The Global Resurgence of Religion and the Transformation of International Relations.* New York and London: Palgrave.

Tilly, Charles 1995. "Globalization Threatens Labor's Rights," *International Labor and Working Class History* 47: 1–23.

Tomlinson, John. 1999. *Globalization and Culture.* Cambridge, UK: Polity Press.

Turner, Bryan. 2008. "Goods Not Gods: New Spiritualities, Consumerism and Religious Markets," in I.R. Jones, P. Higgs, and D. Ekerdt (eds.), *Consumption and Generational Change: The Rise of Consumer Lifestyles.* Edison, NJ: Transaction Books.

Tzur, Eli. 2001. "To Be a Free People: The League against Religious Coercion," in A. Shapira (ed.), *State in the Making.* Jerusalem: Shazar Center (Hebrew).

Verdery, Katherine. 1999. *The Political Lives of Dead Bodies.* New York: Columbia University Press.

Voas, David and Alasdair Crockett. 2005. "Religion in Britain: Neither Believing, Nor Belonging," *Sociology* 39(1): 11–28.

Wald, Kenneth D., Adam L. Silverman, and Kevin S. Friday. 2005. "Making Sense of Religion in Political Life," *Annual Review of Political Science* 8: 121–143.

Wallis, Roy and Steve Bruce. 1989. "Religion: The British Contribution," *The British Journal of Sociology* 40(3): 493–520.

Walter, Tony. 1996. *The Eclipse of Eternity. A Sociology of the Afterlife.* London: Macmillan.

———. 2005. "Three Ways to Arrange a Funeral: Mortuary Variations in the Modern West," *Mortality* 10(3): 173–192.

Walzer, Michael. 1984. "Liberalism and the Art of Separation," *Political Theory* 12(3): 315–330.

Warhaftig, Zerach. 1988. *A Constitution for Israel: Religion and State.* Jerusalem: Mesilot (Hebrew).

Weber, Max. 1958. *The Protestant Ethic and the Spirit of Capitalism.* New York: Charles Scribner's Sons.

Weingrod, Alex. 1995. "Dry Bones: Nationalism and Symbolism in Contemporary Israel," *Anthropology Today* 11(6): 7–12.

Weiss, Linda. 1998. *The Myth of the Powerless State.* Ithaca, NY: Cornell University Press.

Wilson, Bryan. 1985. "Secularization: The Inherited Model," in P.E. Hammond (ed.), *The Sacred in a Secular Age.* Berkeley: University of California Press.

———. 2001. "Reflections on Secularization and Toleration," in A. Walker and D. Martin (eds.), *Restoring the Image.* Sheffield, UK: Sheffield Academic Press.

Winter, Shiri. 1999. "Burial Services in Israel." IASPS, http://www.iasps.org/hebrew/policystudies/PS37heb.pdf (Hebrew).

Witte, John. 1997. *From Sacrament to Contract: Marriage, Religion and Law in the Western Tradition.* Westminster, UK: John Knox Press.

Wuthnow, Robert. 1998. *After Heaven: Spirituality in America Since the 1950s.* Berkeley: University of California Press.

Yadgar, Yaacov. 2010. *Masortim in Israel: Modernity Without Secularization.* Tel-Aviv: Shalom Hartman Institute, Bar-Ilan University, and Keter (Hebrew).

Yaffe, Meir and Michah Rosenthaler. 2005. "The Forum for National Agree-
ment," in U. Dromi (ed.), *Brethren Dwelling Together: Orthodoxy and Non-
Orthodoxy in Israel – Positions, Propositions and Accords.* Jerusalem: Israel
Democracy Institute (Hebrew).

Yahav, Yehudit. 2003. "An Expensive Rest: A Guide for Alternative Burial,"
Ynet, October 24 (Hebrew).

———. 2004. "Secular Burial: There Is Another Way," *Ynet,* February 10
(Hebrew).

Yamane, David. 1997. "Secularization on Trial: in Defense of Neosecularization,"
Journal for the Scientific Study of Religion 36(1): 109–122.

Yefet, Orna. 2007. "To See the White in the Eyes," *Ynet,* September 2 (Hebrew).

Yemini, Galit. 2003. "Yaakov Mania is Planning to Bite into the New Market,"
Yediot Aharonot, March 1 (Hebrew).

Yovel, Yirmiyahu. 2007. *A New Jewish Age.* Tel-Aviv: Keter (Hebrew).

Zameret, Zvi. 2004. "We Shall Turn our Sabbaths into Bonfires of Culture:
Zionist Non-Orthodox Positions toward the Sabbath," in J. Blidstein (ed.),
Sabbath: Idea, History and Reality. Beersheba: Ben-Gurion University Press
(Hebrew).

Zamir, Israel. 1990. "Winds of War," *Al Hamishmar,* December 21 (Hebrew).

Zerubavel, Eviatar. 1985. *The Seven Day Circle.* New York: The Free Press.

Zomer, Navit. 2002. "Tiv-Taam: a Successful Food Chain," *Ynet,* May 7
(Hebrew).

List of Interviews

A.A., Vice General Manager, Fashion Stores Chain
A.S., Vice General Manager, Sporting Goods Chain
Meir Azari, Rabbi, the Reform Temple of Beit Deniel
Jacky Ben-Zaken, Business Entrepreneur
Eitan Bar-Zeev, General Manager, BIG Shopping Centers
Shlomi Cohen, General Manager, Horashim Cemetery
Eyal Fishman, Businessman
Avraham Gal, Lawyer, Founder of Menuha Nekhona
Yossi Gil, Vice General Manager, Tzomet Sfarim
Nardi Green, Secular Rabbi
Nitzan Hadas, General Manager, H&O Fashion Shops
Maurice Halfon, General Manager, Menuha Nekhona
Yiftach Hashiloni, founder, Center of Secular Ceremonies
Einat Hurvitz, Attorney, Israel Religious Action Center
Amit Kama (Dr.), Researcher and Activist
Gilad Kariv, Rabbi, Executive Director of the Israel Movement for Progressive
Judaism
David Keinan, General Manager, King Tours
Doron Keinar, Ceremony Director
Oded Levi, General Manager, Gan Shmuel Shopping Center
Yaakov Manya, Owner, Ma'adanei Manya
Menachem Maudi, General Manager, Bilu Shopping Center
Kobi Moise, General Manager, AICE

Sagit Mor (Dr.), Havaya Israeli Life Cycle Ceremonies
Pe'er Nadir, General Manager, Azrieli Group
Shalom Naim, General Manager, Einat Cemetery
Alon Nativ, General Manager and Owner, Aley Shalechet
Pini Nissim, General Manager, BIG Shopping Center, Beer Sheva
Yehezkel Ophir, Ministry of Industry, Trade and Labor, Enforcement of Labor Laws
Micah Rinat, Former Director of the Mizra Factory, Kibbutz Mizra
Andrew Sacks, Rabbi, Director of Rabbinical Assembly in Israel and Religious Affairs, the Masorti (Conservative Judaism) Movement
Zemira Segev, General Manager, the Forum for Freedom of Marriage
Rami Shavit, Owner, Mashbir Lazarchan
Yonit Shlain, Attorney, Israel Religious Action Center
Yifat Solel, Attorney, Menuha Nekhona
Kobi Tribitch, Owner and Founder, Tiv-Ta'am

Index

List of Books in the Series